RIGHTS AND OBLIGATIONS IN
NORTH–SOUTH RELATIONS

Rights and Obligations in North–South Relations

Ethical Dimensions of Global Problems

Edited by
Moorhead Wright

St. Martin's Press   New York

First published in the United States of America in 1986

Printed in Hong Kong

ISBN 0–312–682–34–4

Library of Congress Cataloging-in-Publication Data
Main entry under title:
Rights and obligations in north–south relations.
Bibliography: p.
Includes index.
1. Developing countries—Foreign relations—Moral
and ethical aspects. 2. Developing countries—Foreign
economic relations—Moral and ethical aspects.
3. International economic relations—Moral and
ethical aspects. I. Wright, Moorhead. II. Title.
JX1391.R53 1985 172′4 85–22212
ISBN 0–312–68234–4

Contents

v

Notes on the Contributors

Jane Davis is a Lecturer in International Politics at the University College of Wales, Aberystwyth. She contributes a chapter on defence organizations and developments to *The Annual Register* and is writing a general survey of third-world conflicts, which together with international organization is her main teaching field.

Margaret Doxey is Professor of Political Studies at Trent University, Peterborough, Ontario, Canada. Her *Economic Sanctions and International Enforcement*, now in its second edition, is widely regarded as the standard work in the field.

V. G. Kiernan is Emeritus Professor of Modern History at the University of Edinburgh. His books include *Lords of Human Kind, European Empires from Conquest to Collapse* and *Marxism and Imperialism*.

A. I. MacBean is Professor of Economics at the University of Lancaster. He has been an economic adviser in the Ministry of Overseas Development, a member of the Harvard Economic Advisory Service in Pakistan, and a consultant for a variety of organizations. His publications include *Export Instability and Economic Development* and (as co-author) *Meeting the Third World Challenge*.

A. J. M. Milne is Professor of Politics at the University of Durham. He is the author of *The Social Philosophy of English Idealism, Freedom and Rights* and *The Right to Dissent: Issues in Political Philosophy*.

S. C. Nolutshungu is a Lecturer in Government at the University of Manchester. Among his publications are *Changing South Africa* and *South Africa*.

H. W. Singer is Emeritus Professor at the Institute of Development Studies, University of Sussex. He spent twenty-two years with the United Nations and has had wide experience as a consultant for such organizations as FAO, UNIDO, UNCTAD and UNICEF. His many publications include *Rich and Poor Countries, The Strategy of International Development* and *Technologies for Basic Needs*.

Moorhead Wright, editor, is a Senior Lecturer in International Politics at the University College of Wales, Aberystwyth, specializing in the ethical and philosophical problems of the subject. He has edited *Theory and Practice of the Balance of Power, 1486–1914* and co-edited *American Thinking about Peace and War*.

Preface

The global situation has been characterized in recent years by an ever-widening gap between rich and poor countries with a corresponding growth in awareness of the need for a North–South dialogue. The failure of this dialogue to produce many concrete achievements has been due both to the complexity of the problems involved and the tendency for both sides to seek short-term political advantages. Demands by the developing countries for a New International Economic Order, for example, have met with little sympathy among the industrialized nations, who see their traditional superiority threatened.

These developments have prompted a considerable amount of scholarly literature on the ethical dimension of relations between developed and developing countries, but there has been no attempt to provide an overall survey of the moral problems presented by a wide variety of issues. This is the aim of the essays in this book which have been written by experts on their chosen topics and reflect a wide range of viewpoints. The opening chapters provide the philosophical and historical background necessary to an understanding of the various ethical positions and arguments. Subsequent chapters tackle specific issues in current North–South relations and the institutional framework which has arisen to deal with them.

Early drafts of six of the chapters were presented at an interdisciplinary conference sponsored by the Department of International Politics, University College of Wales, at the University of Wales Conference Centre, Gregynog Hall, near Newtown, Powys, 2–4 July 1984. The editor wishes to thank the British Academy for a travel grant which enabled Margaret Doxey to deliver her paper, the Advisory Board which administers the endowment associated with the Department's Woodrow Wilson Chair for financial support for the conference, Jane Davis and James Piscatori for their helpful suggestions at the planning stage, the warden and staff of Gregynog Hall for helping to make the conference such a pleasant occasion, and the other participants for their lively and well-informed involvement in the discussions. In this last category special thanks are due to the late Professor Hedley Bull, who stepped in at the last minute to introduce and comment upon one of the papers with his usual acumen and wide-ranging knowledge. We dedicate the book to the memory of this outstanding scholar, respected colleague and good friend.

M.W.

Introduction

Like East–West, North–South has become a dominant axis of world politics and has entered into the vocabulary of international relations as an academic discipline. Both expressions verge at times on clichés and as such mask rather than reveal the complex realities of contemporary global politics. What is broadly true, however, is that the northern hemisphere contains a preponderance of relatively affluent countries, and the southern hemisphere contains the majority of the world's poor countries. More sophisticated groupings are, of course, used by agencies such as the World Bank in their World Development Reports, but the binary classification has captured the public imagination and infiltrated the scholarly literature. In a long-term perspective the principal innovation which the North –South division brings to world politics is the emergence of the relations between wealthy and poor countries as a key issue.

The quest for power, privilege and security continues to be at the centre of international relations, but ethical questions have gained a new prominence as a consequence of the North–South division. The basic preconditions for both political and ethical issues – interdependence, moderate scarcity, and partially conflicting interests[1] – exist in the contemporary world. The essays in this book explore these themes with regard to certain aspects of the relations between North and South.

Justice requires equality of treatment in the sense of fair consideration in the allocation of powers and capabilities to individuals and groups. A just distribution does not imply equality of outcomes, but it must enable everyone to compete fairly for moderately scarce goods and to co-operate for mutual advantage. Capabilities together with entitlements are, as Amartya Sen has convincingly shown,[2] the key to economic development, and from the ethical perspective we can argue that no one should be so deprived of entitlements and capabilities that he or she is unable to maintain a tolerable level of existence. The marked disparities between North and South in this respect give rise to claims of justice.

1

The antithesis between politics and ethics is such a well-worn theme that it needs no review here. Politics, it is argued, is concerned with advantage, self-interest and prudence. Ethics deals with such other-regarding considerations as justice and charity. As such the two are seldom seen to be on good terms with each other. The tendency to draw boundaries around oneself and to regard oneself as an isolated individual has been extended to nation-states and even to groups of nation-states. At each level the 'I' or 'we' is defined at least partly in opposition to, or in contrast with, the other – 'he', 'she', or 'they'. This pluralistic world may have such advantages as cultural diversity but it also has grave shortcomings – intercommunal violence, wars, widespread starvation, and environmental pollution, for instance. That no global 'we' has developed is in part due to the vast distances and cultural diversity itself, but also to the fact that there is no significant 'other' to whom humanity can be opposed.

We are coming to realize, however gradually, the inadequacy of our basic world-picture based on the isolated individual – the 'atomic' self – and by extension exclusive groups with their rival collective egoisms. More profound analysis of the role of language and communication in societies, such as that of Norbert Elias, shows that the personal pronouns do not identify isolated selves or entities but express relations between people.[3] Elias argues against the tendency to reify social entities and advocates the search for relationships, or what he calls figurations (patterns of inter-weavings). This stress on the radical interdependence of persons in society should herald a shift in our thinking about the relations between societies and strengthen the case for an emergent global society of mankind. It alters the focus of contemporary debate from autonomous entities to perspectives on the web of human interdependence.

There are two main obstacles to progress in this direction. First, the extent to which distant and diverse peoples can be said to form a global community, and secondly, the problem of power. The first problem concerns proximity and affinity as the basis for the bonds and consequent obligations between people. These two attributes are virtually absent on a global scale, according to the majority view. But, as Tony Honoré observes, there is clear evidence that a common consciousness has grown in recent years:

Human beings are aware of being engaged in the exploitation of the earth and its surrounding space for their own advantage. They are jointly concerned to make use of the earth's minerals, its animals and plants, for the benefit of the species. They know that we need to defend ourselves against common threats, especially bacterial and virus threats which can cause disease on a global scale. They know that natural and artificial radiation can strike at human survival and that only cooperation can fend off the dangers. They can see the need to avoid the pollution of the atmosphere and the sea.[4]

Although the once fashionable 'global village' never described a true state of affairs, the sense of community among peoples with no direct contacts with one another is now increasing and becoming less opaque with improved knowledge and communications.

It can be argued therefore that the idea of humanity as a source of moral obligations is a valid one, but at the same time we need not abandon the conviction that both politics and morality are based on particular points of view – the 'I' or 'we' standpoint. The recognition that partial moralities are the products of perspectives, and not claimants for the title of universality, is at least a step in the right direction. There is, however, no clear-cut agreement on the methodology of reconciling diverse perspectives. Honoré stresses the 'common aims' of all humanity,[5] but an equally valid approach would be that of compromise among conflicting moral principles.

This will seem hopelessly idealistic to the person who sees nothing but power politics in North–South relations and for whom the following questions seem more relevant: 'Whose potential for withholding what the other requires is greater? Who accordingly is more or less dependent on the other? Who therefore has to submit or adapt himself more to the other's demands?'[6] To a considerable extent the kind of power relations suggested by these questions is ethically neutral, since the pressure or direction can be for the common good as well as for the exclusive benefit of the one who has the favourable power-ratio. The minimum common good is constraint on the misuse of power differentials, for rational analysis suggests that at some future point the power roles may be reversed; this is the crucial question of constitutional democracy and international organization. A truly universal morality would probably stipulate a more demanding criterion such as the 'optimal realization of human potentials'.[7]

Some will contend that the emerging sense of global common interest is not strong enough to provide the basis for North–South co-operation in alleviating the distress of impoverished peoples. The principle of mutual aid, which Honoré commends, is hardly mutual between North and South, so critics argue, since there is little help that the South can provide in return for Northern assistance. Nor is interdependence invariably accepted as sufficiently well advanced to provide the grounds for moral obligations. Such criticisms miss the point that morality in this context requires the imagined reversal of roles or positions. John Rawls has made this famous in his thought experiment of the 'veil of ignorance' and the 'original position', a source of much recent philosophical controversy,[8] and the emphasis on perspectives strengthens the case for this approach to morality. As S.I. Benn puts it:

> Recognizing in someone else the character of a chooser like myself, I would be likely to resent it if, in his conduct toward me, he failed to take account of the impact his actions have on my projects and if he took no account of how they appear from my standpoint. And if that is how I respond to him, I am committed by the universality of reasons, which commits me to seeing the possibility of role reversals, to viewing his projects, and my actions in relation to them from his standpoint. How he sees the world then becomes a proper consideration for me to entertain in answering the question, What is the thing to do?[9]

The major sources of answers to the question 'What is the thing to do?' are rights and obligations, the subject of Alan Milne's opening chapter. He is concerned to recognize the facts of moral diversity without lapsing into ethical relativism, and he articulates a view of 'common morality' which all societies, regardless of culture, must share in order to persist and flourish. He postulates six rights 'which every member of a community necessarily has in virtue of his status as a member, rights each of which all his fellow members have an obligation to respect in virtue of their status as members'. These rights are 'the right to life, the right to justice in the form of fair treatment, the right to aid . . . the right to freedom from arbitrary interference, the right to honourable treatment, and the right to civility'. As Milne shows, these rights apply not only to individuals within societies but also to nation-states within the international community. He therefore envisages no artificial discontinuity between individual and interstate morality. An implication of his analysis is that a legitimate task of states is to see that the rights entailed by the common morality are observed not only within their own borders but in other states as well – a departure from traditional norms of international relations.

That no such common morality existed between European powers and their colonies is made clear by Victor Kiernan's historical account of these relationships. Although he finds much to blame Europe for in the imperial age, there was a positive side as well, notably in the establishment of civil order in areas of local strife and bloodshed, as well as progress towards the abolition of such practices as slavery and suttee.

One of the major ills in the imperial relationship was the exploitation of the colonies' natural resources for the commercial benefit of the metropolitan powers. Alasdair MacBean examines both the economics and ethics of the modern-day version of the problem, in which multinational companies have replaced the colonial powers. He distinguishes between renewable and non-renewable resources, and draws on both utilitarian and Rawlsian theories of justice.

The vestiges of the colonial era also appear in Hans Singer's account of the ethical grounds for foreign aid. He does not find the compensation or reparation of past wrongs a convincing justification for foreign aid, however. More persuasive for him is the charge that there are 'elements in the international economic system which work to the advantage of the rich and the disadvantage of the poor'. It is these structural economic problems which he explores in the central part of his chapter, ending with an eloquent plea for greater emphasis on aid to children.

The use of economic sanctions, the converse of foreign aid in a sense, is the topic of Margaret Doxey's chapter. As she argues, 'resort to deliberate impoverishment of one state by others seems a doubtful proposition even if punitive action might be justified on legal or moral grounds'. She examines the international legitimacy of such measures, the motives and objectives of states initiating sanctions, and the choice of particular measures. She also provides a useful typology of negative non-violent sanctions.

Economic sanctions can be seen as part of the broader issue of intervention, which Sam Nolutshungu explores in his chapter. The form of intervention which in his view arouses the most concern is 'armed intervention involving the dispatch of troops into a country in civil conflict to decide that conflict in favour of one movement or coalition or interest against others'. After expounding three prominent ethical stances with regard to intervention, Nolutshungu sets out the specific features of third world situations which he believes relevant ethical theory ought to take into account, notably the themes of class conflict and revolution.

One aspect of both Doxey's and Nolutshungu's chapters is collective authorization for the measures which they discuss. It is this collective dimension of North–South relations in general which is the subject of Jane Davis's concluding chapter. She is concerned with the extent to which certain institutional developments may contribute to the evolution of an international community and the realization of a more stable and just world order. After exploring the background to North–South institutional developments, she examines the differing attitudes of North and South to international organization. Her chapter then concentrates on three milestones in the evolution of the North–South institutional framework – the United Nations Conference on Trade and Development (UNCTAD), the New International Economic Order (NIEO), and the Third United Nations Conference on the Law of the Sea (UNCLOS III).

The moral imperative which emerges most clearly from this collection of essays is vividly expressed by Kiernan at the close of his chapter. He urges the construction of 'an edifice of social ethics of a more positive cast, uniting humanity in common effort' in order to prevent the potentially disastrous evil of 'two worlds' on one small planet. The principal obstacle to such a common effort is old-style politics, both internal and international. A more rational conception of politics would be what Jon Elster calls the 'transformation of preferences' as an alternative to the suppression or aggregation of preferences. Through public debate there would emerge preferences shaped by a concern for the common good.[10] The progress which has been made so far suggests that such a conception of politics, though far from imminent, is not utopian.

NOTES AND REFERENCES

1. K. Nielson, 'Global Justice, Capitalism and the Third World', *Journal of Applied Philosopy* 1 (1984) p. 181.
2. A. Sen, *Resources, Values and Development* (Oxford: Basil Blackwell, 1984) especially chs 13 and 20.
3. N. Elias, *What is Sociology?* (London: Hutchinson, 1978) p. 124.

4. T. Honoré 'The Human Community and the Principle of Majority Rule', in E. Kamenka (ed.), *Community as a Social Ideal* (London: Edward Arnold, 1982) p. 155. A visually impressive synthesis of global problems is N. Meyers, *The Gaia Atlas of Planet Management* (London: Pan Books, 1985).

5. Honoré, 'The Human Community and the Principle of Majority Rule', p. 155.

6. Elias, *What is Sociology?* p. 79.

7. Ibid, p. 94.

8. J. Rawls, *A Theory of Justice* (Cambridge, Mass.: Harvard University Press, 1971; Oxford: Oxford University Press, 1972). See also MacBean, *infra*.

9. S.I. Benn, 'Persons and Values: Reasons in Conflict and Moral Disagreement', *Ethics* 95 (1984) p. 25.

10. J. Elster, *Sour Grapes: Studies in the Subversion of Rationality* (Cambridge: Cambridge University Press, 1983), pp. 35–6.

1 Human Rights and the Diversity of Morals: A Philosophical Analysis of Rights and Obligations in the Global System

A.J.M. MILNE

INTRODUCTION

This chapter is concerned with four groups of questions. Those in the first are conceptual. What are rights and obligations, what is it to have them, how are they related? Those in the second are concerned with the sources and significance of rights and obligations. How do we come to have them, what is their role in our lives? The questions in the third group are concerned with the idea of human rights. What are such rights and how should we think of them? Those in the fourth group are about rights and obligations in general and human rights in particular in politics, both national and international. They include questions about the global system. What sort of a system is it and how should we think of it? The second group presupposes the first. Before we can answer questions about the sources and significance of rights and obligations, we must know what they are. The third presupposes both the first and the second. If we are to make sense of the idea of human rights, we need to know not only what rights and obligations are and how we come to have them, but what their significance is. The first three groups pave the way for the fourth. In dealing with the questions raised in it, I hope to indicate the appropriate context for the discussion of 'global' ethical issues. In particular, I hope that both the scope and the limits of the concepts of rights and of obligations, and of the idea of human rights in such discussion, will become apparent. They must not be made to carry more weight than they can bear. But neither should their significance be underestimated.

Nowhere in this essay do I mention, let alone discuss, the UN Universal Declaration of Human Rights, the European Convention on Human Rights and Fundamental Freedoms, or the traditional idea of Natural Rights. A word of explanation for these omissions is called for. The key lies in the phrase in my title, 'the diversity of morals'. That diversity and the wider cultural diversity of which it is a part is important in inquiring into the sources of rights and obligations. It is crucial in making sense of the idea of human rights. Any account of that idea which fails to take it seriously cannot be rationally defensible. Unfortunately the UN Declaration, the European Convention and the traditional idea of Natural Rights all fail to do so. As a cursory reading is enough to show, the rights set forth in the UN Declaration are liberal democratic and social welfare rights. They presuppose the values and institutions of modern Western democratic industrial society. The same is true of the European Convention, except that it omits the social welfare rights. Traditional Natural Rights embody the moral and political values of Western culture and civilization. A rationally defensible idea of human rights must be applicable to all cultures and civilizations and therefore must not be linked to the particular values and institutions of any one of them. In the third section I shall suggest such an idea. It is at once less straightforward and more modest than either the historical or contemporary versions but not on that account without significance, or so I hope to show. Finally, a word of caution: my four groups of questions give rise to philosophical problems which cannot be dealt with adequately in a single essay. About these, much which could and in an adequate treatment should be said has been left unsaid. I have confined myself to what is essential for my main purpose, indicating the appropriate context for the discussion of 'global' ethical issues.

RIGHTS AND OBLIGATIONS: A CONCEPTUAL ANALYSIS

The key notion in the concept of a right is entitlement. To say that you have a right to something is to say that you are entitled to it: for instance, to vote, to an old-age pension, to your own opinion, to domestic privacy. To say that rights are entitlements is, of course, only to substitute one word for another. But the substitution is helpful in elucidating the concept of a right. It focuses attention on the sources of rights. If you are entitled to something, either you or someone else on your behalf must be able to answer the question: what entitles you to it? This presupposes that there are ways of becoming entitled to things. Three ways immediately come to mind – law, custom and morality. But more about them and how entitlements come about later. First, let us make use of the notion of entitlement to elucidate the concept of a right.

If you are entitled to something, for you to be denied it by the action or the failure to act of someone else is wrong. It is also wrong for other people to penalize you or to make you suffer for having it. This follows from the meaning of 'entitlement'. If it is not wrong for other people to deny you something, not wrong for them to penalize you or to make you suffer for having it, cannot be something to which you are entitled. It is therefore appropriate for entitlements to be called 'rights'. It you are entitled to something, it is right for you to have it. The role of other people is crucial in having a right. No wrong is done to you if you are denied what you are entitled to, not by the action or failure to act of other people, but by a natural event. If illness keeps you from a meeting which you are entitled to attend, that is unfortunate but no one is to blame. No right of yours has been violated. Not so if someone forcibly prevents you from attending. He is violating one of your rights and thereby doing wrong to you. This shows that what there can be rights to is limited to what can be affected by actions and forbearances for which people are responsible. No one can have a right to have fine weather on holiday or to have a talented son. These are cases of good fortune, not of entitlement.

It follows from all this that for any right it must be possible to say what action or failure to act would constitute a violation of it. If no such action or inaction is conceivable, there cannot be a right. A distinction drawn by D.D. Raphael is helpful here. According to him, rights are of two kinds, rights of action and rights of recipience.[1] To have a right of action is to be entitled to do something or to act in a certain way. To have a right of recipience is to be entitled to receive something or to be treated in a certain way. A right of recipience is violated when someone from whom you are entitled to receive something refuses to provide it, or when someone fails to accord you the treatment to which you are entitled, for example, if you are refused your old-age pension or treated with discourtesy. There is also a violation if you are made to suffer for demanding what you are entitled to receive, or abused or threatened for protesting against being denied the treatment to which you are entitled. A right of action is violated when someone intentionally stops you doing what you are entitled to do, or threatens you with dire consequences if you do it, for instance, if someone forcibly prevents you from voting, or tries to intimidate you into remaining silent when you are entitled to speak.

It is widely held that for every right, there must be some correlative obligation. What has been said about rights being limited to what can be affected by action and inaction for which people are responsible suggests that this is true. But some amplification is necessary. The key notion in the concept of obligation is that of an unconditional imperative. To have or to be under an obligation is to be subject to such an imperative. There is a general obligation to refrain from doing wrong. To violate anyone's rights is wrong. Everyone is therefore under a general obligation to refrain from doing anything which would violate anyone else's rights. It follows that at least one obligation is correlative to every right. This is an obligation upon everyone to refrain from doing anything which would violate the right. It is the only obligation which is necessarily correlative to every right of action. If you have a right to do something everyone else must have an obligation not to stop you doing it, not to interfere with you while you are doing it, and not to penalize you or make you suffer for having done it. The same obligation is correlative to rights of recipience. Everyone is under an obligation not to harass, abuse, penalize, or injure anyone for either demanding or receiving what he is entitled to. But in addition to this general obligation of forbearance, there are specific positive obligations which are correlative to rights of recipience. If you are entitled to receive something, there must be someone who is under an obligation to provide it. If you are entitled to certain treatment, there must be others with an obligation to accord it to you.

It is, however, also wrong for anyone to do anything which prevents anyone else from meeting an obligation, or which impedes or interferes with his meeting it. Equally it is wrong for anyone to be penalized or made to suffer for meeting an obligation. The general obligation of forbearance which is correlative to every right is also correlative to every other obligation. The general principle behind this is that it is wrong for what is right to be penalized, obstructed, threatened, or prevented. Hence, because it is right for people to have what they are entitled to, it is wrong for them to be denied it or penalized for having it. Equally, because it is right for people to meet their obligations, it is wrong for them to be prevented from or penalized for meeting them. But if it is right for people to have what they are entitled to and for them to meet their obligations, where does the difference between having a right and being under an obligation lie? A *prima facie* difference is this: when you are under an obligation, you must meet it unless some more pressing obligation supervenes, in which case you must meet the latter. Subject to this qualification, you do not have a choice about whether or not to meet an obligation. Not so in the case of a right. When you have a right, you are not obliged to exercise it. You have a choice. To be entitled to do something is also to be entitled to refrain from doing it. To be entitled to receive something is also to be entitled to decline it, or to acquiesce without protest if it is refused. There is, however, a difficulty about taking choice with respect to their exercise to be a universal characteristic of rights as such. There are at least some *prima facie* rights of recipience about the exercise of which there is no choice. I shall return to that in a moment, but first more needs to be said about obligation and the absence of choice.

To say that there is no choice about whether or not to meet an obligation is not to deny that it is physically possible not to meet it. In most countries the law imposes an obligation upon car-owners to insure their cars. It is physically possible for a man to drive his car without insuring it, but if he does so he does wrong. The obligation legally excludes choice but cannot physically exclude it. No human law can do that. By the same token, if I have made a promise, I am under a moral obligation to keep it. It is physically possible for me to break it but that would be wrong. The obligation morally excludes choice but cannot physically exclude it. No action can be either right or wrong unless it is one which it is physically possible for the agent either to do nor not to do. Choice is normatively excluded in the sense that a right action is one which must be done and a wrong action one which must not be done. To choose to do a wrong action or not to do a right one, while physically possible, is wrong. That to have a right is to have a choice is straightforward in the case of rights of action. If I have a right as distinct from being under an obligation to attend a meeting, I am entitled to choose whether or not to attend. Choice is normatively provided for, as well as being physically possible. This is also true of most rights of recipience. If I have made you a promise, not only am I under an obligation to keep it, you have a right that I should do so. But your right entitles you, if you choose, to release me from my obligation. It does not oblige you to insist that I do what I promised.

This is not so in all cases, however. The right of children to be looked after by their parents is a right of recipience from which choice is normatively excluded. Children are not entitled to decline parental care. Even if they do not want it, they must put up with it. It follows that if to have a right is to have a choice, children do not have a right to parental care but an obligation to submit to it. This is at variance with ordinary language. We do not say that children have an obligation to accept parental care but that they are entitled to it. This can be dealt with by distinguishing between elective and non-elective rights. Elective rights normatively confer choice, non-elective rights do not. The latter are those rights of recipience which entitle the rightholder to something but do not entitle him to decline it. But there is still a difference between having a non-elective right and being under an obligation. It lies in the fact that non-elective rights are essentially passive in character. Nothing is required from the rightholder. He is simply the beneficiary of certain treatment which others have an obligation to accord to him. Because they have an obligation to accord it to him, he can properly be said to be entitled, i.e. to have a right to it. Not only children but the mentally defective have non-elective rights to care. Animals have non-elective rights to humane treatment. These are, however, special cases. All the rights of sane, adult human beings are elective.

The distinction between rights of action and rights of recipience is between two different kinds of rights. Nevertheless, according to Wesley N. Hohfeld, there are not two but four different kinds of rights. Or rather, according to him, the term 'a right' is used for four different things which are conceptually distinct and which therefore need to be distinguished.[2] Hohfeld was concerned with legal rights, but according to at least one contemporary writer, the significance of his analysis is not confined to legal rights but extends to rights as such.[3] I shall use it here to supplement my own analysis. The four different kinds of rights are: claim-rights, liberty-rights, power-rights and immunity-rights. In terms of my analysis, they are all entitlements but to different kinds of things. Examples of claim-rights are the right of an old-age pensioner to receive a pension and of a promisee to have a promise kept. Examples of liberty-rights are the right of a man to spend his leisure as he chooses and his right to grow a beard if he wants to. A power-right entitles the rightholder to require other people to do certain things at his discretion. Examples are the rights of a landlord to alter the rent paid by his tenants and the right of a policeman to question those present at the scene of a crime. An immunity-right entitles the rightholder to be exempt from something, e.g. an MP to be exempt from the law of libel for what he says in Parliament, or a conscientious objector to be exempt from military service.[4]

According to Hohfeld, rights are advantages to their possessors. Such advantages entail 'correlates' in the form of disadvantages to second parties. The correlate of a claim-right is a duty. If you have the right to an old-age pension, there must be some agency with a duty to pay it to you. You can have the right to a sum of money from me only if I owe it to you and so have a duty to pay it to you. The correlate of a liberty-right is what Hohfeld calls a 'no-right'. If I have the right to spend Saturday afternoon as I please, no one has a right to require me to do anything during that time. If I have the right to grow a beard, no one can have a right requiring me to shave every day. The correlate of a power-right is a liability. A landlord has the right to determine the rent and his tenants are liable to pay what he requires. Witnesses are liable to be questioned by the police. The correlate of an immunity-right is a disability. Everyone is disabled, that is, lacks the power-right to sue an MP for what he says in Parliament. The military authorities are disabled from conscripting conscientious objectors, namely, they lack the power-right to conscript them. Apart from the case of claim-rights, these correlates are not identical with the obligations correlative to rights but they implicitly contain them. (The correlate of a claim-right is a duty or, in my terminology, an obligation.) Thus in the case of a liberty-right, everyone has an obligation to refrain from interfering with its exercise. Those subject to a power-right have an obligation to do what it makes them liable to do whenever the rightholder decides to exercise it. Those disabled by an immunity-right have an obligation to respect the immunity it confers.

Hohfeld's analysis preserves while amplifying the action-recipience distinction. Claim-rights and immunity-rights are respectively rights of positive and of negative recipience. In the language of John Stuart Mill, liberty-rights are rights of self-regarding action, while power-rights are rights of other-regarding action.[5] In speaking of rights as 'advantages', Hohfeld must have been using the term in its non-competitive sense. But to avoid misunderstanding it is better to say that a right is an entitlement to a presumptive 'benefit', because the point of any right is that having it is in some way for the rightholder's good; 'presumptive' because having and exercising the right cannot guarantee that the intended good will materialize. Raising the rent may mean that the landlord loses his tenants. If rights are entitlements to presumptive benefits, their correlates are better described simply as 'requirements' than as 'disadvantages'. A merit of Hohfeld's analysis is to call attention to the complexity which the simple term 'a right' may sometimes conceal. Take the case of the right to vote. At first sight it is a straightforward liberty-right. The rightholder has a right to vote according to his own choice and everyone else has an obligation not to interfere with him. But this entails that he has a claim-right upon the police to protection from interference, a claim-right which it is their duty to meet. If the ballot is secret, he has an immunity-right not to answer questions about how he voted. He is entitled to the privacy of the polling-booth and therefore has a claim-right upon the officials at the polling-station to provide him with this privacy. What initially appears to be a single right turns out to be a cluster of rights.

ON THE SOURCES AND SIGNIFICANCE OF RIGHTS AND OBLIGATIONS

How can the assertion that you have a right be justified? What entitles you and obliges me? In the case of a legal right the answer is this: this right is conferred and its correlative obligations imposed by a particular law which is part of the legal system in a community to which you and I both belong. As members we are both subject to the law, and it is because the law says so that, for example, you are entitled to compensation for an injury due to my negligence, and I am under an obligation to pay up. But custom as well as positive law is a source of rights and obligations. The queue is a familiar custom in British life. According to this custom, when you are at the head of a queue you have the right to be served next, and I as the shopkeeper or official have an obligation correlative to your right to attend to you next. The custom, which as fellow Britons we both accept, confers the right and imposes its correlative obligation. Morality is also a source. An example of a moral right given by A.I. Melden is that of a father to receive preferential treatment from his grown-up son.[6] Another is promise-keeping. You have a right that I keep my word, and I have a correlative obligation to do what I promised. Morality consists of virtues which there is an obligation to practise, principles upon which there is an obligation to act, and rules which there is an obligation to follow, these being the expression of shared moral convictions, i.e. convictions about human life and conduct. It is because you and I share certain moral convictions and acknowledge the virtues, principles and rules which they embody, that on appropriate occasions you are morally entitled and I am morally obliged.

It is often said that rights are essentially social in character. This is obviously true of legal and customary rights since law and custom are social institutions. Every system of law is the system of a particular community, and the same is true of every body of custom. It is therefore as members of communities that people have legal and customary rights. This is also true of the rights which go with membership of associations such as clubs, trade unions and universities. These rights are quasi-legal in the sense that they are conferred and their correlative obligations imposed by the rules of the association. It is as members of the association that people come to have them. But is it true of moral rights? Moral convictions are convictions about human conduct, not merely the conduct of the members of a particular community. They are not always and everywhere the same. Different traditions of culture and civilization give rise to different moral convictions, which give rise to different ideas about the nature and significance of human life and are reflected in different moral virtues, principles and rules. Our own Western culture and civilization is only one of several such traditions in the world today. Others are the Islamic, the Hindu and the Buddhist, to name only three, each of which is centred round a great religion.[7] This suggests that while moral rights may not be social, they are essentially 'culture-bound'. Or rather that there can be 'cross-cultural' moral rights only to the extent that there are moral convictions which are common to more than one tradition.

There is however an important respect in which morality itself is social. Without it, there could be no trust, and trust is necessary for social life as such. Without trust, people cannot live together. They need to be able at least for the most part to rely upon one another to be truthful and honest, to refrain from unprovoked violence, and more generally not to take unfair advantage of one another. This mutual reliance is possible only between people, each of whom acknowledges that it is right to act in such ways and believes that the others acknowledge it too. They must, that is to say, be moral agents who share, and are aware that they share, common convictions about right and wrong conduct. This does not mean that morality is instrumental in character. It is not a means to the end of social living but rather part of what is involved in living socially. A person becomes a moral agent as he grows up in and becomes a member of a community. Early in his life, he learns that he cannot simply do as he likes. Certain ways of acting are right, others are wrong, and he is morally required, i.e. has a general obligation, to do whatever is right and to refrain from doing whatever is wrong.

As a member, however, he not only has obligations; he also necessarily has rights. Having both rights and obligations is part of the concept of social membership. Part of what it is to be a member of any social group, whether it is a community, an association or a family, is to have both certain things which are due to you from fellow members and certain things which are due from you to them. As a member you must be morally entitled to share in whatever benefits accrue to the group, as well as being morally required to contribute to securing them, and more generally to whatever is necessary to maintain the corporate existence of the group. If you have only obligations but no rights, if while certain things are due from you nothing at all is due to you, your status is that of a slave rather than a member. So far as the group is concerned, you are merely a means to be used for its benefit, not yours. On the other hand, if you have only rights but no obligations, if while certain things are due to you nothing at all is due from you, again you do not have the status of a member. You are a beneficiary of the group's activities without being morally required to make any contribution to them. All this shows that moral rights are social as well as cultural. They are social in the same respect as morality is social. But their cultural character remains significant. The particular moral rights which a member of a community has will be informed by ideas, beliefs and values from the tradition of culture and civilization of which his community is a part.

Many moral rights arise out of social institutions and roles which differ from one community to another. In contemporary British society a girl has a moral right to decide for herself whether or not to accept an offer of marriage. Not so an Indian girl in traditional Hindu society. The offer is made not to her but to her parents, and she has a moral obligation to accept their decision. The right to form and join trade unions is a moral right arising out of moral convictions about industrial relations. But there can be such a right only where there is an industrial economy with a system of contract labour. It is inapplicable in a nomadic community or in a tribal community with a subsistence economy. The rights of patients in relation to doctors and of clients in relation to lawyers are moral rights which are usually embodied in codes of professional ethics. Clearly there can be such rights only where the professions of medicine and law have developed to a relatively advanced stage. Or again take the rights of constituents in relation to their MPs or their elected representatives. These too are moral rights. They arise from convictions about how people should treat one another in the special context of representative government. There can be such rights only where there are representative political institutions, and many communities do not have them. These are cases of moral rights which are social in the sense that people can have them only as members of particular communities. They presuppose certain kinds of institutions and roles which are not found in every community.

It is important to appreciate the complex relations between law, custom and morality. In the first place, morality is logically prior to law. While there can be morality without law, there cannot be law without morality. While law can create particular obligations, it cannot create the general obligation to obey law. To enact a law prescribing obedience to law would be pointless. It presupposes the existence of the very thing it is intended to create: the general obligation to obey law. That obligation is necessarily moral. Law can come into being only in a community whose members *ex hypothesi* are moral agents and who are therefore able and willing, at least for the most part, to meet moral obligations. A community in which it has come into being benefits from it. Law can protect many moral rights from violation. It provides greater security for persons and property. It also enables a community to organize and regulate its affairs for the benefit of all its members. Through law, public ends can be attained which either could not be attained at all without it or only attained with partial success. The logical priority of morality to law means that law should conform to moral requirements. In a homogeneous community whose members share substantially the same moral convictions, this does not pose major problems. Matters are different in a pluralistic community whose members have moral convictions drawn from different cultural and especially different religious traditions. Where there is moral controversy, the effectiveness of law as a vehicle of social co-operation is inevitably reduced. In morally contentious matters, for instance divorce, contraception, abortion and euthanasia, personal choice rather than legal prescription may be socially less divisive. But this will be the case only if there is a tolerant attitude on the part of those who hold contrary moral convictions, and that cannot be counted on.

Custom provides continuity and predictability in social life. Both are in the interest of any community. Hence there is a moral obligation on the part of members, and also on the part of visitors, to observe existing customs. 'When in Rome, do as the Romans.' A waiter is entitled to a tip not merely because he has served me but because in our society it is customary for waiters to be tipped by diners. But while custom is a good servant, it is a bad master. If a community is to survive, its members must respond positively to changed circumstances and to the moral and social implications of new knowledge and better understanding, if necessary by abandoning some long-standing customs. Legislation can help by enacting new rights and altering or abolishing existing ones, i.e. by deliberately changing the presumptive benefits to which members are legally entitled. But this must be met by a positive response from the members, and that may not always be forthcoming. People are often reluctant to accept reforms which change what they are used to, for example, new legal rights for women or for ethnic minorities which enlarge their career opportunities, but which conflict with the customs which hitherto have defined their status and roles in society. While the importance of enacting new legal rights must not be underestimated, the limitations of such enactments must be appreciated. New legal rights can facilitate social reforms to the extent that the potential for such reforms already exists. To the extent that it does not, new legal rights can only be palliatives.

THE IDEA OF HUMAN RIGHTS

If the adjective 'human' is to be taken seriously, the idea of human rights must be the idea that there are certain rights which, whether or not they are acknowledged, belong to all human beings at all times and in all places. These are the rights which they have solely in virtue of being human irrespective of nationality, religion, sex, social status, occupation, wealth, property, or any other differentiating ethnic, cultural and social characteristics. Now we have just seen that people have rights as members of particular communities and through their commitment to particular traditions of culture and civilization. What rights can they have solely in virtue of being human? A man becomes the person and the human being that he is through growing up in a particular community, learning to speak its language, and learning to participate in its life. There must be some community for him to grow up in if he is to be a person and, in more than a purely zoological sense, a human being at all. But what community it is makes a difference to who and what he is. If his native community had been different, in important respects he would have been a different person from the one he has in fact become. His native language would have been different. So would have been many of the ideas, beliefs and values in terms of which he has been brought up to think, feel and act. Human beings cannot be culturally and socially neutral. Every human being is necessarily largely made what he is by his particular cultural and social environment. Different traditions of culture and civilization are different ways of being human. These considerations point to difficulties in the idea of human rights. It appears to ignore moral and cultural diversity and to take no account of the social and cultural basis of personal identity.

These difficulties do not arise if the idea of human rights is interpreted as being the idea of a minimum standard. More fully stated, this is the idea that there are certain rights, respect for which is required by a universal minimum moral standard. But must not such a standard necessarily be drawn from a particular tradition of culture and civilization and so fail to be universal? Not if it has its roots in certain requirements of social life as such, irrespective of the particular form it takes. That would make the standard applicable to all cultures and civilizations, regardless of the differences between them. Such a standard does not deny that every human being is largely made what he is by his particular cultural and social environment. It does not presuppose human beings who are culturally and socially neutral. Rather it presupposes moral and cultural diversity but sets minimum moral requirements to be met by all societies and all cultures. These requirements set moral limits to the range of diversity but in no way deny its existence. The universal applicability of the minimum moral standard entails that the rights for which it requires respect should be universally acknowledged. In an intelligible sense they are the moral rights of all human beings at all times and in all places, i.e. universal moral rights, or human rights properly so-called. But can it be shown that there is such a standard? In the limited space available, I shall indicate how the idea of it is rationally defensible.

Moral diversity cannot be total. This is because certain moral principles are necessary for social life as such, irrespective of its particular form. Of these, seven are sources of rights and I shall confine my discussion to them. It is convenient to divide them into two groups, the first containing two, the second five. The two in the first group are respect for human life and justice: the five in the second, fellowship, social responsibility, freedom from arbitrary interference, honourable treatment, and civility. Respect for human life in the limited form of respect for the lives of all fellow members is essential in any community to provide internal security. It forbids wanton killing and requires that no member's life should ever be unnecessarily endangered. The principle does not mean that no member's life can ever be taken. But it requires that this must always be justified as, for instance, a legally prescribed punishment, self-defence, or a vindication of personal honour. Justice in the general form of 'to each his due' is also essential in any community. It requires that each member should render what is due from him to his fellow members and should receive what is due to him from them. Without this principle, there could be no such status as that of member and hence no community. What in detail is due to and from each member depends upon the particular community, its social order, institutions and values. But there is one thing which is always due to and from every member whatever a community's particular form. This is fair treatment, the classical formulation of which is contained in Aristotle's principle of 'proportionate equality'.[8] If a community is not to be torn apart by internal dissension, benefits and burdens must be allocated according to need and capacity, while praise and blame, reward and punishment, must be apportioned according to desert. When interests compete, the terms of the competition must be fair, i.e. afford tó each an equal chance of success.

Justice in its general form of 'to each his due' includes the five principles in the second group because acting upon them is due from every member to every member in all their relationships. But they need to be distinguished both from justice and from one another. From justice because they are not the same as fair treatment; from one another, because it is for different reasons that each is essential for social life. Fellowship requires members to assist any among them who are in distress. People who are totally indifferent to one another's well-being cannot constitute a community at all. Social responsibility requires every member to give precedence to the interest of the community over his personal self-interest whenever they conflict. Without this principle, the community's interest would go by default and its survival as a community would be endangered. Freedom from arbitrary interference is necessary to enable members to go about their business without molestation and in safety. Interference with the freedom of action of any member is arbitrary unless it can be morally justified, i.e. shown to be specifically necessary for the good of the community. Honourable treatment forbids all duplicity. It requires members to keep their agreements and to deal honestly in all their transactions. Without it, there could be no basis for trust and no possibility of systematic co-operation. Civility forbids unprovoked violence and requires all members to treat one another with respect in all their relationships. They must refrain from shocking, insulting, or humiliating one another. On the positive side they must treat one another with respect and with courtesy, which means not only observing conventions of good manners but showing consideration and sensitivity. A community can tolerate both dishonourable behaviour and incivility on the part of some of its members, but it cannot survive if all its members reject the obligations to behave honourably and with civility.

It is convenient to refer to these seven principles as principles of 'common' morality because they are common to every community, whatever its particular form, its social order, institutions and values. We have already seen that having both rights and obligations is part of the concept of social membership.[9] Part of what it is to be a member of a community is to have certain things which are due to you from fellow members and certain things which are due from you to them. Now acting on the seven principles is due from every member of a community to every other member. Each principle puts every member under an obligation to meet its requirements in all dealings with fellow members, and with one exception confers upon him a right to have its requirements met by them in all their dealings with him. The exception is social responsibility. It confers a right not upon the members individually but upon the community corporately to regulate its members' conduct for the sake of the community's interest, a right exercised by agents authorized to act on the community's behalf.[10] There are therefore six rights which every member of a community necessarily has in virtue of his status as a member, rights each of which all his fellow members have an obligation to respect in virtue of their status as members. They are the right to life, the right to justice in the form of fair treatment, the right to aid in the sense of the right to have so far as possible his distress relieved, the right to freedom from arbitrary interference, the right to honourable treatment, and the right to civility. Justice in its general form is the moral foundation of all these rights because it requires that every member should receive what is due to him. There is injustice whenever, owing to the intentional action or inaction of some other member, he does not receive it, and therefore injustice whenever any one of his six rights is violated.

A community's actual morality is never confined to common morality although it always includes it. This is because every community is an individual community with its own distinctive way of life, social order, institutions and values. These generate further virtues, principles and rules, together with specific rights and obligations connected to them. I shall call such virtues, principles and rules, with their associated rights and obligations, 'particular' morality. The actual morality of any community is always a union of common morality with a particular morality. The former consists of the general moral principles which in virtue of being a community it has in common with every other community. The latter comprises the specific virtues, principles and rules which constitute its particular way of life and make it the individual community it is. It is differences between the particular moralities of different communities which give rise to the diversity of morals. That diversity is the moral dimension of cultural diversity. Because the principles of common morality apply to every community, their detailed requirements must be contextually interpreted, i.e. interpreted with reference to an individual community's particular morality and the particular culture which generates that morality. The same is true of the rights conferred by the principles of common morality. Thus what these rights entitle people to is not always and everywhere the same. The right of Muslim women to freedom of action is much more restricted than is the corresponding right of contemporary Western women. But the restrictions to which Muslim women are subject are not arbitrary. They are justified by Islamic religious morality. They would, however, be arbitrary if imposed upon Western women because they are not justified by contemporary Western secular liberal morality.

My argument so far shows that common morality is applicable within every community to all dealings between members but not that it is universally applicable. To show that it is a universal moral standard, I must show that it is applicable not only within but between communities and to human relations as such. That means showing that there are rational grounds for not confining it to fellow countrymen and co-religionists but for extending it to foreigners, infidels and heretics. If the scope of common morality is confined to fellow countrymen, it follows that so far as they are concerned, foreigners have no rights. Fellow countrymen have no obligations to them and need have no scruples about exploiting, enslaving or killing them. Foreigners have no moral status and in Kantian language can be treated merely as a means.[11] Now there is an elementary but fundamental principle of practical reason which requires that cases which are alike in all relevant respects must be treated alike. There should be differential treatment only where there are relevant differences and in accordance with those differences. Let us apply this to the scope of common morality. Is the difference between fellow countrymen and foreigners a relevant difference, i.e. a difference which justifies any of the former treating any of the latter 'merely as a means'?

There are obvious differences, of which fellow countrymen are well aware, between foreigners and themselves. Foreigners live in other communities, speak 'foreign' languages, and have different cultural traditions, values, institutions and customs. But whether or not fellow countrymen take account of it, there are other respects in which they and foreigners are alike. Like fellow countrymen, they value their own existence and possess the distinctively human capacity for formulating and pursuing purposes of their own. No less than fellow countrymen, they are susceptible to suffering. They too have hopes and fears, joys and sorrows. Within their own communities they are moral agents who have rights and obligations which include, but are not confined to, those of common morality. If fellow countrymen treat foreigners merely as a means, they are denying these fundamental respects in which they and foreigners are alike. Foreigners are not their fellow countrymen but they are their fellow human beings, that is, they are people who like themselves act within their own communities upon the principles of common morality, and with whom association and co-operation is possible. I conclude from all this that there are rational grounds for extending the scope of common morality to include all human beings. This can be done by incorporating into common morality the principle that all human beings are fellow human beings, which I shall call for brevity the 'humanity principle'.

Thus foreigners no less than fellow countrymen have the six rights conferred by the principles of common morality. As a fellow human being, a foreigner no less than a fellow countryman is entitled not to be wantonly killed and not to have his life unnecessarily endangered. He is entitled to be treated fairly, to have his distress relieved, not to be arbitrarily interfered with, to be dealt with honourably, and to be treated with civility. To violate any of these rights in the case of a foreigner while respecting it in the case of a fellow countryman, is not to treat like cases alike but to treat them differently in the absence of relevant differences. What is true of foreigners is equally true of all those who, while living within a community, are denied moral status within it, e.g. slaves, serfs and 'untouchables'. They too are fellow human beings. The denial to them of moral status and of the six rights of common morality, rights which by the humanity principle are human rights properly so-called, cannot be justified. Historically the humanity principle has all too often been honoured in the breach rather than the observance. But that does not invalidate it. To the extent that the particular morality of any community endorses institutions such as slavery and serfdom which deny moral status to certain human beings, the humanity principle shows it in that respect to be morally defective.

The incorporation of the humanity principle into common morality converts it into a universal minimum moral standard. It is 'universal' because it is applicable to all human relations; 'minimum' because provided that its requirements are satisfied, it has nothing to say about moral diversity. Its requirements set moral limits to the range of moral diversity by excluding as morally indefensible any institution or practice which denies moral status to any human being. But within these limits the range is considerable. Different religious moralities, e.g. Christianity, Judaism, Islam and Buddhism, are compatible with its requirements. So is secular humanism. Its requirements include the universal acknowledgement of the six rights conferred by the principles of common morality. In an intelligible sense, these are the rights of all human beings at all times and in all places, i.e. universal moral rights, or human rights properly so-called. But like the principles which are their source, they must be contextually interpreted. We have already seen this in the case of the right to freedom from arbitrary interference. What counts as 'arbitrary' is different in Islamic and in contemporary Western society. In the case of the right to life, what counts as 'wanton' killing is not always and everywhere the same. The taking of life involved in the 'blood-feud', euthanasia and abortion, is justified or at least permitted according to some moral codes, unjustified and therefore wanton according to others. What in detail the other rights entitle people to is equally subject to contextual interpretation.

This last point is of crucial importance. Earlier I pointed out that different traditions of culture and civilization are different ways of being human. There are no culturally and socially neutral human beings. That is why human rights must be contextually interpreted. They are the rights which people have not as human beings in the abstract but as human beings living in particular traditions of culture and civilization. They must therefore be interpreted in terms of a particular morality grounded in a particular tradition with its characteristic institutions and values, if they are to have content. Time was when the various traditions were relatively self-contained, contact between them being limited and sporadic. But modern science and technology have changed all that. Our era is one of global interdependence. There is now continuous contact between the various traditions, contact which has often generated conflict. That it should have done so is not surprising in the absence of a common framework within which to interpret human rights and the requirements of the universal minimum moral standard. This brings us back to relations between fellow countrymen and foreigners. It is up to both to create and maintain procedures and practices in the contexts in which they have dealings which will serve as a common framework. That calls for mutual respect, tolerance and above all the acknowledgement that, despite their differences, they are fellow human beings. Not withstanding conflicts of interest, mutual suspicion and fear, there has been at least some progress in that direction. In the age of nuclear weapons and increasing danger to the natural environment, common self-interest is an incentive to further progress. An understanding of the requirements of the universal minimum moral standard and of human rights properly so-called can also help.

RIGHTS AND OBLIGATIONS IN POLITICS AND INTERNATIONAL RELATIONS

Human rights are moral rather than political rights. More accurately, it is only if contextual interpretation requires it that any of them can become political rights. People not only can but have lived together without formal political organization, namely, in tribal communities of food-gatherers, hunters and nomads. There are no political rights which people have solely in virtue of being human, no political rights which belong to them at all times and in all places. But anarchists to the contrary notwithstanding, government has much to contribute to social life. Today virtually all human communities are governed communities, i.e. formally organized political communities. These take the form of nation-states, of which there are now more than 150, and this political organization of social life has implications for the contextual interpretation of human rights. The justification for the authority of government is that the governed benefit from its exercise. One way in which they benefit is that their rights as members of the governed community, including those conferred upon them by the principles of common morality, can be better protected than would be the case without government. The universal minimum moral standard requires this benefit to be extended to all human beings who are subject to a government's jurisdiction. It must therefore protect the human rights of all of them, whether or not they have the formal status of members of the community. Furthermore, in the case of all human beings who are not subject to its jurisdiction, a government is morally required never deliberately to violate, and always so far as it can to respect, their human rights.

But governments, like all things human, are both fallible and corruptible. They notoriously abuse their authority and the coercive power which reinforces it. But there are legal remedies for this abuse when the government is constitutional, that is, subject to the rule of law. Where this is so, the scope and limits of the government's authority are prescribed by law. All human beings subject to that authority have two constitutional rights. One is the right to the equal protection of the law. The other is the right to freedom under the law, i.e. the right where the law is silent to act according to personal choice and decision. But if human rights are to be protected, there is an important proviso about the content of the law. It must not itself violate human rights, for instance, by maintaining slavery, serfdom or racial segregation. The latter violate the right to fair treatment because they require like cases to be treated differently. Purely physical differences such as colour cannot count as morally relevant differences. The law must also do what it can to protect human rights. The honest, impartial and efficient enforcement of the criminal law is clearly vital here. It is logically possible for a government not subject to the rule of law, for instance an enlightened absolute monarchy or a benevolent dictatorship, not to violate the human rights of its subjects and to protect them effectively. But under such a government, human rights are always at risk because there are no legal remedies for the abuse of political authority. If they are not to be at risk, the government must be constitutional. All subject to its jurisdiction must have the two constitutional rights, and the content of the law must satisfy the minimum moral standard when that standard, in Collingwood's words, is 'transposed into the key of politics'.[12]

The two constitutional rights are the political analogues of two human rights. These are the right to fair treatment and the right to freedom from arbitrary interference. They are what the latter become when interpreted in political contexts. Violations of them are violations of the two human rights. To be denied the equal protection of the law is to be treated unfairly. To suffer illegal interference is to be interfered with arbitrarily. There are no political analogues of the other four human rights. There are, that is to say, only two political rights which directly embody human rights, and they are the two constitutional rights. There is much to be said for liberal democratic and social welfare rights wherever social, cultural and economic conditions make their legal recognition possible. But they do not embody human rights and are not required for their protection. The majority of humanity have never enjoyed liberal democratic and social welfare rights. For the foreseeable future, they will have to manage without them for economic and cultural reasons, quite apart from political obstacles. Nor can Bills of Rights, characteristic of the constitutions of many democratic states, be declarations of human rights properly so-called unless they are confined to the two constitutional rights. They are better described as declarations of the fundamental rights of the citizens for the states concerned. All too many governments today are not subject to the rule of law. But to require that they should be, that all subject to their jurisdiction should have the two constitutional rights, and that their legal systems should satisfy the proviso are not utopian demands. Nor need talk of human rights in political contexts be utopian so long as it is confined to the two constitutional rights.

As a principle of common morality 'social responsibility' is applicable in every community and association. But it can be applicable to human relations as such only if there is an intelligible sense in which humanity constitutes a genuine community. International law presupposes the idea of an international community. Today we have in the United Nations a practical expression of that idea. But there is an objection to equating an international organization such as the UN with a single community of humanity. This is that the members of the former are nation-states, which in practice means national governments. Individual human beings are members only in virtue of their membership of individual nation-states. This means that any human beings who because of race, colour or creed, or for any other reason, are denied membership of the nation-state in which they live, or who do not live in a nation-state at all, are thereby denied membership of the international community. As members of that community, national governments are committed to common morality in all their dealings with one another. The universal minimum moral standard extends that commitment to their dealings with all human beings. But their membership of the international community does not of itself entail this wider commitment. A national government can meet the requirements of common morality in all its dealings with other governments while violating the universal minimum moral standard in its treatment of some of its own subjects – by maintaining slavery, promoting racial segregation, or simply not acknowledging the two constitutional rights. A despotic government can be a responsible member of the international community.

This objection is not, however, decisive. Humanity today consists of more than 4,000 million human beings. It can therefore constitute a genuine community only as some form of international community, i.e. as a universal community of communities. The objection shows only that the UN today is a far from perfect embodiment of such a universal community. This is not because of any inherent defects in the structure and organization of the UN.

Rather it is because of moral defects within its member nations, and because of a less than complete commitment by many of them to the UN as an international community. 'Social responsibility' is applicable in an international community. The interest of that community is in establishing and maintaining conditions which will enable every member nation not only to survive but so far as possible to prosper. International 'social responsibility' therefore requires all national governments to co-operate in the pursuit of that interest, subordinating the pursuit of national self-interest to it wherever necessary. Two conditions which are obviously in the interest of an international community today are the preservation of world peace and the conservation of the natural environment. Others include checking the growth of the world's human population and the reduction of poverty. The UN is a far from perfect embodiment of a universal human community. But it is sufficient to provide a global context for the application of 'social responsibility' as a principle of common morality extended to human relationships as such. The humanity principle, the principle that all human beings are fellow human beings, requires national governments to interpret their responsibilities as members of the UN in ways which will make it a better embodiment of a universal human community.

To the extent that national governments are committed to common morality in all their dealings, they have the rights and obligations conferred and imposed by the principles of that morality. But these must be contextually interpreted to fit the circumstances of an international community. The right to life is the right to national existence. This includes both an immunity-right and a power-right. The former is the right to immunity from foreign conquest, the latter the right to resist it when it is attempted. The right to fair treatment includes a claim-right to impartial ajudication in international disputes and an immunity-right to non-discrimination in international trade. The right to aid includes a claim-right to help in natural disasters and to assistance in establishing and maintaining a viable national economy. The right to freedom from arbitrary interference includes immunity-rights to non-interference in internal affairs and to non-aggression, together with power-rights to resist both. It also includes a liberty-right to pursue domestic national policies of the government's own choice, this being a corollary of the right to non-interference. The right to honourable treatment includes claim-rights to the observance of treaties and international agreements and an immunity-right to be free from foreign subversion. The right to civility includes a claim-right to be treated according to established diplomatic procedures. The obligations correlative to these rights consist of the acts and forbearances necessary to respect them. As a member of the international community, every government is under these obligations in all its dealings with other governments while itself having the rights to which they are correlative.

In connection with the relations between fellow countrymen and foreigners, I referred to the need for a common framework to interpret human rights. In the case of an international community, there is a similar need since the rights of member nations must be interpreted. International law and the conventions of diplomacy provide the rudiments of such a framework. But while this can help to contain international conflicts, it can provide neither the authority nor the power to settle them. Hence the ubiquity of war as the ultimate arbiter of international conflicts. The existence of an international community does not mean that international conflicts cease to arise. In the economic sphere, national self-interest and the international community's interest are not identical. A nation's interest abroad is in conditions which will enable it to prosper, not in conditions which will enable all nations to prosper. There is no pre-established international harmony which guarantees that what promotes one nation's prosperity necessarily promotes the prosperity of all. But while there is often an economic dimension, not all international conflicts are economic in origin. Many arise from deeply felt grievances about alleged past wrongs, long-standing religious and (especially today) ideological hostility, and the consequences of domestic revolution. International law and diplomatic conventions may be insufficient to enable the parties to a conflict to agree about the interpretation of their respective rights and obligations. What to one nation is aggression to another is the legitimate defence of its vital national interests, or the justified rectification of a past wrong. When what is fair is in dispute, appeals to the right to fair treatment will be unavailing.

Earlier I referred to a pluralistic community and to the moral controversies which arise within it.[13] An international community is a pluralistic community 'writ-large'. Not only are there many conflicts of national interest, but also and often different traditions of culture and civilization generate different conflicting particular moralities in different national communities.

While nation-states formally acknowledge the rights and obligations of membership in an international community, too much should not be expected of that formal acknowledgement. Nor should too much be expected of human rights, the more so because national governments notoriously violate them in the case of their own subjects. But the significance of the idea of human rights as a minimum standard should not be underestimated. In international conflicts it can serve as a check to the worst excesses. In war, it requires acknowledgement of the distinction between combatants and civilians, of the rights of prisoners of war to honourable and civil treatment, and of the immunity-rights of neutrals. There is widespread, if not universal, recognition of these requirements today. There is also international recognition of the right to aid of victims of natural disasters, of refugees, and of others who are casualties of war and revolution. Previously I said that the humanity principle requires national governments to interpret their responsibilities as members of the UN in ways which will make it a better embodiment of a universal human community.[14] The idea of human rights as a minimum standard is the basis for that interpretation. How best to act upon it is a challenge to creative international statesmanship.

NOTES AND REFERENCES

1. D.D. Raphael, *Problems of Political Philosophy* (London: Macmillan, 1970) pp. 68–70.
2. W.N. Hohfeld, *Fundamental Legal Conceptions* (New Haven: Yale University Press, 1964) pp. 36.
3. C. Wellman, 'A New Conception of Human Rights' in E. Kamenka and A.E.-S. Tay (eds.), *Human Rights* (London: Edward Arnold, 1978) pp. 48–58.
4. These examples are mine, not Hohfeld's. They include moral as well as legal rights to show that his analysis extends to rights as such.
5. J.S. Mill, *Utilitarianism, On Liberty, and Considerations on Representative Government* (London: J.M. Dent, 1972) pp. 131–49.
6. A.I. Melden, *Rights and Right Conduct* (Oxford: Blackwell, 1959) p. 6.,
7. Until this century, our tradition might well have been described as 'Christian culture and civilization'. Today 'post-Christian' or 'secularized Christian' would be more accurate. I pass over the question of whether there can be said to be a Communist tradition of culture and civilization for two reasons. One is that because Communism has been imposed upon the people who live under it, it is questionable whether it can be said to constitute a tradition. Admittedly, both Christianity and Islam were originally imposed upon many people but over the centuries came to be widely accepted. There has hardly been enough

time since the imposition of Communism for this to happen. The other is that since Communists' ideas and values originated in the West, there is a case for regarding Communism as a Western heresy rather than an authentic tradition in its own right. But that cannot be pursued here.

8. Aristotle, *The Nicomachean Ethics of Aristotle* (London: Oxford University Press, 1959) Book V, p. 106.

9. See pp. 16–18.

10. This is a Hohfeldian power-right. Its correlate is the moral liability of the members to have their activities regulated for the sake of their community's interest and therefore entails a correlative obligation to comply with whatever regulations are made to promote that interest.

11. I. Kant, *Fundamental Principles of the Metaphysics of Ethics* 10th ed. (London: Longmans, Green, 1946), p. 56.

12. R. G. Collingwood, *The New Leviathan* (London: Oxford University Press, 1944) p. 214.

13. See pp. 18–19.

14. See pp. 29–30.

2 Europe and the World: The Imperial Record

V.G. KIERNAN

> Earth is sick,
> And Heaven is weary, of the hollow words
> Which States and Kingdoms utter when they talk
> Of truth and justice.
>
> (Wordsworth, *The Excursion*, Book 5)

A hundred years ago a Lhasa official said to a Briton from India: 'Thibetans like to remain in their own land; how is it that the English are always craving for the territories of others?'[1] It was a question with a very wide bearing, considering that so much of history has been a matter of peoples trespassing on one another's soil. In modern times Europeans have done so most conspicuously. It may be reckoned to them as a sign of grace that they have learned to be capable in some degree of self-criticism over their conduct; it is unlikely that Roman intruders, Chinese, Arabs, or Turks ever acquired this capacity, except over some odd particular outrage. But far louder today than any self-reproaches of Europe are recriminations from the countries that it annexed, or meddled with. Looking back on its collective past, contemplating its present condition, this 'Third World' more and more loudly demands reparation by way of a better share of our planet's good things. Burke could only recommend the suffering and oppressed to await the final proportions of eternal justice; today, the poorer nations are as little inclined to follow such advice as the poorer classes.

Their claims rest on charges of injury, plundering, and impoverishment by the West, not of a material kind alone. On the other side there are benefits, tangible or less ponderable, to be set against what was appropriated. In some ways at least, it is scarcely

34

possible not to recognize a heavy balance against Europe. But to draw up an account-sheet, with every ramifying consequence included, would baffle any but the eye of Omniscience. O'Henry has a story about a well-meaning young man, inheritor of an ill-gotten fortune, who is anxious to make restitution; a carping socialist convinces him that to make good all the secondary and tertiary evils it was responsible for would more than swallow up all his money.

What is most easily discernible among the gains and losses belongs to the material sphere; to translate it into moral terms is harder, and a task historians are little qualified to undertake. Ever since they turned into a regular professional body, a hundred years ago, they have prided themselves on a strict objectivity, eschewing any concern with ethics (though not always with patriotism). What meaning history without regard to morality can possess, they have not explained. Vico thought of men unconsciously fulfilling the purposes of Providence; others in search of a meaning may sometimes feel drawn to a comforting notion of an automatically functioning distribution of good and ill, like the self-adjusting market of the economists. Portuguese and later Europeans descended on Asia and Africa to enrich themselves by fair means or foul, but they brought with them a wide range of useful new plants and animals.

One complication is that Europe through most of its annals has been closely entangled with its neighbours. Rome spread over parts of Asia and Africa as well as much of Europe; Ottoman sultans reigned over parts of Europe and Africa as well as of Asia. A clear-cut antithesis of Europe and its neighbours has only emerged in recent times. Not all its governments were colony-seekers; some were only over a brief span. All countries within the European orbit benefited however, as Adam Smith pointed out, from colonial contributions to a common stock of wealth,[2] bitterly as they might wrangle over ownership of one territory or another. The latest, if not last, colonial wars were fought by single countries, but with enough backing from others to make all the capitalist West their accomplice. Much devastation by the Portuguese in Africa was carried out with equipment supplied by NATO.[3] But since 1917 an always deeply divided Europe has been split in a new way, with the peculiarity of a large expanse of Asia continuing to be linked with Russia and sharing its socialist orientation. Neither camp has failed to put its own interests first, but those of the USSR, and Eastern Europe since

1945, have been substantially more in harmony with those of the Third World, and their dealings with it far less open to censure.

Badly as Europeans might often treat colonial peoples, they were ready to be quite as brutal with one another when conflict broke out between nations, or as in Spain in 1936 between classes. This had its counterpart in the way non-Europeans were accustomed to harry one another, until partially restrained from doing so by the European ascendancy. German propaganda had an axe to grind, when Germany was being deprived of its colonies after the Great War on the ground of unfitness to rule, with its tale of Hottentots – 'doomed to degeneration and extinction by their own vices' – getting into South-West Africa and preying on the villainous Herreros, who in turn, until the coming of the German flag, preyed on the hapless Berg-Damaras.[4] All the same, Africa and most of the Third World really were a *Dar-al-Harb*, a realm of war, no peaceful garden of Eden for the 'merchant-thieves of Frangistan' to break into.

One feature that stands out is the surprisingly high proportion of Africa and Asia, including both India and China, under alien or half-alien rule. West African societies frequently consisted of an intrusive people superimposed on an earlier one, ethnic discord taking the place of Europe's class discord; further south the Matabele dominance over the Mashonas of what is now Zimbabwe was of a similar character. Fanon's dictum that 'it is the settler who has brought the native into existence'[5] overlooks all this. Revolts of many kinds were endemic; so were wars. Most of the black slaves carried off to the Americas were war-captives sold by African kings or chiefs to white dealers for gunpowder or rum. It may, of course, be that this business would not have reached such staggering dimensions without Europe's gunpowder to inflame African strife. Similarly it was with firearms improved by intercourse with the West that Mehemet Ali, the Albanian tyrant of Egypt, got control of most of the Sudan, where 'the slave trade rapidly developed into the major industry', with annual negro-hunting expeditions on a grand scale.[6] It cannot be too surprising if Europeans sometimes felt that nothing they did to them could be worse than what these 'natives' did to one another.

Entities such as we call 'Burma', or 'Holland', are largely fictions or optical illusions. Each name covers a welter of jarring groups, and among these some on both sides might do well or badly out of the operations of imperialism. A good many who came to grief fully deserved their fate. The vicious Oriental potentate or the barbarous tribal chief was not always a figment of Western imagination; there were many ruling classes that their peoples were far better off without. Numerous Europeans were enriched by their empires; many others who took part in the building of them travailed or perished, as little rewarded as Egypt's pyramid-builders of old. European forces suffered appreciable losses in fighting one another for colonies before 1815, and though their losses in battle with Afro-Asian antagonists were nearly always small compared with the other side's, they underwent all the torments of hunger and thirst, and were swept off in multitudes by disease.

How does the account stand between England and Wales, and how might a free Wales have turned out? We cannot guess how many promising new beginnings may have been crushed underfoot by juggernauts like the Roman legions; and we must ask whether, even if most of the old world from China to Peru was to all appearance in a sorry condition, there may have been enough vitality here and there to throw off the winding-sheet of the past. Many of its spokesmen in recent years have thought so, and some have endorsed 'development theory' arguments that their countries are 'underdeveloped' only because Europe made them so. It is soothing to a poor country's self-esteem to be assured that its poverty has been due to foreign exploitation, not to any defects of its own; and its well-off classes will welcome the assurance as removing any share of the blame from them. Yet to believe that any countries outside Western Europe were capable of moving forward on their own is not easy; the dead weight of ages lay heavily on them. Japan was able to advance by imitation of the West; it must seem unlikely that any others, or more than a very few, could have emulated it, though some made fitful efforts.

Most of Asia outside the Far East and Turkey, and nearly all Africa, were brought under European occupation. Among the survivors, some lost part of their territory, as Siam did to France, Persia to Russia, Mexico (most flagrantly of all) to the United States. The term 'semi-colonial', in vogue in the later nineteenth century, suggests aptly enough the status of nearly all. It was the creed of the Old China Hands, the Western traders at Hongkong or Shanghai, that China existed to furnish them with quick fortunes, and that their governments' duty was to make sure that it did so. There is not much in the condition of these countries, while they had freedom of action, to favour belief in their capacity for progress. A French observer in Afghanistan soon after the first British occupation in

1838–41 testifies that the feudal lords and clerics denounced the British 'because under them they could not practise their iniquities'; commoners rose against them because blinded by prejudice, but soon regretted them.[7] Spain had reacted similarly to the Napoleonic occupation, Afghanistan is reacting similarly now to the Russian. In an account of the disorderly state of Turkey about the same time, we read of a governor of Mosul who 'rushed out one night, mad with drink, to murder at pleasure'; Stratford Canning, the British ambassador, who 'took a very elastic view of his responsibility', was exerting himself to save Jews, Greeks, Armenians from massacre.[8] This may seem a highly coloured picture, but it remains true that the Ottoman empire's endeavours at reform were spasmodic at best, interrupted by many backslidings, and wholly inadequate in their outcome.

Conquest and occupation were grievous experiences; whatever beneficial results might ensue, the cure was at best a harsh one, like old-style surgery without anaesthetics. Only in the light of their tragic vision of history could Marx and Engels contemplate conquest as sometimes a chapter of human progress. Conservatives have been fond of warning us that human nature is not good enough for socialism, but they have judged it quite good enough for imperialism, which must put a far heavier strain on it. No evidence could contradict more flatly than imperialism's record the judgment of Dr Johnson that a man is never more innocently employed than when he is making money. The first modern empires, or in the case of Spain's empire what was left of it after the early nineteenth century, remained to the end unregenerate, much as Spain and Portugal made only laggard progress at home. Their worst consequences were unintended, the work of germs exported from Europe along with its human marauders. Diseases assisted the acquisition of Spanish America, though they reduced its value, by inflicting on a vulnerable population a demographic disaster beside which the Thirty Years War, or even the Black Death, was a trifle.[9]

Spanish and Portuguese greed wore a religious cloak; bourgeois Holland and England represented a new society that took naked class division for granted, without holy water or feudal camouflage, and could regard a frank confrontation of higher and lower races as no less natural. It was in the worst days of tooth-and-claw philosophy that the newest empires were hatched. King Leopold's Congo marked the lowest depth that European behaviour outside Europe could reach; it cast before it the shadow that was to turn into

Hitler's empire inside Europe. Ugly happenings have accompanied all conquest; it may be said for modern Europe that whereas Assyrians or Romans boasted of their worst doings, Europeans have preferred to throw a veil over them. They were guilty of nothing worse than many things perpetrated at the same time within the non-European world by its own men of might, during the Abyssinian expansion in the nineteenth century for instance, or the reoccupation of Sinkiang by a Chinese army after the Muslim rebellion. At times, European example may have done something to inflame the ferocity of others. Western conduct during the joint campaign of 1900 in China against the Boxers cannot have had a wholesome influence on the Japanese taking part; but there was seldom much need of the white man's tuition.

A complex society like Europe's could not for ever be content with crude spoliation: other and better motives were felt, or had to be simulated and might come to acquire real meaning from force of repetition. In one form or another they had floated for very long on the surface of empire. They are readily discernible among Romans or Chinese, and in religious guise among Muslims. In Europe other refining and softening influences were at work. Among them Enlightenment thinking, with its interest in other races and its humanitarian leanings, has been recognized as a forerunner of the anti-slavery movement.[10] In addition, social friction in Europe, with the French Revolution as its loudest eruption, and the religious revival it did much to bring about, stirred misgivings about rights of exploitation, and helped to inspire the principle that colonial rule ought to be beneficial to both sides.

As the nineteenth century went on the civilizing mission became an article of conventional faith. It could be clothed, as it was in France, either in spiritual drapery, to satisfy Catholic voters, or cultural and scientific, for secularists. Macaulay cherished the thought that if Britain should some day lose India, its gift of civilization would be imperishable. In the midst of their quarrels among themselves, Europeans could praise one another for improving conditions in their colonies. Russian expansion east of the Caspian, an Englishman wrote in 1883, had been 'of immense benefit to the country . . . an unmixed blessing to humanity': slave-raiding and brigandage had been suppressed, commerce protected.[11] Inveterately anti-tsarist as he was, Karl Marx concurred; he could sound so robust a civilizer as to be termed by a recent commentator 'merely another mid-Victorian'.[12]

It became clear very early to some of the best European minds that if Europe was to civilize other races, it must look to its own blemishes. Enslavement of native peoples was the evil that stirred up most controversy. Debate began in the first days of the Spanish coming to America, a triumph hailed by the contemporary historian López de Gómera as the greatest event since Christ, bringing the blessing of baptism and release from a long catalogue of vices like idolatry, sodomy, and polygamy.[13] It threatened the recipients with the more dubious blessing of reduction to serfdom on the settlers' *encomiendas* or feudal estates, or in the silver mines. Las Casas, the missionary bishop whose book *The Destruction of the Indies* came out in 1539, was only the most eloquent of the Indians' defenders. Men like him wanted natives to be accepted and treated as human beings, and it was their doctrine that prevailed in Spain, officially at any rate, over the rival thesis of Sepúlveda that they were scarcely human, natural slaves whom it was proper to treat as chattels.

In its own, however distorted fashion, Europe often really was a civilizing presence, and its aspirations could be authentic, if never unmixed with less lofty impulses. But they could readily fall into self-deception, or serve as a mask for hypocrisy. Profession and practice were never the same, and might be grotesquely far part. Milton's manifesto composed in 1655 on behalf of the Protectorate, to justify the war with Spain which led to the seizure of Jamaica, rehearsed standard national and imperial themes, among them sympathy with the downtrodden inhabitants of the Americas, and religion as England's primary incentive, one that ought to unite Englishmen of all parties.[14] Next year an English translation of Las Casas was prefaced by a condemnation of Spanish crimes and an assurance that any English acquisitions, by contrast, would bring liberation.[15] In the West Indies of the era that followed it might have been said, as in England in the time of Stephen and Matilda, that God and His angels slept.

'There can be no doubt', one of the buccaneers invading what was to be Rhodesia declared, 'that the Mashonas will improve immensely under the civilising influence of our rule.'[16] Japan was quick to pick up Western catchphrases, and made 'celestial salvation of the oppressed' its warrant for occupying Korea. When Italy was attacking Libya in 1911 there was a cascade of rhetoric about the Crusades and Lepanto, in a style, as an Italian historian of the war writes, which today seems bewildering.[17] Professor Zimmern thought of the Great War as putting the coping-stone on 'the principle of the trusteeship of the ruler on behalf of the ruled', and quoted the Kenya White Paper of 1923 on England's 'mission' to train the inhabitants ' "towards a higher intellectual moral and economic level" ', part of its 'benevolent despotism' everywhere in the colonial empire.[18]

There were always sceptics who declined to take at its face value the imperial password of being cruel only to be kind. Livingstone saw many things more clearly than they could be seen from Europe, and derided the optimism of 'minds enlightened by the full jet of the oxyhydrogen light of modern civilization'.[19] At the end of the nineteenth century, Winston Churchill, in his younger and better days, inveighed against the hollowness of imperial rhetoric, the distance 'from the wonderful cloudland of aspiration to the ugly scaffolding of attempt and achievement', a gap 'filled with the figures of the greedy trader . . . the ambitious soldier, and the lying speculator'.[20]

Goodwill during a great part of the nineteenth century was concentrated on abolition of the slave trade and colonial slavery. It was most vigorous in Britain. Agitation about the plight of blacks might sometimes be, as objectors like Dickens suspected, a substitute for reform at home; but it is quite as likely that by educating public opinion it helped to pave the way for social amelioration at home as well. It may be viewed as part of the all-round advance of the middle classes; this advance slowed down later as the millocracy joined forces with the landed aristocracy and its confederates in the City, whose ambitions were turning increasingly toward colonial gains. Campaigning for the rights of other races was carried on by bodies like the Aborigines' Protection Society, or the opponents of the opium trade. But the support they received did not come up to what the anti-slavery movement had been able to arouse.

Public protest against imperial misrule never disappeared. It belonged to a European tradition stretching back through Burke and the trial of Warren Hastings to Cicero and the Verrine orations; it was something inconceivable in any non-European empire. At the beginning of the nineteenth century Sir Thomas Picton was recalled from his governorship of Tobago and convicted of allowing a woman suspect, under old Spanish law, to be tortured. He was acquitted on appeal, and lived to die at Waterloo. In the far graver scandal over Governor Eyre of Jamaica in 1865 'the intellectual flower of the country' joined in the protest, with J. S. Mill in the lead;[21] though it is noticeable in this case that while the thinkers were on the right side, the men of feeling and fancy – Carlyle, Ruskin, Tennyson – were on the side of the criminal, and carried majority opinion with them.

Mitigation of the harshest features of German rule in Africa was the outcome of remonstrances by both Catholics and Socialists. But an enlightened public opinion broad enough to be effective was rare. A Commons speaker in 1814 lamented that in the British mind far-away Hindus were mysterious beings, 'as if they were not composed of flesh and blood, nor had passions and desires, as the rest of the human species'.[22] Old Mr Willet in *Barnaby Rudge* was not much different from the run of his fellow countrymen in thinking of all remote lands as 'inhabited by savage nations, who were perpetually burying pipes of peace, flourishing tomahawks, and puncturing strange patterns in their bodies'.[23] At a superior social height we hear from Osbert Sitwell of a London house in 1914, soon after the Delhi Durbar, 'sumptuously frescoed by Sert, with designs of elephants and howdahs and rajahs and pavilions and melons and bulrushes in sepia and gold'.[24] In these hues India offered a theatrical backcloth for the gambollings of a plutocracy; to the many it brought an occasional thrill. In a great measure empire and its heroic trumpet-calls were 'pure escapism';[25] an imaginary empire would have served the stay-at-homes almost as well, and when the Hollywood film dawned, an alternative outlet for fantasy became available.

With a public mind so frivolous, adequate scrutiny of colonial affairs was not to be expected. A critic of Dutch rule emphasized the incapacity of voters in Europe to weigh questions about territories on the other side of the globe;[26] and their possession by Europe's leading democracies could have a stultifying effect on parliamentarism. Gladstone in opposition found fault with a Tory MP for asserting that 'the people of India were most happy and contented', and proving it by the absence of complaints in a heavily censored press.[27] From the Treasury bench he would see India through the other end of his telescope. As colonial nationalist movements grew up, it usually seemed to them that parties of the left and right in Europe had the selfsame deaf ear for their appeals, however noisily they might disagree on domestic issues. In the climacteric years of the revolt of Afro-Asia the average Westerner's response was at best indifference. Little notice was taken of the horrific massacres by the French at Sétif in Algeria in 1945 or in Madagascar in 1947;[28] after eight years of the Algerian war a conspiracy of silence still prevailed in France, the disgusted Sartre wrote.[29]

Peer Gynt in old age, looking back on a lifetime of racketeering and slave-dealing, epitomizes modern Europe's ransacking of the other continents. Individual Europeans could be sensitive to fine issues through an awareness of Europe's pre-eminence and responsibility; on far more, the political or psychological effects must have been mostly bad. Bitterli points out that the Portuguese entering Africa were encountering societies where slavery was habitually practised,[30] and the same is true of the British and other slave-traders who followed in their footsteps. In the early nineteenth century four-fifths of the revenue of Angola came from a tax on export of slaves.[31] Europe was in danger of being barbarized by its contact with barbarism. In our own day, the grisly epidemic of police torture infecting so much of the world has had some of its starting-points in attempts to subdue colonial unrest by terror.

During the nineteenth century imperialism was, as W. J. Mommsen says, convenient for 'deflecting the attention of the rising middle classes from the constitutional issues they should have been coping with';[32] while colonial possessions enhanced the prestige and self-confidence of ruling classes, and helped them to keep their ground. Materially investors often did very well out of the Third World, morally far less well. About the end of the century, G. E. W. Russell drew a gloomy picture of upper-class luxury, depravity and decadence. 'The power of the purse is everywhere felt, if not seen,' he wrote with the occupation of Egypt and the Boer War in mind. 'It regulates our journalism. It pollutes our domestic politics. It governs our foreign relations.'[33] Corruption in high places must be reckoned among the causes of the reckless policies which brought about the Great War; for Europe the war brought retribution, but a good share of the cost and suffering fell on its dependencies.

Some part of the mediocre success of the civilizing mission can be ascribed to mutual incomprehension, i.e. the difficulty or impossibility of any meeting of minds within the unnatural walls of an empire. Like the triumvirs in *Julius Caesar*, colonial rulers were always prone to suspecting 'millions of mischief' behind loyal smiles. Failure to penetrate the native mind nagged at the all-powerful white man. 'Every person with any knowledge of the African soul', according to an official German statement, 'knows how well the negro is able to conceal his real feelings' from his master.[34]

With the gulf separating ruler and ruled, it is not to be wondered at that civilizing missions were envisaged chiefly in negative form, as the freeing of benighted peoples from bad rulers, and then from bad habits. Spain might be said to have liberated Mexico from its Aztec tyrants, much as Turks at the same moment were liberating Hungary from its seigneurs; both had a firm conviction of bringing deliverance from the bonds of superstition. Suppression of abuses could fit in better than positive measures of improvement, even famine relief, with Europe's nineteenth-century faith in *laissez-faire*, most assertive in Victorian England. There such evils as public hangings, boy chimney-sweeps, or cock-fighting, were being put a stop to. All peoples have indulged in regrettable customs, from 'ploughing by the tail' in Ireland to cannibalism, a blemish of various climes including, it has been suggested, Aztec Mexico,[35] and parts of the Pacific, where it was a stumbling-block to Robert Louis Stevenson's sympathy with the islanders.

India's Muslim overlords had frowned on suttee, but did not effectively ban it; British rule ended it, though less promptly than could be wished. Like other social reforms this required the support of progressive Hindu thinking, but such thinking derived primarily from foreign ideas, and without foreign law-makers and policemen would for an indefinitely long time have been impotent. Further steps came sluggishly, and the blame is not easy to apportion. There was always a legitimate doubt as to how far outsiders could interfere with practices sanctioned by religion, like child marriage. For government to tamper with them might be risky; not to do so might make it seem to be washing its hands of responsibility. In the twilight of the Raj the book *Mother India*, by an American admirer of British rule, Katherine Mayo, was vituperated by Indian patriots as a compendium of imperial and racial prejudice. A British heretic in India observed that if the place was really like that, after so many years of British management, it was time for his countrymen to go away.[36] A tacit answer was that the Caliban-disposition of its inhabitants made it impossible for any Prospero to do much with them, beyond preventing them from biting and scratching one another.

Apart from hesitant social reform, the gift that Western rule prided itself on bestowing was order, that watchword of governors in the colonies as of Metternich and the Holy Alliance in Europe. It had more of an affirmative and novel quality in Asia because it implied a guarantee of private rights, seldom safe under any of the old regimes; above all, security of life and, almost as important to the European mind, property. Administration in Calcutta, one of

Britain's new urban creations, might have many vices, but 'the god Property was respected here as it was everywhere that people spoke English', and wealthy Indians were happy to take up residence in the city.[37] When William Hickey quarrelled with a native broker he owed money to, and fiercely ordered him out of the house, the Bengali went straight to a lawyer and took out a writ of *capias ad satisfaciendum*.[38] Needless to say, British or other Western law benefited chiefly those who could learn how to manipulate it; to the rustic its niceties were a mystery, and he hankered for old modes of dealing out justice, rough and ready but at least comprehensible. In less sophisticated Africa, even so civilized a representative of Europe as Hammarskjöld might seem to share with ordinary Europeans a conception of order as first and foremost the safeguarding of *their* property and interests.[39]

Functions undertaken, as a rule inadequately, by colonial authorities included those concerned with what is known today as 'nation-building'. In some measure they were helping to build nations by the simple act of bringing together heterogeneous communities, subnationalities like India's or principalities like Malaya's. There were, on the other hand, cases of deliberately opposite tactics, as when the French split up Vietnam into separate compartments, or cut off Lebanon from Syria. But the birth of a nation could be hastened in either case by colonial rule provoking resentment, and national movements being launched. For these, or for any progress, ideas were as indispensable as economic change; also institutions, administrative or legal or political, in harmony (or not too much out of harmony) with them. Administrators were not likely to think of trying to release popular energies and to help men and women to expand more fully into human beings. Still, such schoolrooms as they provided might at least open new horizons to a minority. Printing was a newcomer everywhere except in the Far East, and newspapers, even though never allowed to operate without interference (they suffered from it in most parts of Europe too), could help to kindle a political spirit; towns, the cradles of nascent nationalism, could begin to acquire a civic quality they had never possessed outside Europe.

Without Western infusions, colonial discontents could have found no better expression than the sterile *jihadism* which had failed to avert European usurpation. Nationalist movements infallibly met with an unfriendly official reception, but its sharpness varied widely. British reactions were on the whole the mildest, and the eventual

British withdrawal was far less bloodstained than most others. All the same, it was preceded towards the end by a shrinkage of liberal principles and a stiffening of police activity, in face of the challenge of nationalism and of trade unionism. Leonard Barnes was writing in 1939 of a drastic curtailing of African civil liberties by new penal codes, and of authorities licensed to intern or deport at their own whim.[40] In 1947, a Fabian writer with experience of Africa portrayed the frigid manner of bureaucrats of 'the sullen, somnolent, dyspeptic type', and remarked that conventional officialdom could function not too inadequately while things were quiet, but that 'as soon as a "native" turns dynamic and intellectual, he becomes an enemy'.[41]

It was clear to Fanon that there were urban dwellers in northern Africa – workmen, shopkeepers, petty-bourgeois – who could enjoy a modest prosperity under their foreign rulers, so that the nationalist parties they adhered to were not excessively militant; a true revolutionary force, he believed, was to be looked for only among the peasantry. In some fields colonial power was assisting, not merely allowing, its wards to flourish – or some of its wards: it may be salutory to recall the warning of a seasoned witness that there is 'no necessary connection for good or ill between public works and native welfare'.[42] In India its salient achievements were irrigation canals, roads and railways; it left behind a relatively good infrastructure of communications and transport. But beyond this, and some investment mainly in the extractive enterprises of mine or plantation, there was far too little in British or other colonial territories of the material progress that Marx had looked to as the second phase of the civilizing mission.

After thirty-six years in Somalia, it had to be admitted, no more had been accomplished than establishment of order; economic growth was nil, and taxes were stiff.[43] Writing in 1909, Sir G. Molesworth was indignant at Indian disaffection. 'The Government of India is the purest administration in the world, and forms a brilliant contrast to the Parliamentary administration of Great Britain, which day by day grows more corrupt.' Yet he was constrained to regret that Indians in spite of their wonderful government were woefully poor, and industrially retarded; Britain ought to have encouraged their cotton mills, instead of hampering them.[44] Pressure from Lancashire had too much to do with policy; there was besides what an Indian historian calls 'a nagging fear of the industrialisation of the Eastern peoples'.[45]

Lack of rapport between government and people was another

handicap. Public works like canals could be constructed by fiat; where public confidence and co-operation were required, bureaucracy fumbled. Its measures to combat cholera in western India early in this century aroused resentment, because there were no channels through which they could be explained to the man in the street. At Lyallpur in the Punjab it set up an impressive agricultural research station, but to persuade illiterate, suspicious peasants to take its good advice was another matter. A local man employed in public relations told me of the method he had devised: he sat under the village tree dispensing hints about aphrodisiacs, a topic of never-failing interest to the rustic, and then led the discussion to improved seeds or tillage.

Hammond called his book on Portuguese Africa 'a study in uneconomic imperialism', and C. Southworth concluded that colonies had been 'an unprofitable venture' for France.[46] Not, however, for a good many Frenchmen; advocates of colonialism had private nests to feather, and many of the losses and gains of empire meant a transfer of wealth from pocket to pocket within the colony-owning country, and by other circuits within the colonies. How much the common man in Europe shared in the profits is a disputatious question. Gollwitzer's opinion is that on the whole imperialism helped to improve conditions in Europe, in part directly, in part through international rivalry making better health and efficiency acceptable national goals.[47] This might, of course, have come about otherwise; and colonial greeds had much to do with the feuding that led to both World Wars.

How much, again, the Third World contributed to capital accumulation and industrialization in Europe has long been argued. Many have suspected that the white man's burden of riches had its start in colonial plunder; for example, not a few Indian scholars have urged that loot from India was the prime motor of modern England's prosperity. Against this it may be recalled that loan-capital was plentiful in eighteenth-century Europe; anyone could borrow, from Holland especially, at low rates. By the time of the Industrial Revolution very large reserves had been built up in England itself. Admittedly colonial tribute helped to swell them. Fernand Braudel lends his weighty support to those who stress its importance, for industrializing Britain in particular. 'It was this extra share which enabled Europeans to reach superhuman heights in tackling the tasks encountered on the path to progress.' On the other hand, he calls attention to the price this exacted from the

British masses.[48] Here, once more, 'Britain' might be enriched, but a great many Britons impoverished. Multitudes were condemned to starvation, more still subjected to traumatic change. From this point of view, West Indian rum, sugar, tobacco, Chinese and then Indian tea, can be seen as tranquillizers, at least as efficacious as Methodism, which helped to reconcile Europe's poor to their lot. Desire for these luxuries could make men want better wages to buy them with; this might make for discontent, but also for harder work.

In the colonies costs of empire fell most heavily on peasants, almost everywhere the majority. In India taxation, chiefly of the villager, was already severe before the British advent, and land tax continued throughout the nineteenth century to provide a disproportionately large part of the revenue required for running the administration and for maintaining a powerful professional army, Indian and British, which not only policed India but shared in imperial campaigning far and wide. In Egypt under the British soldiers went on being conscripted as before; it was the French who relied most on this system, especially in Africa. Any such practice carried with it inevitable abuses, worst of all when it came to conscripts being brought to Europe and the Middle East to fight in the battles of the Great War.

Too often Europeans were parasites on colonial peoples; in addition, their rule gave fresh opportunities to swarms of local predators, to whom indeed its profits quite largely went. Old forms of slavery continued to be widespread in Asia,[49] and some of their beneficiaries could be useful auxiliaries of foreign power. Hereditary debt bondage lingered on in the Indian countryside all through the British period. Newer types of parasite might be generated by the new order; frequently they came from outside. Indian moneylenders found their way into Burma, and much Burmese land found its way into their hands; in French Indochina rice-milling and most other commercial activities were cornered by Chinese,[50] who would be an awkward legacy of colonial rule after it came to an end. Transformed into a mercantile (and very loyal) community by the magnet of Bombay, Parsees had a lucrative share in the smuggling of opium into China, on which British India's balance of payments for so long depended.

In such a case the native predator shaded into the collaborator, of whom every empire stood in need. All administration had to be carried on, more or less, through local intermediaries, who often could be only loosely controlled; they might be an obstruction between even a well-intentioned government and its subjects. At their best they were of a type most in evidence in India, trained as understudies of British officials and gradually winning equal status, public servants with standards of conduct unimaginable in the India of any earlier times. Far less wholesome was the employment of sections of earlier ruling classes as assistants, or as buffers between government and people. After the Mutiny the remaining Indian princes were kept on under British patronage; analogous procedures were adopted in Egypt and Malaya, by the French in Indochina and Morocco, and by the Russians in Bokhara. Where suitable collaborators were not forthcoming they might be created, like the landlords set up in India, first of all by the Permanent Settlement in Bengal, whose consequences were an incubus to the province until after independence.

More straightforwardly the required middlemen might be produced in some colonies by the coupling of white men and native women, whose offspring occupied a middle ground in terms of race as well as of rank. Commandeering of women was one of the many species of tribute levied by the white man, most blatantly in the slave-plantation areas of the Americas, and in southern Africa. It had been another accompaniment of conquest all through history; modern Europe was the first to abandon it, if never completely.

Churchill in Africa was alive to the perils threatening native peoples 'abandoned to the fierce self-interest of a small white population', full of 'the harsh and selfish ideas which mark the jealous contact of races and the exploitation of the weaker'.[51] It was in settler regions that ethnic groups which could be dubbed 'primitive' came most easily to be classed as 'superannuated races', and to be expected to go under in the struggle for survival. That 'savage tribes disappear before the progress of civilized races' was deemed by a Revd Thomas Atkins, who visited Tasmania in 1836, 'a universal law in the Divine government'.[52] To expedite their departure might be reckoned a kind of euthanasia. Mrs Bates, who spent half a lifetime studying and caring for Australian aborigines, was convinced that there could be no future for them.[53] 'History' was often invoked, most loudly by American expansionists, as equivalent to destiny or heavenly decree, in order to justify things that might cause qualms of conscience. 'We can't stop history in full course,' the British statesman in Cary's novel declares. 'And history is going all against the primitive – it always did.'[54]

Communities not wiped out were disrupted in many ways, some

of which might in the long run prove beneficial; the worst disruption took place where Europeans were allowed to settle and deprive cultivators of their land, reducing them to helotry as many of the smaller peasantry of Europe were being reduced. This happened in parts of Africa suited to white settlement, but also here and there in Asia where plantations were being laid out – in Ceylon and the Indian hills, or in Indochina. A British writer on Africa praised the Convention of London of 1884, after Majuba, because it sought to shelter Africans from 'the unscrupulous aggression of the Boers'.[55] In reality such protection could amount to very little, and when the Union of South Africa was set up in 1910 any attempt to shield the other races against the whites was virtually abandoned. Since then British capitalism has taken an energetic hand in their exploitation.

Refusal to be drilled into fixed work-habits, useful chiefly to settlers, was a leading criterion of 'primitiveness'. In one guise or another, labour was an essential part of the dues exacted from colonies. Taxation might take the form of corvée work. When slavery was given up its place was taken by the 'coolie emigration' from India and China,[56] often not much better than slave-dealing under a new name. West Indian plantations and Malayan tin mines were ready customers. More irregular modes of recruitment, like the 'blackbirding' that went on in the Pacific, added to the total. That natives should be summoned to work seemed so obvious that it could be endorsed by some socialists. Fourrierist plans for settlements in north Africa not infrequently hinged on conquests followed by obligatory labour services.[57]

Asians and Africans were called on not only to toil, but to do so with vigour and enthusiasm. A gospel of work, with Carlyle for one of its authors, became an essential part of the civilizing mission. Like the quality of mercy, work had the double merit of blessing both him who gave and him who received; for the giver it was educational, and usually the only education that came his way. 'Multatuli,' in his novel, invented a Revd Mr Twaddler of Amsterdam who was fond of preaching on the conversion of the Javanese, now happily rescued by Dutch power from heathen darkness and only needing to be 'led to God by labour'.[58] A German ex-governor and apologist for his country's methods quoted with relish the words of Joseph Chamberlain: 'I believe it is good for the native to be industrious, and we must bend every effort to teach him to work.'[59] There must be suitable penalties, in the German view, for 'the frequent laziness and insubordination of native workers or servants'; masters must be authorized to exercise 'a light paternal correction'.[60] Smuts accused

Milner of failing to grasp, unlike Rhodes, that unless an African is 'compelled to work by firm persuasion he is very likely to prefer a life of ease, lying happily in the sun'.[61] Depravity indeed, which the white man could feel a clear duty to banish, but which his forceful tutoring was only too likely to deepen.

The term 'race' came into Europe in the sixteenth century; appropriately, in view of its hazy meaning, its origin is unknown. It has been asserted that racialism as we know it is no older than modern nationalism and imperialism. There is some truth, though not the whole truth, in Freyre's claim for Brazil of 'racial democracy'; Portuguese emigrants were too few to avoid blending with other breeds, and this could lead to such fusions as Brazil's musical idiom and dances. It has been said too that belief in racial inferiority is an intellectual rather than a moral error, and its being shared in some degree by a man like Marx goes to confirm this. But it was also very much an extension of belief in the inferiority of the lower classes within Europe; this helped to make it a ubiquitous component of European thinking. A curious reflection can be found in that popular fable *The Wind in the Willows*, with its clear-cut demarcation between the civilized animals who sing Christmas carols or doze by the fire over a sheet of rhymes, and the vicious denizens of the Wild Wood. Its climax is a barbarian invasion, repulsed after a heroic fight. It came out in 1908, the year when Kenneth Grahame retired from the secretaryship of that sacred fane of civilization, the Bank of England.

Exponents of racism like Sir Richard Burton were fond of saying that Africans themselves admired light complexions.[62] In India too such a feeling can be traced to a long-continuing drift of incomers and conquerors from north to south; so also in Europe after the Romans. Somalis could be credited with 'proud bearing and a superb carriage bespeaking their consciousness of a racial superiority over their neighbours'.[63] The white man *par excellence*, the Englishman, stood at the summit of a hierarchy. When a British proconsul ascribed to his countrymen 'that power of government which . . . is the prerogative of their Imperial race',[64] the pride of rule of an aristocracy was being democratized into a virtue of a whole people, mostly perfectly innocent of it. The Labour party when it appeared on the stage was not free from some comparable underlying assumptions; its thinking about areas like the West Indies showed marks of a 'racial typology' when their fitness for self-government had to be weighed up.[65]

According to a Frenchman who knew India, the English were less good than the French at getting on with Asiatics, because of 'that stiffness, punctilious etiquette, and domineering tone, which they adopt everywhere'.[66] According to an Englishman, French manners were stamped by 'absolute ignorance and insolent disregard' of the character and feelings of subject peoples.[67] Dutchmen were apt, as they themselves were aware at times, to alienate notables by their contemptuous attitude.[68] British rudeness may have had the excuse of serving as a substitute for the violence more habitually indulged in by most other colonialists, a relief for the bottled-up irritations of a life of exile. Britons in India seldom went much beyond beating their servants, in the style of the apoplectic Major Bagstock, retired to London with his dusky attendant, in *Dombey and Son*. Unwillingness to be on social terms with 'natives' could have the good result of compelling those who smarted under it to turn to their own countrymen instead, thus giving national movements a broader base.

Conservatives in France or Britain today like to suppose that their former subjects remember them with esteem; however, the gratitude felt by educated Asians or Africans has not been to Western bureaucrats, businessmen, policemen, but to Shakespeare – India's national poet, as he has been called – or J. S. Mill, or Descartes. But what these men gave might have to be paid for by a diminished vitality of old cultures. Success inflamed the West with a 'naïvely egocentric' conviction that 'civilization and culture were synonymous with the Western varieties'.[69] Complaints of European misrepresentation of the character and way of life of other peoples have multiplied of late, adding a new chapter to older charges of imperial abuse of strength. Edward Said condemns, too sweepingly, the 'Orientalism' of travellers, explorers and scholars writing about the Middle East; Alatas pursues a similar theme in further Asia.[70] It is hard to specify the harm done. Unflattering accounts of Afro-Asian life may have paved the way for occupation of more territories by preparing Western opinion to think it always justified. Lamartine evoked an Orient conscious of its failure and longing to be taken under Europe's wing.[71] Asian self-respect may have been undermined only among those few who could read what was said about them, but these may have been rendered more anxious to westernize themselves, at the cost of cutting themselves off further from their own kin.

Yet 'Orientalists' initiated fruitful studies in many fields, introduced nations to their own past and taught them to think of their future. A similar ambivalence pervaded religious thinking. In the anti-slavery agitation the churches in Britain distinguished themselves, with Nonconformists the most zealous; so did missionaries from many lands in educational and medical work in the colonies. It was a common suspicion among white men that 'Christianity might produce dangerous notions of democracy, of human equality';[72] between missionaries and settlers or officials there was only limited intercourse. On the other side of the medal, they could be regarded in Afro-Asia as agents of imperialism, and so in fact they often were, as in the Spanish and Portuguese empires, which always relied heavily on ecclesiastical machinery, or in the French penetration of Indochina. Some Protestants in China could welcome war, even an Opium War, as a battering-ram to break down obstacles to the Gospel; in 1900 some punitive expeditions against Chinese villages were led by American missionaries.[73] It was as hard for mission workers as for other white men and women to feel much patience with a traditional life that appeared to them nasty, brutish, and short, as it still too often does to visitors. Such impressions throng the record, for instance, of the Scottish Presbyterian mission in the Punjab, where the inner 'darkness of superstition and sin' seemed to match 'the abhorrence of soap and water', 'the accumulated filfth', of the outward man.[74]

It was part of Fanon's case that colonialism quickly subverts inherited culture, and seeks to 'dehumanize' by stifling it without offering a satisfactory replacement, and by merely subjecting a useful minority to an education modelled on its own. To detach an élite from the mass was a strategy not unknown inside Europe; Slovenes in Hapsburg Hungary who wanted education had to turn themselves into Magyars. The colonial intellectual's groping for a national identity, so poignantly felt by Fanon, must have been still more tormenting for Africans, with their non-literate background; although Asia's literature, philosophy, and useful knowledge, apart from being little shared in by the masses, were in some respects worn out and sterile before contact with the West galvanized the Chinese and others into revitalizing them. North Africa was in a similar but more forlorn state. In sub-Saharan Africa art and myth were more a heritage of entire communities, but this meant that they were bound up with the noxious as well as the more admirable features of communal life.

Still, Europe should be better able today to sympathize with regrets over cultural disruption, because industrialism and modernism have had the same blighting effects on its own life as European ascendancy is accused of having had elsewhere. A few Europeans have been learning to appreciate the arts and practical skills of other climes, Indian classical music for example; far more have been having their wits addled by a counter-invasion, as in Roman times, of Eastern astrology and mumbo-jumbo, while a vacuum in popular art has been filled up by the synthetic jazz culture of America.

'Cultural imperialism' could be displayed most blatantly in elementary education. To keep their subjects docile, it has been said, rulers present them with an image of the world meant 'to increase their alienation and passivity', by showing it as 'a fixed entity', incapable of change.[75] South African school-books are compiled in this spirit; in Namibia children are taught that the Germans were 'invited by warring tribes' to come in and establish peace among them.[76] More broadly, empire ideology combined with arrogance has been well calculated to convince its underlings of their inadequacy. No record, perhaps, of the painful psychological trauma this can inflict is more graphic than the Tunisian writer Memmi's *Portrait du colonisé*. Alatas is indignant at the hangover of colonial mentality in his Malaya.[77] At the 1984 meeting at Tashkent of the Afro-Asian Writers' Association a spokesman recalled that this body had been set up in 1958 because of a growing consciousness of 'the incredibly difficult, sometimes agonizing process of "spiritual decolonisation"'.[78] Intellectuals must have been the most directly affected, but the diffusion of plagues like alcoholism suggests widespread damage.

Sooner or later conditions in many colonies brought to the front new or half-new classes which could lead the way, fumblingly enough, towards independence. Where imperialism nurtured, as it was only too well able to, an indiscriminate hated of everything associated with it, the struggle might be blind and unconstructive, or fall back into religious bigotry. Muslim countries have been more than usually prone to such regression. Mahdism – that 'new poor emerging out of the African darkness', as it seemed to Europe[79] – made a deep impression on them in the late nineteenth century. The present 'Islamic revival' contains many questionable ingredients; they are most obtrusive in the clerical regime in Iran since the fall of the Shah, who with his huge foreign armoury and backing had been proof against any more rational opposition. By the West, always two-faced in such matters, fanaticism in Iran is loudly condemned, because a nuisance to Western interests, but in Afghanistan loudly applauded, because there it embarrasses only Moscow.

Some countries formerly under Western sway have reached genuine independence, such as India by one path, Vietnam by another. Many more have passed since 1945 into the limbo of neo-colonialism, whose affinities are with the 'indirect rule' cultivated in some colonies, and with the handling of 'semi-colonies' or 'spheres of influence'. It could be resorted to with little harm to imperial concerns, because colonialism had left both a material infrastructure and a human basis in westernizing groups willing to co-operate and in a position to benefit. Europe prepared the ground, the United States reaps more and more of the harvest. Its hegemony has, on the one hand, quickened the shift away from direct colonial rule, on the other, done its best to frustrate any further advance towards real freedom.

Hopeful observers have counted on Western capital to help to develop the backlands for the sake of worthwhile markets. On the whole it seems content rather to dump surpluses and extract raw materials. Things are steadily worsened by the population explosion: the negative bent of most of the good done by Europe shows in the curbing of epidemic disease without the economic development needed to absorb and check the resulting numbers. Emigration confers opportunity on a few, at the cost of some loss of human resources. New York is crowded with Indian and Filipino doctors and surgeons who ought to be working at home.

Shortcomings of both rulers and ruled in colonial times must be blamed for the poor calibre of political leadership in most newly freed countries. Imperialism chose some dubious associates, a habit carried much further by the United States. Colonial rule was superimposed on earlier, deep-rooted patterns, so that it cannot bear sole blame. Governments like the British in India may have reinforced some mischievous legacies of the past by making so much use of 'martial races'. Some armies they left behind have a deplorable political record, and some of the dictatorships thrown up by them have reverted to the habits of aggression so rife in Afro-Asia before the Europeans: the Sudanese in the non-Arab south, the West Pakistani in east Bengal, and the Indonesians in Timor. In each of these cases there has been an accompaniment of wholesale bloodshed. We are very far from fulfilment of Fanon's vision of the Third World coming into the van, utilizing Europe's ideas but remembering its high crimes and misdemeanours, and 'starting a new history of Man'.[80] For some years China purported to be doing this, but those years have gone by.

How cogent is the claim of ex-colonies for compensation, or how likely to carry conviction to Western publics? In recent times Germany has acknowledged a debt to the Jews; ironically, payment has been made to the state of Israel, whose debt to the Palestinians it has displaced is equally undeniable. So is the compensation promised but not paid by the United States to Vietnam. When we look further back into history things become more puzzling. State debts can be transmitted from age to age, and the sins or follies of the fathers thus visited, with Biblical warrant, on the children. But it would be difficult to say how far back responsibility for acts of conquest and spoliation can be assigned or measured; and if restitution is due from European conquerors it must be due from others as well. There were Persian and Afghan invasions of eighteenth-century India as well as European. India, it may be remarked, has exerted itself to make amends for age-old cruelty to its aboriginal peoples by reserving places for them in colleges and government service.

Another way of looking at the question may be to say that if humanity was ever to break out of the ruts it had got stuck in, some region had to lead the way. Europe led, and if it ransacked other continents it subjected itself to centuries of wars, upheavals, and religious furies – calamities which may well have been a necessary ordeal, the initiation rites of industrial society. Any benefits of this ordeal the rest of mankind now has a chance of sharing at far lesser cost, and far more quickly. If Bengal helped to foot the bill for Britain's industrial revolution, in the long run India would be among the gainers. An album in the India Office Library of Pictures of Kashmiri craftsmen at work in the 1850s shows a goldsmith with spectacles on his nose. The blessing represented by the spread of this single, simple invention round the globe is incalculable.

A corollary is that the West, having no real need now to squeeze the Third World, ought to free itself from the continuing temptation to do so by eliminating from its social structure the factors making for exploitation of other peoples. In every social order throughout history there have been such elements, stimulating aggression in one or other of its countless forms. In the case of modern Europe and its American offshoot it is capitalism that has been most to blame. Human nature is not totally depraved, as Christianity has taught, but it is extraordinarily mutable or malleable in this raw youth of its evolution; how it shapes depends, as that great Welshman Robert Owen was one of the first to perceive, on the environment it is exposed to. Colonialism has an analogy in the ill-treatment since history began of women by men. The men of today cannot make up for this, but they can join with women in reforming the institutions which guaranteed their subjugation.

Urban man everywhere has adopted European clothes; more important, something like a common moral code has made its way everywhere, in the limited sense at any rate that such evils as the slave-market, which Europe renounced and by example or compulsion brought others to renounce, today have few if any defenders; and that others such as torture have few confessed though many secret practitioners. On the open space thus cleared there is room for an edifice of social ethics of a more positive cast, uniting humanity in common effort. It is long since the malady of 'two Englands', rich and poor, side by side, began to be deplored; 'two worlds' on one small planet would be the same evil disastrously magnified.

NOTES AND REFERENCES

1. *Asiatic Quarterly*, July 1866 ('Summary of Events').
2. *The Wealth of Nations*, Book IV, ch. 7 ('Of Colonies'), part 3 (opening).
3. Bruno da Ponte, *The Last to Leave: Portuguese Colonialism in Africa* (London: International Defense and Aid Fund, 1974) pp. 60–1.
4. German Colonial Office, *The Treatment of Native and Other Populations* (Berlin: 1919) p. 31.
5. Frantz Fanon, *The Wretched of the Earth* (1961; trans. C. Farrington, Harmondsworth: Penguin Books, 1967) p. 68.
6. M.D. Theobald, *The Mahdiya. A History of the Anglo-Egyptian Sudan, 1881–1899* (London: Longmans, Green, 1951) pp. 7–8, 10–11.
7. J.P. Ferrier, *Caravan Journeys and Wanderings* (English ed. by H.D. Seymour, London, 1857; reprint, Karachi: Oxford University Press, 1976) p. 186.
8. S. Lane-Poole, *The Life of Lord Stratford de Redcliffe K.G.* (London: Longmans, Green, 1890) pp. 199, 201.
9. C.M. Cipolla (ed.), *The Fontana Economic History of Europe: The Sixteenth and Seventeenth Centuries* (London: Collins, 1974) p. 10n.; F. Braudel, *Civilization and Capitalism 15th–18th Century*, vol. III, *The Perspective of the World* (1979; trans. S. Reynolds, London; Collins, 1984) pp. 393–4.
10. E.g. U. Bitterli, *Die 'Wilden' und die 'Zivilisierten'* (Munich: Verlag C.H. Beck, 1976) pp. 426–7.
11. C. Marvin, *The Russians at Merv and Herat* (London: Allen, 1883) pp. 269, 276–7.
12. R. Robinson, in F. Madden and D.K. Fieldhouse (eds), *Oxford and the Idea of Commonwealth* (London: Croom Helm, 1982), p. 31.

13. L. Hanke, 'More Heat and Some Light on the Spanish Struggle for Justice in the Conquest of America', *Hispanic American Historical Review*, 44 (1964) pp. 296–7.
14. *The Prose Works of John Milton*, ed. J.P. St. John (London, 1848), vol. II, pp. 349ff.
15. Translated by J. Phillips (new ed., New York: Oriole Editions, 1972). Much can be learned about the ancestry of the civilizing mission in England from J. McVeagh, *Tradefull Merchants: The Portrayal of the Capitalist in Literature* (London: Routledge & Kegan Paul, 1981).
16. W.A. Wills and L.T. Collingridge (eds), *The Downfall of Lobengula* (London: African Review Offices, 1884) p. 306.
17. G. Malgeri, *La Guerra Libica (1911–1912)* (Rome: Edizione di Storia e Letteratura, 1970) p. 48.
18. Sir A. Zimmern, *The Third British Empire* (London: Humphrey Milford, 1926) pp. 13, 40, 53.
19. I. Schapera (ed.), *Livingstone's Missionary Correspondence 1841–1856* (London: Chatto & Windus, 1961) p. 282 (13 September 1855).
20. *The River War* (London: Longmans, 1899) pp. 26–7.
21. M. St.J. Packe, *The Life of John Stuart Mill* (London: Secker & Warburg, 1954) p. 469.
22. *The Speeches of Robert Rickards, Esq. in the Debate in Parliament on the Renewal of the Charter of the Hon. East India Company . . . 1813* (London, 1814) p. 50.
23. Ch. 28.
24. *Great Morning* (1948; London: Reprint Society, 1949) p. 257; cf. p. 215.
25. W.S. Hamer, *The British Army: Civil-Military Relations 1855–1905* (Oxford: Clarendon Press, 1970) p. 217.
26. 'Multatuli' (E.D. Dekker), *Max Havelaar* (1860; English ed., New York: Alfred A. Knopf, 1927) pp. 235–6.
27. *Hansard*. vol. CCLI, 1880, col. 922ff.
28. Fanon, *The Wretched of the Earth*, p. 62.
29. Ibid., preface by J.P. Sartre, p. 25.
30. U. Bitterli, *Die 'Wilden' und die 'Zivilisierten'*, p. 96.
31. R.J. Hammond, *Portugal and Africa 1815–1910* (Pao Alto, Cal.: Stanford University Press, 1966) p. 46n.
32. W.J. Mommsen, in T.W. Moody (ed.) *Nationality and the Pursuit of National Independence* (Belfast: Appletree Press, 1978) p. 128.
33. *Collections and Recollections*, Series 2 (London: Nelson, 1909) p. 63; cf. pp. 275ff.
34. German Colonial Office, *How Natives are Treated in German and French Colonies* (Berlin, 1919) p. 29.
35. M. Harris, *Cannibals and Kings* (1977; London: Fontana, 1978) ch. 9.
36. Lt. Col. Arthur Osburn, *Must England Lose India?* (London: Alfred Knopf, 1930) p. 11.
37. A. Calder, *Revolutionary Empire: The Rise of the English-Speaking Empires* (London: Jonathan Cape, 1981) p. 590.
38. *Memoirs of William Hickey*, ed. A. Spencer (London: Hurst & Blackett, 1913) vol. III, pp. 151–2.
39. C.C. O'Brien, 'The Congo, the United Nations, and Chatham House', in *New Left Review*, no 31 (London, 1965) p. 8.

40. *Empire or Democracy?* (London: Gollancz, 1939) pp. 165–6.
41. L. Silberman, *Crisis in Africa* (London: Fabian Colonial Bureau, 1947) pp. 5–6.
42. J.S. Furnivall, *Colonial Policy and Practice* (Cambridge: University Press, 1948) p. 322.
43. D. Jardine, *The Mad Mullah of Somaliland* (London: Herbert Jenkins, 1923) p. 30.
44. Sir G. Molesworth, *Economic and Fiscal Facts and Fallacies* (London: Longmans, 1909: Popular ed., 1910), ch. 41.
45. P.S. Gupta, *Imperialism and the British Labour Movement, 1914–1964* (London: Macmillan, 1975) p. 154.
46. Hammond, *Portugal and Africa*; C. Southworth, *The French Colonial Venture* (London: P.S. King & Son, 1931) p. 131.
47. H. Gollwitzer, *Europe in the Age of Imperialism* (London: Thames & Hudson, 1969).
48. Braudel, *Civilization and Capitalism*, pp. 386–7, 581, 641.
49. See B. Lasker, *Human Bondage in Southeast Asia* (Honolulu: Institute of Pacific Relations, 1950).
50. Southworth, *The French Colonial Venture*, p. 100.
51. *My African Journey* (1908; London: New English Library, 1972) pp. 25, 118.
52. A. Montagu, *The Nature of Human Aggression* (1976; London: Oxford University Press, 1978) pp. 84–5, 169.
53. Daisy Bates, *The Passing of the Aborigines* (1938; London: Panther Books, 1972).
54. Joyce Cary, *Prisoner of Grace* (London: Readers' Union, 1954) p. 280.
55. E. Sanderson, *Africa in the Nineteenth Century* (London: Seeley, 1898) p. 282.
56. See P.C. Campbell, *Chinese Coolie Emigration to Countries within the British Empire* (London: P.S. King, 1923); H. Tinker, *A New System of Slavery: The Export of Indian Labour Overseas 1830–1920* (London: Oxford University Press, 1974).
57. See M.N. Mashkin, *Frantsuskie Sotsialisti i Demokrati i Kolonialnii Vopros 1830–1871* (Moscow: 'Nauka' Publications, 1981).
58. 'Multatuli', *Max Havelaar*, p. 129; cf. p. 239.
59. A.H.H. Schnee, *German Colonisation Past and Future* (English adaptation, London: Allen & Unwin, 1926) p. 135. Cf. Hammond, *Portugal and Africa*, pp. 156, 160.
60. *The Treatment of Native and Other Populations* (see n.4) p. 125.
61. J.C. Smuts, *Jan Christian Smuts* (London: Cassell, 1952) p. 93.
62. Christine Bolt, *Victorian Attitudes to Race* (London: Routledge & Kegan Paul, 1971) p. 134.
63. Jardine, *The Mad Mullah of Somaliland*, p. 19.
64. Lord Cromer, cited by Sir A. Colvin, *The Making of Modern Egypt* (London: Nelson, 1906) p. 350.
65. P.S. Gupta, *Imperialism and the British Labour movement*, p. 260; a recurrent theme of the book.
66. Ferrier, *Caravan Journeys and Wanderings*, p. 341; cf. p. 372.
67. Sanderson, *Africa in the Nineteenth Century*, p. 101.
68. C.R. Boxer, *The Dutch Seaborne Empire 1600–1800* (Harmondsworth: Penguin Books, 1965) pp. 259–61.

69. M. Leiris, 'Race and Culture', in *The Race Question in Modern Science* (Paris: UNESCO, 1956) p. 97.
70. E. W. Said, *Orientalism* '(London: Routledge & Kegan Paul, 1978); S.H. Alatas, *The Myth of the Lazy Native* (London: Frank Cass, 1977).
71. Said, *Orientalism*, p. 179.
72. Bolt, *Victorian Attitudes to Race*, p. 118.
73. Jane Hunter, *The Gospel of Gentility: American Women Missionaries in Turn-of-the Century China* (New Haven: Yale University Pres, 1984) pp. 6, 171.
74. Revd J.F.W. Youngson, *Forty Years of the Panjab Mission of the Church of Scotland* (Edinburgh: R. & R. Clark, 1896) pp. 252, 276–7.
75. Paulo Freire, *Pedagogy of the Oppressed* (Harmondsworth: Penguin Books, 1972) p. 109.
76. Ann Harries, in *Anti-Apartheid News* (London), April 1984.
77. S.H. Alatas, *Intellectuals in Developing Societies* (London: Frank Cass, 1977).
78. *Soviet Weekly* (London), 1 October 1983.
79. W. Baird, *General Wauchope* (Edinburgh: Anderson & Ferrier, 1900) p. 89.
80. Fanon, *The Wretched of the Earth*, p. 254.

3 Economics and Ethics in the Development of Natural Resources

A.I. MACBEAN

INTRODUCTION

Natural resources of all kinds from the air we breathe to the zinc we mine have been a major source of conflict among people and societies for as long as human wants have exceeded their capacity to satisfy them. Perhaps eviction from the Garden of Eden dates the beginning of such conflict as much as the need for economics. The emergence of the independent nations of the South highlights certain types of conflict and raises economic and moral issues which are of importance, not only to us, but to future generations. This paper seeks to identify the areas both of conflict and of common interest between the various actors in North–South relationships in the exploitation of natural resources. Because the subject is both wide and complex, this chapter concentrates mainly on two principal actors – the managements of multinational corporations (MNCs) and the governments of developing or less-developed countries (LDCs) – and on their role in the development of mineral resources. Although the nations of the North have often been involved directly or indirectly in disputes with the South over natural resources, especially oil, it is generally the MNCs and the governments or public enterprises of the LDCs which have been engaged in the front line.

Economics is concerned with growth, welfare, distribution and especially efficiency, without which none of the others can be maximized. A central concern of politics is justice. Does the exploitation of natural resources in poor countries which requires the expertise of large foreign companies constitute a *prima facie* conflict between efficiency and justice, and if so is there any way of resolving it satisfactorily?

The key characteristic of natural resources is that nature provides them. Mankind makes use of them, depletes them and even exhausts them. The fear of exhaustion of key natural resources is one of the main causes of worry both for mankind as a whole and for some societies which are heavily dependent on specific minerals or fish. It is one cause of conflict.

There exists a near infinite variety of natural resources with their own specific characteristics. One cannot hope to capture the many and diverse problems to which each can give rise. One categorization is particularly important – the division between renewable and non-renewable resources. In the end, however careful our conservation, however much we recycle, the reserves of minerals must be used up. Forests of trees and populations of animals and fish do renew themselves biologically and can be preserved, provided the nations want to and can evolve the institutions to govern their exploitation. While recognizing the variety and the overlaps which characterize the real world, we can capture the essential flavour of the problems by organizing the discussion around these two basic forms of natural resources.

ECONOMIC THEORY OF NATURAL RESOURCES

A prime concern of economics is efficiency. It is not the only concern as any reading of the extensive literature of welfare economics or applied economics would show. But a good deal of economic theory is concerned with defining the most efficient way of achieving given objectives. This is studied both from the viewpoint of the individual organization and from the viewpoint of society as a whole. A major interest is how far existing institutions, such as a relatively free market system, promote efficiency in the operation of firms and from the viewpoint of society.

The economic theory of natural resources has itself been something of a boom industry in the last ten years. The discussion has taken a very techical form, and indeed the arguments of the major study by Professors P.S. Dasgupta and G.M. Heal[1] are largely expressed in mathematics. In order to focus on the issues likely to be most important in the North–South context, we should concentrate on minerals which are non-renewable, and discussion of the economics of a renewable resource is relegated to an appendix.

Optimal Management of a Non-renewable Resource

The basic argument in this field derives from a classic article by H. Hotelling in 1931.[2] Assuming perfect competition, but also making a special assumption of constant costs of extracting and selling a Representative Mineral (REM) we conclude that the equilibrium price of REM will rise annually at a rate equal to the rate of interest. Why? Because as far as the owners of the REM mines are concerned REM in the ground is a good as a bond in the financial market. If they expect its price to rise by less than the rate of interest they will hasten to dig up REM, sell it and put the resulting revenues into bonds. This has the effect of increasing current supplies and reducing future supplies of REM, thus lowering its current price and raising the price that can be expected for it in future. If they overshoot by excessive extraction so that this year's price is lowered too much and next year's price is then expected to exceed this year's by more than the interest on a bond, they would call a halt; for now, by holding REM in the ground for sale next year, they can make more money than by holding bonds. These actions will ensure that the expected price will always tend to exceed the current price by a rate which equals the rate of interest.

Note that this is independent of changes in demand. If demand were constant the price would rise at a constant rate, and quantities demanded would fall by amounts dependent on the price elasticity of demand for REM. If population growth and rising incomes raise the demand for REM the quantities demanded will expand, though not by as much as if there had been no rise in price. But the crucial point is that the rate of increase of the price is independent of demand and fixed purely by the rate of interest so long as supplies of REM remain.

The implication of this analysis is that even if there were constant extraction costs we should have constantly rising prices for minerals. If minerals vary in quality and difficulty of recovery, competition will ensure that the REM whose cost of extraction is lowest will be mined first. Then prices will have to rise to cover the increased costs of extraction plus the rate of interest. So, with diminishing returns to mining, prices ought to rise a good deal faster than the rate of interest.

One might note, as an aside, that the real world behaviour of mineral prices does not accord in the least with the predictions of this very simple static model. Prices, far from rising steadily, fluctuate wildly around a fairly stable long-run trend in real terms.

This is for two reasons. First, the model assumes a fixed stock of the resource. While the physical reserves of non-renewable natural resources must be finite, the known reserves have, up to now at least, kept on increasing faster than the growth of world demand. The following table shows examples of this tendency for five major minerals:

Ratio of Reserves to World Demand

	Zinc	Oil	Lead	Tin	Copper
1950	18.8	13.8	9.8	14.4	27.9
1976	19.2	26.0	26.4	36.0	38.0

Source: US Department of Interior Mineral Statistics (1978).

United Nations statistics show that between the late 1940s and the late 1960s the published reserves of almost every major mineral apart from tungsten increased by amounts ranging from 10 per cent for tin to 2,360 per cent for potash.[3]

Secondly, the model makes no allowance for advances in technology, which have significantly lowered the real costs of extracting and delivering minerals. You can see why the economist is described as 'The person who knows tomorrow why the things he said yesterday didn't happen today'.

The problem is the general one of uncertainty. When working out its mining strategy the management has to make estimates of future prices and costs. Both of these must take account of changes in resources and changes in technology, but the size and impact of such changes are so uncertain that they make the activity of mining one that involves very considerable risks. The way different parties view these risks can be a source of conflict to which we shall return.

The theory says that a rational management of a mine operating in a competitive environment should seek to maximize the present value of the stream of expected net revenues given the discount rate. The standard rule for maximizing profits is to operate at the point where price and marginal cost are equal. But for the mine-owner there has to be allowance for the effect of current sales in reducing the stock of REM and so future sales. The manager has to consider not only whether producing an extra unit adds to this year's profit but also whether that would outweigh the reduction in future profits. This leads to the rule that the discounted value of marginal profits must be constant over time. Otherwise shifting profits from a year where the discounted value is lower to one where it is higher would raise the sum of the net present values. This in turn implies that marginal profit must rise at an annual rate equal to the rate of interest.

The rate of extraction and therefore of depletion is sensitive to the rate of interest. If it is raised mining will be speeded up. If lowered more REM will be left for the future. If society's time preference differs from the market discount rate this will give rise to conflicting objectives.

Monopoly

If the mine were a monopoly one might expect output to be lower than the competitive level. But this is not necessarily so. If the degree of monopoly is the same in each period there may be no point in transferring production from the current period to a later one. A rigorous proof of this has been given by Professor J.E. Stiglitz.[4]

Capital Costs

Mining is typically a very capital intensive activity so that neglect of the influence of capital costs could be misleading. One effect is that output can no longer be considered continuously and costlessly variable. There will be discrete jumps from one level of production to another as new shafts are sunk or new faces opened up. Normally there will be considerable lags between recognition of the need for new investment and completion simply because of the large scale of most modern mining operations. However, at the very general level of this discussion one could maintain that the theory would indicate whether new investment was required or not.

A second aspect of the capital intensity of mining is that it may change the impact of the interest rate. The standard point made earlier that a rise in the investment rate would bring forward extraction is no longer necessarily true. A higher interest rate both encourages depletion and discourages investment in the equipment needed to increase extraction.[5]

CONFLICTS BETWEEN PUBLIC AND PRIVATE INTEREST

All I have done so far is to give something of the flavour of theorizing in the economics of natural resources. However, even at this level of abstraction, several points have emerged where the theory indicates potential sources of conflict between a market solution or the aims of a private management and the objectives that might be expected to be held by society.

If there were no conflicts of interest in the exploitation of natural resources there would be no need to appeal to justice. Harmony displants morality. But can even perfect markets provide that harmony? An important contribution of classical economics is the demonstration that most economic activity is not a zero-sum game. Trade, both within and between nations, normally occurs because both sides to a transaction expect to gain from it. More gains may accrue to one or another side. The distribution of the gains may be unjust, but both normally do gain. That conclusion may seem trite, but appears to be quite widely disbelieved as far as trade between North and South is concerned. The operation of a system of free markets may not produce total harmony but it is the best method yet invented for providing people with the information needed to make rational decisions and to harmonize a great deal of economic activity. Nevertheless, there are a number of issues where the signals given by market forces may lead to inefficient and/or inequitable results when regarded by the government of a developing country.

I shall assume that the government is a representative one both able and willing to make a rational assessment of the needs of its citizens. Its aim would be to maximize the present social value of the retained net revenues from exploiting the resource. It may also have political or strategic objectives as well; I leave them on one side for economists have relatively little to say on them. Its economic objective would require that the marginal social value of output should be constant over time. Otherwise it would be possible to raise the sum of the present values by shifting production from periods when its value is low to when it is expected to be high. It would use an accounting rate of interest which reflected its views as to the marginal social opportunity cost of capital or social time preference as opposed to the market determined interest rate.

The differences between government policies and the optimal extraction rate chosen by the model private company would stem from this word 'social'. It has four major implications. The first is a concern for externalities, which are common in natural resource exploitation. The obvious ones are risk of damage to the environment through visual pollution and damage to air, water and land. But, as we noted earlier, the common access problem also belongs to the class of externalities. An individual fishing company does not directly bear the depletion costs and its activities affect the costs of others in the industry. Similar problems arise in mineral extraction when different companies sink oil wells or gas wells into the same underground reservoir. These are all cases where property rights are difficult to define and enforce and where excessive depletion rates are likely to occur.

Secondly, the prices which are paid and received by companies may not reflect marginal social opportunity costs. This is particularly true in developing countries where the effects of taxes, tariffs, subsidies and overvalued exchange rates on prices of inputs and outputs will result in distortions. These and distorted wages and interest rates are problems made familiar in welfare economics, trade theory and cost–benefit analysis.

The third implication relates to income distribution (a) between the LDC and the MNC, (b) between members of society, and (c) between present and future generations. There is no particular reason why market forces should produce a just distribution of income in any of these categories. The first is largely a matter of bargaining power in which access to information may be of key importance. The second may depend on the society's social welfare function and its ability to tax gainers from the mining operation and transfer income to less advantaged groups. If it is capable of doing so the impact of even a large mining operation on income inequality may not be very important. But if that is not the case, one can conceive of situations where the inequitable effects of large-scale mining might, in the collective view of the society, outweigh the benefits of additional national income accruing from it. They might prefer to do without the activity, or prefer to run it in other ways, even if they were much less efficient.

As for the question of intergenerational income distribution, the free market might be expected to take less care of future generations than would the collective wisdom of society. Their needs cannot be expressed directly in the market place. If the actions of individuals expressing their time preference in the market lead to high interest rates, accelerated depletion rates could be the result. Some see undervaluation of future needs by the market as a world problem. As envisaged by Meadows *et al.*, in *The Limits to Growth*,[6] it leads to catastrophe. But as the theory has shown, the effects of high interest rates upon the rate of mining activity are actually ambiguous because of their effect on investment in a highly capital intensive activity. A standard complaint of economists against the more alarmist writings on this subject has in fact been that many of their gloomy results follow from simple extrapolation of geometric growth rates of demand for resources, without paying attention to the effects of the price mechanism in leading to economizing on resources and in stimulating substitution for resources long before they run out. I share their scepticism, but am also moved to agree with James Meade's comment: 'The disutility of Doom to future generations would be so great, that even if we gave it a low probability and even if we discount future utilities at a high rate . . . we would be wise to be very prudent in our present action.'[7]

Actually the argument can go either way on whether we are leaving too little or too much to future generations. If we accept diminishing marginal utility of income and expect per capita incomes to grow over time, we should approve relatively high discount rates, which encourage more consumption today. The more faith we have in technology's ability to come up with resource substitution and resource saving, the less concern we feel for future generations. Nor is it clear, in practice, that governments look after future generations better than private companies. Governments are often the most eager to extract and sell minerals at the highest possible rate because their time horizons are very short, or they are desperate for foreign exchange, or they are afraid of the political effects of unemployment in a key sector.

The fourth implication of the word 'social' is the potential conflicts arising from different evaluations of risk. From the various viewpoints of a private company, a nation or the world society as a whole, the same risks may be evaluated quite differently. For the owner/operator of REM mines both the future prices and quantities of REM rates are unknown. REM may become obsolete or boom as technology devises substitutes which can replace it or creates new uses for it. There are no adequate futures markets or any other means for insuring market risks. Nor are such markets likely to develop much beyond the relatively short-term markets for trading in futures which already exist. The existence of such uncertainty could lead to more or to less depletion depending on whether REM owners are risk averse or natural gamblers. As an unsophisticated but quite common method for allowing for risk in business is to add a risk premium to the discount rate or the required internal rate of return when evaluating an economic strategy, it would be likely to accelerate current extraction rates but reduce exploration and development work by the private industry.

Many nations are likely to have fewer eggs in one basket than a mining company has since their economies may be diversified quite broadly. Even within the mining sector there may be several companies operating in different areas so certain classes of risks are much less bothersome, for example, dry wells, aborted seams of ore, and other random failures, for the disaster of one company may be matched by the unexpectd rich vein opened up by another. But this general situation may be of little comfort to some developing countries which happen to be highly specialized in one or two minerals. Several copper producing nations, e.g. Zambia, Zaire and Chile, tin exporters like Bolivia or Malaysia, and many of the oil exporters are likely to be much more dependent on the fortunes of their mines or oil wells than are most of the multinational companies who typically operate in minerals. The oil giants and companies like Amax, RTZ, Alcoa and Alcan are often quite widely diversified, both in the location of their production and in their activities. They are also able to internalize some risk through vertical integration from mine to finished product: what one stage loses another gains.

A specific risk which has loomed large in recent decades is political risk. For the companies this includes: nationalization without adequate compensation, unilateral changes in agreements governing their operations in a country which affect their profitability (tax changes, foreign exchange rules, insistence on opening managerial positions to local citizens), revolutions, civil war, and terrorism. Evaluation of these risks is creating new job opportunities for students of politics. Even for large MNCs with great financial resources and political leverage, increases in these risks are taken seriously. Some years ago Amax almost completely ceased investing in LDCs and directed its exploration and development efforts to the United States and Canada as a result of its experiences in LDCs and their effect on its estimates of future political risk. The World Bank sees this as a general problem:

> Foreign mining companies and investors have hesitated to commit large funds to mining ventures located in countries that appear politically unstable or where there is a serious risk that the terms of investment agreements may be changed by the host government. Uncertainty on this score is perhaps the main reason why mineral investment, particularly equity investment, during the last two decades has taken place largely in developed countries.[8]

From the viewpoint of global economic welfare, it is a matter of concern that political risk may result in inadequate exploration and development of the mineral resources of the South. It will reduce their incomes, employment and foreign exchange earnings in future and may mean that the world will go short of resources which could have been available at lower cost than the alternatives from the mines or the chemical industries of the North.

Above and beyond issues of economic efficiency lie considerations of justice. For help in analyzing and resolving these we turn naturally to the philosophers.

THEORIES OF JUSTICE

The purpose of a theory of justice is to reduce the need for the use of moral intuition in deciding whether a particular institution or act is fair. What is required is a set of general principles or guidelines which can be applied to most situations.

These principles have to be ones which the reasonable person judging impartially would accept as fair. Utilitarianism and the theories of John Rawls are examples of ones which are influential today.

In general, such theories have been developed to provide criteria for evaluating social institutions and behaviour within a society. This is particularly true of those which have been based upon the idea of an implicit contract. The extension of such rules for behaviour to relationships between states has been regarded by many commentators as illegitimate.

One school of thought exemplified by Hobbes and Machiavelli would regard justice as inseparably connected with the existence of a sovereign state. It only exists within the state because it is only enforceable there. Between states there are no general contracts. If states are viewed as being in a 'state of nature' in Hobbes' terms, there is no international sovereign authority to ensure that reciprocal compliance which Hobbes views as an essential basis for behaviour which is both self-interested and moral. The duty of their governments, then, is simply to pursue the national interest. This is imposed by an appreciation that other states will be pursuing their national self-interest, by force where necessary and without concern for the interests of other actors or of the international community. Many scholars in the field of international politics appear to take this sceptical view of morality among nations.[9]

Hans Morgenthau encapsulates their views: 'The state has no right to let its moral disapprobation get in the way of successful political action, itself inspired by the moral principle of national survival.'[10] Reasons of state are assumed to override the normal moral standards which guide human conduct. It is not difficult to think of examples of state behaviour which conforms to Morgenthau's prescription.

The only basis that such sceptics can accept for an international morality for states is enlightened self-interest. But then some would claim this is the only basis for morality that exists. Seeking a basis for international morality in his recent book, *Political Theory and International Relations*, Charles Beitz argues that this is not adequate: 'It fails to account for certain principles that intuitively seem to impose requirements on our actions regardless of considerations of actual or possible resulting benefit to ourselves. Elementary examples of such principles are the rule not to cause unnecessary suffering or to help save a life if that can be done at acceptable cost and risk.'[11] In his view the test of a moral theory is whether it 'allows us to explain the basis of such natural moral requirements . . . as move us to act even when there is no assurance of reciprocal compliance, and hence no self-interested justification, available'.[12]

Beitz does not deny that enlightened self-interest can explain a great deal of co-operative behaviour or actions of assistance between people or nations. In general, enlightened self-interest and what he would regard as a genuine moral point of view would indicate the same course of action. I suppose Marshall Aid from the United

States to Europe after the Second World War would be an outstanding example of what he means.

It is certainly true that most people do expect nations to take actions which involve them in costs and which bring them no obvious benefit. Governments do mount expensive rescue operations for people who are not their citizens. They do send large amounts of relief to other countries in emergencies such as famines and earthquakes. It is difficult to see that they do this in the expectation of a reciprocal action. The countries they help are often incapable of mounting such programmes of assistance. The media and the citizens of most donor nations seem to approve of these relief operations much more than they do overseas development assistance, even though that is fairly explicitly carried out for political or commercial self-interest.

Suppose a large rich nation with a diversified and buoyant economy had a dispute over fishing rights with a small, low-income nation whose citizens' livelihood depended upon the ability to sustain a fishing industry as far into the future as can be seen. Competition between their fishing fleets is depleting the stock so that the commercial returns to fishing and employment in fishing are falling rapidly in both countries. Now this might be a situation in which the large nation would concede the rights to the small one because it could see some future gain which would compensate for its present loss – perhaps a vote in the UN or support in some other important forum from the small nation. But let us assume this is not so. To surrender the rights would bring no foreseeable gain. Let us assume further that to police any treaty dividing and controlling the quantities fished would be too costly. The small country is too poor and has such foreign exchange problems that there is no way that it could pay compensation to the rich country for surrendering its fishing rights.

I suspect that in this situation most people would believe it to be morally just for the rich nation to hand over the fishing rights to the small, poor nation. Pragmatically, this would be the only way of ensuring the survival of the stock of fish for future generations, and the loss to the rich nation would seem small compared to the damage that would be inflicted on the poor nation by continuing the competition for the limited and declining stock of fish.

How do we underpin such a moral judgement with principles which would take us beyond the moral intuition, and the culturally determined value systems which are likely to differ significantly between individuals in different nations? It is hardly likely that, the moral judgments of say, the Ayatullah Khumayni and Herr Willy Brandt, both eminent statesmen, would often coincide.

One could appeal to a higher authority – God. But unfortunately past experience suggests that every nation thinks God is on their side It is unlikely that Khumayni and Brandt would be receiving the same signals from the same Authority. There are philosophical theories to which we can appeal for help, however. Here I summarize and, inevitably, oversimplify.

Utilitarianism

Economists have always had a fondness of utilitarianism as a basis for normative economics. At least, since it is not a contract theory, there is no reason to regard its propositions as only relevant within a nation's borders. In its simplest form the basic rule is that actions shall be judged upon whether they lead to the greatest happiness for the greatest number. The calculation of the greatest happiness is arrived at by simply adding together the pleasures and gains across human beings without concern for their quality or their distribution. Actions are good in so far as they maximize the net balance of satisfactions for the particular society with each person's pleasures and pains having equal weight.

The problems posed by this are self-evident. That all pleasures are of equal merit is not universally accepted. Even if their pursuit did not inflict pain on anyone else, societies usually want to condemn pleasures which are self-destructive. But even if quality of pleasures could be allowed for, a more important objection is that the criterion of a net balance of satisfaction could allow changes which make some rich people better off while making some poor people worse off. A simple Benthamite utilitarian theory is consistent with a very unequal distribution of income and with changes which make it even more unequal. But this would not be regarded as just in most societies.

The adoption of the principle of the diminishing marginal utility of income may help solve this problem, but not entirely, for if the gains of the better off from a change were sufficiently large, they would exceed the losses of the poorer unless the relative weights were very different.

The principles of utilitarianism combined with the diminishing marginal utility of income do provide us with some general guidelines for evaluating institutions governing international relations. Probably many of us have some such principles at the back of our minds when making moral judgments about such matters. But a competing set of principles can be found in the work of John Rawls in his monumental work, *A Theory of Justice*.

Rawls' Theory of Justice

Rawls sees society as a 'cooperative venture for mutual advantage' and sees ethical principles as needed to identify institutions that will fairly distribute the benefits and burdens of social life.[13] He deduces these principles by positing an 'original position' in which members decide what principles they would like to see invoked. They make these decisions in total ignorance of what their endowment of intelligence, strength and inheritance would be. If rational, non-gamblers, they would adopt a 'maximum' strategy, i.e. they would want to ensure that society was so organized that if they happened to be in the least fortunate group they would be as well-off as possible. From this basis he deduces the following principles:

(1) Each person should have as much freedom as is compatible with a similar freedom for everyone else.
(2) Social and economic arrangements should provide the greatest benefits to the least advantaged, consistent with adequate savings, and there should be equality of opportunity.

These are ranked in order of priority: liberty comes first, equality second. The latter, however, is qualified by the willingness to allow those inequalities necessary to create incentives to increase total net benefits, provided this brings gains to the least favoured. Rawls puts this together in his general conception: 'All social primary goods – liberty and opportunity, income and wealth, and the bases of self-respect – are to be distributed equally unless an unequal distribution of any or all of these goods is to the advantage of the least favoured.'[14]

It is an attractive theory. It relies purely on rational self-interest as the motive for setting up a social system which produces fair treatment for all. The fact that it stimulates severe criticism from extreme libertarians on the one hand and egalitarians on the other may suggest that he has got the balance about right.

Rawls' theory appears to have been written as if confined to a society within a nation-state where people recognize that they belong in a community within which they can see clear advantages in co-operative behaviour. Does that make it inapplicable as a guide to institutions and conduct in international relations? I do not think that it necessarily does make it irrelevant. Many changes in recent history are likely to have persuaded many people that co-operative behaviour between nations is not only likely to improve their own prospects of liberty and a reasonable standard of living, but may even be the only prospect for survival. Certainly, if they were to carry out the thought experiment of putting themselves into 'the original position' in which the probabilities would be that they would be born as a Chinese or Indian, they would be likely to support a great deal of international co-operation. In a brief passage Rawls does suggest extending the interpretation of the original position to nations (p. 378).

It is hard to believe that nations exist in a Hobbesian 'state of nature'. A great deal of co-operation does already take place through the UN, the GATT, and bilateral and multilateral aid programmes. Some nations are prepared to accept the decisions of the International Court of Justice on international disputes. Even if one views that evidence with some cynicism, it is most certainly true that a great deal of social activity in the form of trade and finance takes place between nations.

Suppose we do reject these approaches towards principles of international ethics. Then our only possible judgments about the action of a nation would be whether it was efficient and whether it was in its national self-interest.

Do the actions of nations in the field of natural resources show adherence to any ethical principles? In the collective expressions which emerge from such bodies as the United Nations do ethical principles have any bearing? Sovereignty, a perennial issue in politics, has attracted a great deal of attention in the relations between multinational companies and host countries in the past, one result being a UN resolution on the subject.

SOVEREIGNTY AND NATURAL RESOURCES

This UN General Assembly resolution asserts that nations have 'permanent sovereignty over natural resources'.[15] It is not self-evident that this is just, since natural resources are quite arbitrarily scattered over and under the surface of the earth. It is not obvious that this distribution is likely to give rise to maximum satisfaction. Nations, in Rawls' original position, would probably want to ensure equal access to important natural resources unless it could be shown that the least advantaged nations would benefit from some other arrangement. Purely from the viewpoint of national self-interest, it is not obvious why nations would accept such a resolution as binding if sovereignty meant the right of each nation to do entirely as it pleased with the natural resources inside its boundaries and territorial waters. If barred from access to an essential resource or if access were made subject to intolerable conditions, nations would be likely to use force to gain access. It is not self-evident that a war fought on these grounds would be unjust. However, the reasons for the UN resolution may change our view of this somewhat.

Both the text of the resolution and the debates concerning it make it clear that the main purpose was to defend developing countries from exploitation by foreign mining companies. It supported the right of the LDCs' governments to expropriate (with compensation) foreign-owned mines and processing facilities. As the developing nations are by definition relatively poor and their governments weak and often thought to lack access to the best information and advice when making contracts with foreign companies, a resolution of this kind may have strengthened their bargaining power *vis-à-vis* the international mining and oil companies. *De jure*, and generally *de facto*, governments have always possessed the power of expropriation with or without compensation.

Even if one accepted a global redistribution principle, apart from the small oil-rich nations of the Gulf, possession of natural resources is not a very significant factor in explaining affluence and poverty. Nations like Japan, Switzerland, West Germany, South Korea and Singapore are relatively poor in resources, but enjoy relatively high and rapidly rising standards of living compared with well-endowed nations like Brazil, Mexico or Nigeria. The wealth of an oil sheik may be offensive when contrasted with the poverty of an Egyptian or Sudanese farmer, but that is more likely to lead to South–South rather than North–South conflict.

International trade is a powerful force for ameliorating the effects of unequally distributed resources. Nations with vast mineral resources have to dispose of them if they are to obtain the products of other nations which they require to enjoy reasonable standards of living and prospects of growth. Embargoes or even effective cartels to control the supply of minerals for political or economic reasons are relatively rare events. We are still suffering from the one outstanding success in this field, but that success may well prove limited in time and circumstance. OPEC's power has diminished greatly since 1979 and no other mineral producing group of nations has succeeded in emulating the oil cartel.

SOUTHERN GOVERNMENTS AND NORTHERN COMPANIES: CONFLICT AND ACCOMMODATION

More than half of the mining operations in developing countries are nationally owned and controlled, through public sector companies, joint ventures in which the government has the majority of shares, or local mining companies. So who needs the foreigners?

Naturally the views of mining company officials and those of politicians and government officials tend to polarize on this question. The argument centres on several issues:[16]

(1) Efficient mining output is more likely to occur the greater the number of experienced mining companies competing with each other in exploring for and developing minerals in a country. Experience suggests that public sector monopolies do not promote efficiency in mining any more than in agriculture or manufacturing.

(2) It is more likely that a government enterprise with top management made up of political appointees will run the industry so as to attain national objectives than would competing enterprises operating within a legal framework which was designed to promote national objectives.

(3) A subsidiary of an MNC has access to a large pool of technology and management skills for solving problems. When Chile nationalized the copper mines they had to import an army of technical consultants from all over the world to help solve production problems. Despite this output was low and costly for several years.

(4) Risk-taking may be better handled by MNCs both because of their greater access to finance and their ability to pool risks across worldwide operations.

(5) For some minerals there are no organized commodity exchanges, e.g. bauxite, iron ore and manganese. Vertically integrated MNCs can provide markets. They are also in a better position to arrange long-term contracts for output which are often a condition of loans for development.

(6) The vast sums of money needed for a large modern mine, as much as $1000 million, often make it essential to have equity participation by an MNC. Foreign investors, including the World Bank, usually require the assurance of proven experience in mine management that the MNCs can offer.

Can the contributions provided by MNCs be obtained in other ways? Can the money be borrowed independently and the various skills hired at market prices which avoid paying an excessive rent to the MNCs? This is the notorious 'depackaging' or 'unbundling' issue which frequently surfaces in the context of MNCs and the developing countries' relationships. Many commentators believe that depackaging is possible and that LDCs would gain by it. The attempts to set up a binding code on foreign investment and technology transfer are to a considerable extent motivated by this aspiration.

In the mining field there are numerous firms of consulting engineers who can and do provide many of the services required in mining development. Their services are used widely by the MNCs themselves and also by the state mining corporations of several LDCs, but they do not provide equity capital and only rarely do they manage operations. They clearly do not provide all the services required nor, lacking an equity stake, do they have the same incentives to insure the success of the whole operation from development to marketing. They are also very expensive.

Raymond Mikesell concludes that it is very doubtful that all the necessary inputs can be bought separately. Moreover, he also believes that the resources embodied in the MNC are much more effective than the sum of their parts. His general conclusion is that there is no need for a government to choose between public and foreign private enterprise for all its resource development, but that for the reasons given above a substantial element of foreign participation is likely to be much more beneficial than a state monopoly.

There is, in general, between an MNC and the government of the country in which it operates a considerable area of mutual interest.

Co-operation between them makes possible greater benefits than either would be likely to produce without that co-operation. But there is also conflict, since both are interested in how the benefits are distributed and how the mining operations are carried out. The way in which the benefits are distributed can affect the efficiency of the mining activity: the costs of extraction, the rate of depletion, investment in development, new exploration, training for local management and technicians, and the level and growth of royalties and taxes which accrue to the host goverments.

Historically a good deal of the conflict has arisen because at the exploration stage, when no one knows the development prospects, a bargain has been struck which gives foreign companies rights to extract and sell minerals found on the basis of quite modest payments. If the area turns out to be rich in easily mined resources, the foreign companies make vast profits. This attracts hostility from the local nationals, who may then expropriate or unilaterally change the existing contract to get a larger share of the revenues. Such actions, together with the political instability common in many LDCs, have made it difficult to attract foreign investment into exploration and development. In fact they have led to a sharp fall in new private investment in mining and exploration of the South.[17]

From the companies' side they have been treated unfairly. They took the gamble of exploring for minerals. Many of their surveys around the world turn up nothing. They may sink 100 boreholes to find one viable oil-well. It was their money that was at stake, not the government's, and a high return on the investment in this country is needed to offset their losses elsewhere. The company looks at its overall return from its worldwide activities, which on average could be quite low while a particular mine is making large profits. But the government is concerned to maximize the return to it from the minerals under its soil.

Over time most countries have sought to increase their revenues from mining. In the Chilean copper industry the government's share of pretax profits rose from 16 per cent in 1930 to 28 per cent in 1940, 58 per cent in 1950, and 69 per cent in 1965. But between 1944 and 1955 Chilean copper output fell from 540 000 tons to 400 000 tons per year while world production went up by 20 per cent. The government's receipts from copper actually fell in real terms.[18]

Both MNCs and LDC governments have grave mutual suspicions. The governments feel that they have been taken advantage of in the past because of their lack of information and expertise. They believe companies evade corporation taxes by creative accounting practices and by transfer pricing. For their part the MNCs feel that the governments are so paranoid that they cannot make their minds up on what seem to them simple issues. They do not seem to understand competitive business and the need for prompt decisions. They fear that contracts will not be honoured but changed to their disadvantage in the future.

If as a result of these sorts of difficulties mining developments lag in the South, this will also hurt the countries of the North in a decade or so. No altruism is required to encourage Northern action; self-interest should be sufficient.

Various solutions have been proposed for these problems: international assistance for exploration, equity participation by the host government so that by sharing the risks it becomes entitled to share in economic rents, joint ventures which include investment by international organizations such as the World Bank to help give some guarantee of secure contracts, systems of arbitration acceptable to both parties to mineral contracts. Many innovative schemes have been developed in recent years, and Mikesell reports on several from Papua New Guinea to Indonesia.[19] Each has to be designed to meet the particular circumstances of the mineral and the objectives of the government and the MNC.

One area in which the position of host governments has been greatly strengthened in recent years is in the quality of information and advice, both technical and legal, which they have had at their disposal. The MNCs now complain that they are outgunned by the international experts on the government negotiating team. Greater clarity in legal contracts does help to reduce one area of conflict.

If we are to appeal to the principles of Rawls in this matter, then the egalitarian principle would require that in the absence of any other ways of achieving redistribution most of the gains from mining in LDCs should accrue to them, but this is constrained by the difference principle. The latter requires that sufficient incentives be given to the investors and management of the MNCs to induce them to operate in ways which would maximize the absolute benefits going to the host countries. I am not sure whether, or how, that should be modified in a case where the government of the LDC is itself unjust or where the benefits are likely to accrue to a very few of its richest citizens.

The subject of the economics and ethics of natural resource development is so vast that this paper could not hope to cover it.

Even in the limited areas covered the importance of the conflicts which arise between LDCs and MNCs in the development of natural resources is clear. But solutions which would lead to concrete gains to both the MNCs and the LDCs are possible. What is required is that both examine the issues in terms of their long-run self-interest. This may not produce either the most efficient or the most just solution, but in the real world pursuit of the optimum is often in vain. The achievement of even a small improvement in an area as important as this is a worthwhile pursuit.

APPENDIX

Optimal Management of a Renewable Resource: Fish[20]

Fish stocks actually fluctuate with climate, disease, predators and in-built cyclical processes, but we assume a stable situation in which there is a natural equilibrium stock resulting from a proportionate growth as the number of births rises with population size up to a point at which the environment (food limits and predators) slows and eventually stops natural growth. Up to that equilibrium point births exceed deaths. This means that at any stock below the natural equilibrium it is possible to take quantities of fish so that natural loss plus captures are equal to the natural additions and the stock remains in equilibrium.

For this representative fish population there exists a set of constant levels of catch and stock which are each consistent with a stable stock at that rate of fishing. If stocks are less than a critical level an equilibrium stock would only be possible with negative catches, i.e. artificial additions to the stock, say adding young trout to a trout fishery. The reason for this is that below that stock level natural forces would lead to the extinction of this population (as has happened with some animal species). They may be too widely dispersed to allow adequate breeding to maintain the population or insufficient to survive random calamities.

There would be a particular stock level which would allow the largest catch consistent with maintenance of the stock. This is the maximum sustainable yield (MSY). But it would only be an optimum if fishing were costless and there were no preference for consumption today over consumption tomorrow, i.e. no positive discount rate.

Fishing Costs

Clearly the activity of fishing must involve costs of equipment, wages, fuel, etc. These costs will be related to the size of the catch (more time, more distance and over the longer run investment in more equipment), but also to the size of the stock, i.e. the same catch can be obtained more easily when the stock of fish is large.

As fishing is expanded from a low level of fishing with a large stock average costs will fall at first as overheads are spread over larger volumes of fish caught. But as the level of catch is increased unit costs rise as more ships, fishermen and fuel are needed and as stocks are depleted, more time and distance is involved in searching for and catching the fish. Before the maximum sustainable yield is reached average costs would be rising very sharply. Beyond the MSY the catch falls with the reduced stocks and the unit costs continue to rise. One actually has a backward bending long-run average costs curve. The point chosen will be where price obtainable for fish equals the long-run marginal cost of catching the fish. Given these conditions, that will occur before the MSY level is reached i.e. the effect of introducing costs of fishing is to reduce the optimum catch below the maximum sustainable yield.

Time Preference

As argued above when costs are included but time preference ignored, the optimal fishing strategy produces a catch less than MSY. Any greater catch involves reducing stock and causes higher costs next period. This is only true if there is indifference between present and future benefits. If one introduces a discount rate the firm does better to reduce the stock gradually because the consequent lower catch next period carries less value than the current increased catch. The present value of the sum of sales of fish would be raised by increasing present catches at the expense of future catches. If the discount rate is sufficiently high it will pay to fish beyond the MSY point provided the price of fish is high enough.

If scale economies are strong it may pay to alternate between periods of intense fishing followed by zero fishing while the stock recovers. This is particularly likely where a fishing fleet can be switched between one area and another. It is rather like slash and burn cultivation or leaving fields fallow to recover from intense farming.

Another possibility is selective culling. This can maintain the stock with an increased offtake because the fleet avoids the breeding seasons or grounds, or uses large mesh nets to leave the smaller, faster growing, fish in the sea.

The Problem of Common Access

If there is unrestricted access the following problems arise: (i) catches exceed socially desirable levels; (ii) stocks are more likely to be exhausted; (iii) cost may be unnecessarily high due to depleted stocks and the consequent loss of scale economies and increased search costs.

The basic reason is that the individual fisherman cannot control user costs, the loss of future profits due to excessive fishing today. It is the result of the sum of the activities of all. Individually he neglects user cost and maximizes short-run profits by equating short-run marginal costs with price. The effects can be dramatic and are the source of international disputes in whaling, fishing and mineral exploitation of the sea bed.[21]

NOTES AND REFERENCES

1. P.S. Dasgupta and G.M. Heal, *The Economic Theory of Natural Resources* (Cambridge: Cambridge University Press, 1979).

2. H. Hotelling, 'The Economics of Exhaustible Resources', *Journal of Political Economy* 39 (1931) pp. 137–75.
3. R. Bosson and B. Varon, *The Mining Industry and the Developing Countries*, World Bank Research Publication (London: Oxford University Press, 1977) p. 63.
4. J.E. Stiglitz, 'Monopoly and the Rate of Extraction of Exhaustible Resources', *American Economic Review* 6 (1976) pp. 655–61.
5. R. Lecomber, *The Economics of Natural Resources* (London: Macmillan, 1979) pp. 55–6.
6. D.H. Meadows *et al., The Limits of Growth* (London: Earth Island, 1972).
7. J. Meade, 'Economic Policy and the Threat of Doom', in B. Benjamin *et al.* (eds), *Resources and Population* (London: Academic Press, 1973).
8. World Bank, *Annual Report* (Washington, DC, 1978) pp. 20–1.
9. C.R. Beitz, *Political Theory and International Relations* (Princeton, NJ: Princeton University Press, 1979) chs. 2 and 3 for summaries of their views and criticisms; R. Aron, *Peace and War: A Theory of International Relations* (New York: Doubleday, 1966) p. 580; G.F. Kennan, *Realities of American Foreign Policy* (Princeton, NJ: Princeton University Press, 1954) p. 47: H.J. Morgenthau, *Politics among Nations*, 5th ed. (New York: Alfred A. Knopf, 1973) p. 10; T. Hobbes, *Leviathan* (1651) in Sir William Molesworth (ed.), *The English Works of Thomas Hobbes*, vol. 3 (London: John Bohn, 1841); N. Machiavelli, *The Prince and the Discourses* (New York: Random House, 1950) p. 65.
10. Morgenthau, *Politics among Nations*, p. 10.
11. Beitz, *Political Theory and International Relations*, p. 56.
12. Ibid., p. 58.
13. J. Rawls, *A Theory of Justice* (Cambridge, Mass.: Harvard University Press, 1971; Oxford: Oxford University Press, 1972) p. 4.
14. Ibid., pp. 302–3.
15. Resolution 1803 (XVII), quoted in Beitz, *Political Theory and International Relations*, p. 142, n. 31.
16. Most of the following points are drawn from R.F. Mikesell, *New Patterns of World Mineral Development* (British North American Committee, 1979) and Bosson and Varon, *The Mining Industry and the Developing Countries.*
17. Mikesell, *New Patterns of World Mineral Development*, pp. 23–4.
18. Bosson and Varon, *The Mining Industry and the Developing Countries*, pp. 140–1.
19. Mikesell, *New Patterns of World Mineral Development*, pp. 53–60.
20. Main sources are Dasgupta and Heal, *The Economic Theory of Natural Resources*, and Lecomber, *The Economics of Natural Resources.* This exposition draws mainly on Lecomber, ch. 3.
21. I am grateful to V. Balasubramanyam, Walter Elkan, Robert Rothschild, and participants in the conference on 'Rights and Obligations in North–South Relations' for comments and suggests on an earlier draft.

4 The Ethics of Aid

HANS W. SINGER

In the ethics of aid there are two separate problems. The first concerns the *motives* or *reasons* for which aid is given. Are they in the field of ethics, i.e. aid given for humanitarian or charitable reasons or because of a sense of global responsibility (all of which are presumably in the field of morals or ethics)? Alternatively is aid given for reasons of self-interest or politics (both of which presumably would not qualify as moral)? The second problem relates to the *effects* of aid rather than its motives. If the aid is both intended to be and is effective in reducing the poverty of poor people, feeding hungry children, coping with emergencies, or helping a struggling poor country to make better provision for its citizens, then presumably there is a strong moral basis and moral justification for this aid. On the other hand, if the aid is both clearly given for reasons of politics or self-interest and if its effect is to help an oppressive and vicious government to maintain its control over its citizens with widespread violation of human rights, then such aid would clearly be immoral or at least non-moral. But what about the mixed cases? In one type of mixed case the aid is given for humanitarian and good reasons with an intention to help poor people, but in fact the benefits of the aid are leaked away from the intended purpose and support a bad government or an opulent élite in the recipient country. Another mixed case would be where the aid is given – as is usually the case – from a variety of motives in which self-interest, politics, global responsibility, charity and human-itarianism are all hopelessly mixed up together and impossible to disentangle. The effects of aid can be equally mixed: some of it (through 'trickling down') will benefit poor people directly or indirectly but another part will leak away to the rich or powerful or oppressive. For reasons of theoretical completeness we might list another mixed case, i.e. where the aid is given for non-moral reasons

84

(let us say to prop up a friendly government or secure air bases or simply to spoil the game of the Russians, etc.) but where in fact the aid is used in such a way that it benefits poor people in the recipient country.

There are no statistics which would enable us on the basis of such a rough classification to decide how much aid is moral and how much aid is not. My own guess is that perhaps 20 per cent of all aid is morally supportable, about 20 per cent is clearly not moral, and 60 per cent belongs to one or other of the mixed cases. Whether or not such a record justifies aid at the present or an increased level is a matter of judgement, according to what weight we attach to the moral case for aid as against other justifications. What is clear is that those making a moral case for aid should be concerned to change the mixture so that more aid is clearly morally justifiable both as to motives and as to effects, and perhaps more important in the big bag of mixed cases the morally desirable element becomes stronger.

The ethical or moral case for aid may also be contrasted with the mutual benefit case. The first Brandt Report, even before stating its specific recommendations, nails its flag to the mast in a chapter on 'Mutual Interests' by stating in the first paragraph: 'The principle of mutuality of interest has been at the centre of our discussion.'[1] Yet we may notice that as this chapter develops, the mutual benefits which it proclaims become increasingly qualified. In fact, it concludes with a section entitled 'The Moral Imperatives' and the statement that 'we do not suggest that the measures we propose are without cost to the North'.[2] Not without some justice, Dudley Seers has entitled his review of the Brandt Report 'Muddling Morality and Mutuality'.[3]

Yet the Brandt Report is not inconsistent, for the ethical–moral case and the mutual benefit case for aid are in no way incompatible. If they are both true, they mutually reinforce each other. In that case we have a happy coincidence of self-interest and morality. This is, of course, an extended version of Adam Smith's 'invisible hand'. By following their self-interest, individuals or firms or countries also satisfy the moral principle of the common good of the community, country or world as a whole. We can also put it in the opposite way: by following such moral principles as reducing poverty, feeding the hungry, sharing wealth and income more equitably between countries, etc., it will turn out that we have also served our own interests and are better off as a result. It is an extended version, because Adam Smith applied the principle to trade, not aid.

Moreover, he was clearly sceptical of any unqualified international application of his principle, for he wrote of trade with the 'new continent' of America:

> A new set of exchanges, therefore, began to take place which had never been thought of before, and which should naturally have proved as advantageous to the new as it certainly did to the old continent. The savage injustice of the Europeans rendered an event, which ought to have been beneficial to all, ruinous and destructive to several of those unfortunate countries.

So the 'invisible hand', when combined with immoral 'savage injustice' on one side (the stronger side), does not bring forth the common good, but rather the ruin of the other (weaker) partner.

Here, by the way, we also have in a nutshell a controversial aspect of the moral case for aid. If it is really accepted that we have behaved in the past with 'savage injustice' to the inhabitants of 'new continents', do we then have a moral duty to atone for our past guilt by offering aid to the successors of those we wronged? This raises a Pandora's box of questions. Were we in fact guilty of such injustices in the past? And are we today responsible for the guilt of our ancestors? Have the present inhabitants of these countries a claim to compensation? And is aid a suitable form of such compensation?

Let me say straight away that I do not believe that the atonement of past wrongdoing as a moral case takes us very far. Excepting some special and more recent cases – German aid to Israel would be a clear example – I do not think that guilt feelings over past injustices can be invoked as a moral basis of aid today. In this respect, I agree with P.T. Bauer (Lord Bauer) when he argues against accepting the undoubted fact of present inequalities as constituting in itself evidence of past injustice. He probably exaggerates the importance of the 'restitution' motive when he declares it to be widespread among the advocates of aid – particularly the clerical advocates – and even more powerful subconsciously, never far below the surface.[4] He is certainly right in arguing that inequality has many origins and reasons; that not all inequalities by a long stretch are evidence of exploitation, past or present; that not all exploitation is across international boundaries and thus susceptible to the aid approach; and that aid may be ineffective in reducing inequalities, or even add to them. When exploitation is indigenous, aid *may* but need not assist the exploiters rather than their victims.

Yet when all this is admited, there is more in the restitution argument than Lord Bauer admits. There are elements in the international economic system which work to the advantage of the rich and the disadvantage of the poor. To have a near-monopoly of technological capacity, research and development (R&D) capacity, know-how, financial power (at least up to the emergence of OPEC), investment resources, entrepreneurial capacity, information, and briefing and negotiating techniques, will give the richer industrial countries an edge in trade, investment, growth capacity and indeed in all the bargaining and negotiations relating to economic contacts. It is a matter of terminology whether such built-in advantages represent 'exploitation' or not. I myself would avoid such terminology as misleading and prefer to stick to 'built-in advantages'. I would also readily admit that the developing countries and their governments could do a lot more to reduce and cope with such built-in disadvantages by more effective domestic policies and also by better co-operation with each other. Yet the built-in disequilibrium in advantages *does* constitute a *prima facie* moral (and perhaps also economic) case for compensatory action, i.e. aid in one form or another. Such aid in the broader sense – 'in one form or another' – may, of course, take the form of tariff preferences, better prices for their export commodities, liberalized migration, etc., rather than aid in the narrower direct sense, but it remains 'aid' in the sense of unilateral concessionary action.

In terms of mutual benefits, the existence of built-in advantages and disadvantages raises the question of the distribution of such benefits. Even if there are mutual interests or mutual benefits, this does not necessarily mean an equal or fair distribution of these benefits. The third-world countries tend to argue that mutual benefits within an unequal power structure will normally mean a correspondingly unequal distribution of benefits. There is some evidence for this. For instance, a well-known study of the effects of buffer-stock programmes to stabilize the prices of primary commodities has found that the gains to the developed countries from price stabilization were at least three times the size of the gains to the developing countries.[5] From the point of view of Brandt, this would be a positive finding since his plea is addressed to the developed countries. But if one of the global objectives is the reduction of gaps between rich and poor countries – the reduction of international inequality in this sense – then such a distribution of benefits will not help to improve matters.

The natural conclusion would then be that what is needed are measures to strengthen the capacity of developing countries to participate more equitably in the world economy, but this involves changes in the power structure which would more directly conflict with the principle of mutual interests. While the unequal power structure continues, however, there is a case for compensatory action. This leaves open the question whether in specific cases the aid actually is an effective transfer of resources from the beneficiaries of unequal advantages to the victims of unequal disadvantages, or whether it is ineffective or possibly perverse (counterproductive) in its effect. The existence of built-in advantages in terms of know-how, R&D, technological capacity, management, information, etc., is already a pointer as to the forms of aid most likely to be effective, with some degree of emphasis on technical assistance. In this case the aid is morally right because it represents compensation for the injustice of returns to developing countries from participation in the world trading and financial system. But what is a 'just' or 'fair' return? The 'just return' has notoriously been a difficult item of debate, among theologians as well as economists.

The question of colonial responsibility, in whatever attenuated form, still has a lot to do with the geographical distribution of much of bilateral aid. British aid still goes predominantly to the Commonwealth, the survivor from the old colonial relationship. The attenuated form which colonial guilt feelings take is usually described as something like 'a special sense of responsibility, arising from historical association and shared language and institutions'. Similarly, French aid is still largely concentrated on the former colonial empire in Francophone West Africa; and Japanese aid on the old Japanese 'co-prosperity sphere' in Eastern and South-East Asia. In the case of Japan, this is perhaps still more clearly a case of surviving colonial and wartime guilt feelings; this applies particularly to continuing Japanese aid to South Korea, which was a direct and heavily exploited Japanese colony. The critics of aid describe such concentrations of aid as 'neo-colonialism', i.e. as a perpetuation of the old colonial relationshp in new forms. Other critics of aid say that although a sense of responsibility and a concern for safeguarding of old historical associations may be basically creditable and moral motives, in an immoral world order among unequal partners the end effect is inevitably to strengthen dependency.

There is a similar ethical problem for the aid recipients. For the donors the question is whether we today are responsible for any sins of our ancestors and must make restitution. For the recipients it takes the form of whether the present inhabitants, or even more so the present governments, are entitled to be compensated for harm done to *their* ancestors. It is tempting to answer this question with a straight 'no', especially in the case of governments, most of which came into power by violently overthrowing previous governments; but further reflection may make us doubtful about such a straight negative answer. There *is* an economic linkage between generations which may take several forms, of which we may mention just two:

(1) If my grandfather was malnourished and uneducated as a child, as a result of oppression, or exploitation, or land alienation, his brain and muscle development and his efficiency as a producer would have been undermined. This means that he ends up as a poor man so that my father and I in due turn are undernourished and uneducated as children and cannot develop *our* full productive potential.

(2) If my country two generations ago was deprived of physical capital, industries, transport, higher education, health services, etc., as a result of exploitation, this would lower productive efficiency all round and reduce the potential for further capital accumulation, which could affect generation after generation.

These are just two examples of the existence of a historical continuum. There is no radical disjuncture between past and present.

Perhaps we have pursued the argument of guilt feelings for past unequal relationships too far, for it is by no means certain that the net effect of the colonial relationship was in fact one of exploitation. The record of many developing countries since independence, particularly in Africa, does not provide clear proof that independence in itself provides a better basis for development than a colonial relationship. Certainly the case of Hong Kong does not suggest that the status of a colony is necessarily harmful for economic development. But there is another form of guilt feeling which has a lot to do with the moral argument surrounding aid. This is the feeling of guilt of the rich when confronted with the poverty of the poor. There are many elements in such guilt feelings which have been applied by one school or another to international relations: I may feel guilty because I believe that my riches must be the result of some form of exploitation; this leads us back to the previous argument. Or I may feel that my riches and the other man's poverty are due to unequal opportunities; that I have been lucky in my opportunities, or in my choice of ancestors, or in choosing the place where I was born (if choice is the right word), compared to the poor man who was unlucky in one or all of these respects. This being a case more of luck than of merit, it establishes a moral case for aid to help the poor to improve the opportunities open to them.

The force of this argument appears in public opinion polls. In 1977, one such survey in the UK[6] suggested that, while the average elector believed expenditure on aid to be some three and a half times its actual level, the electorate's support for aid was based for the most part on altruistic grounds. Thus, on being asked why aid should or should not be given, 52 per cent of the sample cited a 'moral' or 'humanitarian' obligation to help the less well off, against 4 per cent who thought aid would improve Britain's trading position and 3 per cent who said it would improve political relations with developing countries. There may also be a guilt feeling involved in knowing that the last pound of my income as a rich man means very little to me and the sacrifice of doing without it is very small, whereas the additional pound to a poor man might mean the difference between life and death for him or his children. I would then feel guilty in not increasing the social value of this pound by transferring it to the poor. This last argument has been one of the bases of the national welfare states which we have created in our western democracies. It then takes a relatively simply moral appeal to human solidarity or the unity of mankind to extend this principle from our fellow citizens to our fellow beings in other countries.

A contrasting view of international inequalities is that they are not a matter of unmerited good luck or exploitation but of merit, and that by giving aid to the poor you are rewarding and encouraging their failure to utilize the opportunities open to them. On this view, you should direct aid not to the poorest countries and poorest people but to those who are successfully climbing up the ladder, assuming that they need the aid to climb even faster. This moral support for industry and success will also be more readily combined with self-interest, since the successfully expanding countries – the Koreas and Singapores of this world, Ivory Coast and Malawi rather than Ghana and Zambia – will also be more effective partners in international trade and will present better markets. Presumably the argument does not justify aid where 'success' is clearly due to good luck rather than merit, as in the case of Saudi Arabia's oil wealth. One can, of course, hold that our higher standards of living are a matter of merit rather than good luck or exploitation, and yet at the same time argue that there is a moral case for supporting those who have shown less merit in the past, specially in the case of children where lack of merit cannot mean more than choosing the wrong parents or place of birth. The case becomes tricky, however, if you hold (like Peter Bauer and others) that aid is an actual disincentive to industry and success.

The critics of aid would, of course, deny the ethical basis of any such guilt feelings.[7] They argue that if we are better off than others this is unavoidable since economic growth and development must start somewhere rather than everywhere simultaneously; that improvement is largely in the hands of poorer countries themselves; that the receipt of aid undermines incentives to improve your own condition by your own effort; that much of the aid does not in fact benefit the poor but benefits the rich, powerful and oppressive in the recipient countries, while much of the cost of aid is borne by the poorer people in donor countries. Certainly there is evidence that a significant proportion of project aid benefits does not 'trickle-down' from the richer to the poorest groups, and it is argued that 'if those poorest groups are to be reached by development aid then it must be done direct, and not by hoping for indirect spin-off'.[8] This last argument, with much justice, is often elaborated in showing that targeting on the poor is extremely difficult in practice, and that much aid, while intended to reach the poor, in fact ends up in the pockets of the rich: the World Bank, for example, stresses that, in spite of overall success, several of its programmes which have been targeted on the very poor, in particular food subsidy and special credit programmes, have on occasion been 'highjacked' by higher income groups.[9] However, unless it is argued that targeting on the poor is an impossibility, this seems more an argument for improvement and changes in the nature and structure of aid (for example, by relying more on OXFAM and CARE types of aid and trying to bypass 'bad' governments as much as possible) rather than an argument against aid as such.

A true guilt feeling which would be accepted by many critics of aid as constituting a moral case for giving aid, in spite of its alleged shortcomings, is a result of our protectionism against the trade of developing countries. This is both economically and morally inexcusable, yet very widespread and clearly intensifying under the impact of unemployment and recession. If we look at such a conservative and understating publication as the IMF's 1984 'World Economic Outlook', we find the following statements:

> resort to protectionist measures continued to increase in 1983 . . . Despite the acknowledged need to reverse the drift toward protectionism, efforts at liberalization were limited. Although Tokyo Round tariff reductions negotiated under the auspices of the General Agreement on Tariffs and Trade (GATT) continued, little progress was made in many industrial countries in removing the non-tariff trade barriers introduced in specific sectors since the mid-1970s . . . the adoption by industrial countries of non-tariff barriers negotiated on a bilateral basis outside the GATT framework has further weakened the open multilateral trading system; extension or intensification of trade restrictions by the industrial countries in such sectors as steel, automobiles, textiles and clothing, electronics, and agriculture.

The report identifies three broad categories of protectionist measures facing developing countries: (1) measures directed specifically at developing countries, as in the textile and clothing sector, by means of which restrictions against them have been steadily tightened, despite general freedom from non-tariff restrictions in intra-industrial country trade; (2) measures not directed solely at developing countries but which affect products of direct interest to them, as in agriculture, footwear and other leather products, and steel: and (3) measures in other sectors such as automobiles and high-technology industries which have adverse indirect effects by increasing distortions and creating uncertainty in investment decisions, and which discourage export diversification efforts and the pursuit of outward-oriented growth strategies by developing countries. The report states that 'overall access to foreign markets for developing countries has deteriorated in the past few years'.[10]

Obviously the situation described in these quotations calls for redress; since direct redress in the form of reduction of protectionism is so obviously impossible in spite of rhetorical affirmations, any indirect compensatory redress through aid could clearly be considered a moral commitment. With this most of the critics of aid would also agree since they continue to proclaim trade, not aid, as the right policy. One may wonder whether some of them do not do this insincerely, knowing that they bang their heads against a wall asking for reduced protectionism. Generally speaking, trade liberalizationists are also in favour of aid (the Brandt Report would again be an example), while most of those who are protectionists are also opposed to aid. The slogan 'Trade Not Aid' was already current in the 1950s, and one is reminded of the honest answer given by Senator Taft, the leading conservative Republican spokesman at the time. When asked what he thought of this slogan 'Trade Not Aid', he replied: 'I agree with the second part of it.' Perhaps he was more candid than some of today's critics of aid who tell us that we should liberalize trade instead, even if the ranks of this latter group have recently been joined by the leader writers of *The Times*.

It should be noted here that ethical (as well as economic) disapproval of aid is not monopolized by the far right. Indeed, similar conclusions are drawn by otherwise diametrically opposed camps. While Bauer's ethical opposition to aid is based on the view that aid, in attempting to create more egalitarian social conditions, in fact generates 'distortions' of the 'naturally' hierarchical world order, Theresa Hayter's opposition, coming from the left, has predictably different roots.[11] She argues that aid is merely a way of maintaining a common interest between the élites of developing and developed countries and furthermore that aid is a 'bribe' to make it worthwhile for developing countries' élites to continue to co-operate with the drain of resources from their countries. As a further comparison, Bauer considers aid to be a positive barrier to development (which in his view is equated with the free operation of market forces), while Hayter argues that aid promotes a particular kind of development which is in accordance with the interests of the West (or North). Thus President John F. Kennedy is cited as saying that 'foreign aid is a method by which the US maintains a position of influence and control around the world and sustains a good many countries which would definitely collapse or pass into the Communist bloc'. President Richard N. Nixon, less elegantly, is claimed to have said: 'Let us remember that the main purpose of American aid is not to help others but to help ourselves.'[12] That is not even mutual interest, but only self-interest.

Though both arriving at negative conclusions as regards the suitability of aid, the two voices of Bauer and Hayter are obviously expressing fundamentally antithetical world views, each with its own vision of what is ethical or moral. Both sides present a highly simplistic picture of what is a very complex question. They are concerned with the objectives of aid rather than the efficiency with which these objectives are fulfilled by aid. For the latter question, it is not sufficient to ask whether aid is a 'good' or 'bad' thing. What is also needed is to look at the way in which it is allocated and administered. But when morality is the issue at hand, the first point to be raised is that of motives. Concern with the 'effectiveness' of aid on the part of donor countries is a very recent preoccupation. Some observers have noticed that aid supporters tended to regard the practice as so clearly right that any investigation of the efficiency with which it was used appeared superfluous, if not somewhat mean-minded.

The new concern with effectiveness coincided with the onset of world recession. The perceived need for economic contraction corresponded to a parallel belt-tightening in charitable disposition. Nobody would dispute the common sense of wanting aid to be efficient and effective, but at the same time it appears legitimate to doubt whether some of the increased questioning of the effectiveness of aid does not really conceal a weakening of the moral motives of aid donors.

In this way, the blame for an ever greater reluctance to donate aid during the last decade has been placed on the Third World. These countries are charged with not making optimal use of funds, squandering them through corruption and inefficiencies. There is, of course, an element of truth in this, but at the same time a cynic might add that the perceived self-interest of donors in reducing aid may constitute a prime cause of their heightened concern with such failings on the part of the recipients; it is not clear that such failings are new or that they have sharply increased recently.

The question of effectiveness nevertheless remains an important ingredient in donor countries' decision-making. Arguments, such as those put forward by the Brandt Report, that quantitative levels of aid should be increased have become more and more unpalatable at a time of international recession. Indeed, at such times emphasis on the quantity of aid may be misplaced. As Mosley stresses, when national income growth of most aid donors is constrained, to persuade their governments to increase public expenditure of any sort, let alone on such a 'luxury' item as foreign aid, is very difficult.[13] The implication here is that limited resources are much better spent for national purposes than 'wasted' as 'charitable handouts'.

The realistic consequence of this tightening of the national purse-strings is to increase emphasis on what Mosley calls the 'quality' of aid. This he considers to be aid both used more effectively and given through more altrustic concerns for the development of the recipient countries themselves and, in particular for the 'Wretched of the Earth', in other words the very poorest. Such an 'aid quality index' is, of course, a subjective matter, depending on our view-point. In terms of reducing international inequalities, targeted grant aid is unarguably of 'higher quality' than much tied loan aid. If the opinion polls are to be believed, there is the added advantage that targeted aid for the poorest is a potential vote catcher for the donor government.

Recent changes in development economics, i.e. in thinking about development problems, have served to highlight ethical problems at the expense of 'structural economic problems'. In the 1950s and 1960s, the process of development (under the influence of Keynes) was treated as a matter of physical capital accumulation, investment, savings and the productivity of capital (the so-called capital–output ratio). Yet from the very beginning there was always an indication that the real sources of development had as much or more to do with the quality of human resources ('human capital') as with physical capital; empirical and econometric studies confirmed that for instance in the history of the United States physical capital accumulation could not explain much of the rising incomes, and that the 'residual' was largely explained by such human factors as better health, longer life, better education, more skills, more training, more knowledge, and better management. These findings were also applied to the developing countries, and it was found that the health, nutrition and education of young children was a key factor in economic growth and subsequent productivity. This emphasis on 'human capital' went hand in hand with a gradual redefinition of the purpose of economic development, moving away from emphasis on rising GNP (Gross National Product) towards emphasis first on employment creation and then towards more equal income distribution, reduction of poverty and the satisfaction of basic needs.

It will be readily seen that such changes in thinking put emphasis on the ethical or moral basis of aid. If the purpose of aid is to promote development, and if development is defined as a reduction of poverty and the satisfaction of basic needs for those now deprived of it, the purpose of aid-giving converges quite clearly with the charitable, humanitarian or moral imperative of relieving poverty, both directly or more effectively indirectly by 'helping the poor to help themselves', i.e. to develop the productive capacities and increase the economic opportunities open to those now living below the poverty line.

There are thus sound theoretical reasons for the incorporation of income distributional or poverty alleviating objectives within any approach to the measurement of economic performance. While the theoretical literature of welfare economics and welfare measurement is quite general in its application, it has recently been applied most vigorously in the context of the developing countries. Analytical credibility now requires that the impact on poverty and distribution be directly incorporated in discussions of stabilization and adjustment as well as in project analysis.

This is particularly striking in relation to children. To begin with, by concentrating on children we almost automatically concentrate on the poor. The average child is always much poorer than the average adult. This is so for a number of reasons, the main one being that large family size is itself a major cause of poverty. Also by concentrating on children we build for the future. The direct cost of improving the nutrition, health and education of children is relatively small; in fact some of the most effective measures cost nothing or are cost-saving in relation to present arrangements.[14] The returns to expenditure on early childhood nutrition and health, education and other social services, according to World Bank and other sources, are very high. Deterioration in child welfare does severe damage to medium-term and long-run productive potential. According to World Bank data, the social returns to expenditure for primary education in developing countries are as high as 27 per cent; this is much higher incidentally than returns to education in intermediate or advanced countries and also much higher than returns to secondary and higher education in developing countries.[15]

Yet aid given to children (although to some extent inevitably linked with aid to mothers and the families and communities of the children) also satisfies all possible ethical and humanitarian instincts. Young children cannot in any sense be held responsible for their own condition. In aid directed towards children all the ethical and economic arguments for aid converge. Even the element of enlightened self-interest is there. Some 80 per cent of all children today are born in developing countries. This means that if you believe in a non-racist distribution of human potential, then 80 per cent of the world's potential Einsteins and Newtons are born in developing countries. Yet what chance have these potential Einsteins and Newtons to become actual Einsteins and Newtons? Virtually none at all. If they do not die as children as a result of malnutrition or nutrition-related illness, their brain development is retarded by poor nutrition and the same nutrition/health-related vicious circle (90 per cent of all brain cells are formed before the age of 4); they remain illiterate or ill-educated without stimulation; and they are needed to contribute to the family income and family chores at the earliest possible age. What we lose for the world as a whole by this destruction of potential human genius is incalculable. At a more modest level, if we think in terms of the loss of potential doctors, engineers, architects, teachers, etc., the destruction of human potential and the consequent loss of human welfare for all of us are sufficiently serious to reinforce the moral appeal of this kind of aid.

The way aid is presently handled, it often has the directly opposite effect. Children are the most vulnerable group in the population, both in the physical sense that any reduction in family income and deterioration of social infrastructure in health, education, sanitation, etc., affect the children worst, but also in the political and financial sense that such factors as financial stringency, balance of payments difficulties, and need to reduce inflation, almost inevitably lead to a more than proportionate cutback in services for children. This is usually done either under the inevitable pressure of dealing with immediate problems (whereas action for children obviously relates to a medium-term or long-term future), but also in the mistaken belief that the improvement of the condition of children and the maintenance or expansion of the related social services are 'luxuries' or items of consumption, whereas in times of pressure emphasis must be put on 'productive' sectors, especially on those which immediately earn or save foreign exchange.

The present author has recently helped to produce a study for UNICEF on 'The Impact of World Recession on Children'.[16] This argues that the type of conditionality imposed by the IMF, World Bank and other aid agencies in times of balance of payments and foreign exchange troubles further tends to reinforce the neglect of children, undermining the moral as well as the economic basis of aid, which should protect children from the impact of recession rather than make them the main victims. The study gives many examples from such countries as Zambia, Tanzania, Nigeria, India, Sri Lanka and Brazil of the multiple impact of the recession itself, the national policies adopted to cope with recession, and the conditions imposed by aid givers. These factors all work in the direction of worsening the condition of children and thus undermine the wider future of developing countries. Our report argued for a broader approach to the adjustment process comprising five elements:

(1) First and foremost a clear recognition of the importance of preserving a minimum level of nutrition, household income (in cash or kind), and basic services for all groups of the population, as a means towards protecting and maintaining human investment and welfare.

(2) Second, the maintenance or creation of a network of basic services and support for young children, the most vulnerable group of the population yet also the one most important for the economic, social and political future of a country and, at the same time in most respects, the one least costly to protect.

(3) Third, a serious restructuring within the health, education and related social services to achieve greater cost-effectiveness and internal efficiency in the provision of those services.

(4) Fourth, more use and more creative use of community action and the informal sector, which tend to use more local and low-cost resources and fewer high-cost and imported supplies.

(5) Finally, more concern with income distribution, not less, especially in the sharing of the burden of economic adjustments and cutbacks.

In putting forward such a broad approach we argued on behalf of UNICEF that it would not only add up to a more conscious concern with the human dimensions of adjustment but should also be supported by international action, for which we put forward the following five suggestions:

(1) A greater measure of co-ordinated action by the main industrial countries to stimulate a higher level of world economic activity, to lower interest rates, and to reduce import barriers and trade restrictions, especially for the poorer countries.

(2) A change in international financial institutional arrangements to prevent the main burden of adjustment from falling on the deficits of poorer countries and to introduce a broader approach to adjustment and conditionality that protects the living standards of the poorer and more vulnerable sections of the population.

(3) Measures to reduce the risk of war and to achieve some shift from military and armaments expenditures to development, in both developed and developing countries.

(4) A higher level of official development assistance to developing countries: in the early 1960s this averaged 0.5 per cent of the GNP of the industrial countries but by 1981 had dropped to 0.35 per cent, comparing even less favourably with the long established international target of 0.7 per cent.

(5) Expanded and more effective co-operation between developing countries.

The emphasis on the satisfaction of basic needs as the ultimate objective of development has also brought with it a more direct link between development economics and ethical factors. This relates to what is to be included among 'basic needs'. We are all agreed that food, shelter, access to water, sanitation, health, education, employment, etc., form part of basic needs. But should basic needs not also include human rights, e.g. freedom from persecution and arbitrary arrest, freedom to order your own life, and freedom of migration. In the debate among development economists quite a number have tended to extend the concept of basic needs to include such human rights. Naturally there is a danger that economists – and others – of different ideologies may hold different views on what human rights are and which human rights are important. For this reason, and also because of their well-known preference for matters which can be quantified and measured by 'social indicators', development economists have tended more recently to fight shy of such a widening of the concept of basic needs; but the debate continues.

Apart from aid for children (which we have just looked at in some detail as an example), aid for refugees, emergency aid, aid given to the very poorest countries, and perhaps more generally aid given in the form of food are cases where the moral basis for aid can be more generally presumed. Similarly, aid generated through non-governmental organizations (NGOs) and going directly to the poor and vulnerable groups in the recipient countries, to some extent bypassing the recipient government, could be presumed to have a better chance of being morally supportable. Perhaps one could also add that aid channelled through UN and other multilateral organizations is likely to have a stronger moral element than bilateral aid. This in itself constitutes a list of changes in global aid which those supporting it on moral grounds should be putting forward (and are putting forward).[17] But perhaps by far the most important reform would be to reduce the leakages which now divert well-intentioned aid away from its intended targets. This is an extremely difficult but not impossible task and perhaps the most important item on the aid agenda for those advocating aid on moral grounds.[18]

NOTES AND REFERENCES

1. *North–South: A Programme for Survival* (London: Pan Books, 1980) p. 64.
2. Ibid., p. 76.
3. *Third World Quarterly* 2 (1980) pp. 681–93.
4. P.T. Bauer, *Reality and Rhetoric* (London: Weidenfeld & Nicolson, 1984) chs. 3 and 5.
5. J.E. Behrman, *International Commodity Agreements: An Evaluation of the UNCTAD Integrated Commodity Programme*, Monograph, No. 9, NIEO Series (Washington, DC: Overseas Development Council, 1977).
6. Cited by P. Mosley, 'The Political Economy of Foreign Aid: A Study of the Market for a Public Good', University of Bath, Papers in Political Economy, Working Paper 1181.
7. See, for instance, Bauer, *Reality and Rhetoric.*
8. P. Mosley, 'Can the Poor Benefit from Aid Projects: An Empirical Study of the Trickle-Down Hypothesis', University of Bath, Papers in Political Economy, Working Paper 0983, p. 25.
9. World Bank, *An Element of the Attack on Rural Poverty: Meeting Basic Needs* (Washington, DC: IBRD, 1980) p. 14.
10. The above quotations have been taken from the summary of the IMF report in the IMF *Survey*, 8 May 1983, pp. 135–6.
11. T. Hayter, *The Creation of World Poverty: An Alternative View to the Brandt Report,* (London: Pluto Press, 1981).
12. Ibid., pp. 83–4.
13. P. Mosley, 'The Quality of Overseas Aid', University of Bath, Papers in Political Economy, Working Paper 0982.
14. The best example, of course, is the substitution of breast feeding for bottle feeding or other artificial weaning foods. UNICEF has produced a well-known four-pronged, low-cost child policy called GOBI: G for growth charting, O for oral rehydration (a simple salt and water packet to combat diarrhoea), B for breast feeding, and I for immunization.
15. *World Development Report 1980* (Oxford: Oxford University Press, 1980).
16. Summarized as Chapter IV of the latest UNICEF Report on *The State of the World's Children 1984* (Oxford: Oxford University Press, 1984). For the full study see 'The Impact of World Recession on Children', *World Development* 12 (1984) pp. 171–391.
17. C. Elliott, *Real Aid; A Strategy for Britain.* (London: Independent Group on British Aid, 1982).
18. I am indebted to my colleague, Robert Cassen, and to Dr Paul Mosley of Bath University for their valuable comments.

5 International Sanctions: Ethical and Practical Perspectives

MARGARET DOXEY

In a world beset with economic difficulties and marked both by wide discrepancies in living standards within individual countries and a huge gap between rich, developed countries of the 'North' and poor, developing countries of the 'South', resort to deliberate impoverishment of one state by others seems a doubtful proposition even if punitive action might be justified on legal or moral grounds. Progress in economic development, not economic retardation, is a universally shared goal and the theme of this book not only suggests positive rather than negative approaches in international relations, but also prompts questions about the ethics of economic sanctions being applied to developing countries by those better placed on the economic ladder. And what of the possible harmful effects of such measures on innocent, bystander states, and indeed on the international system as a whole? Outcomes must obviously be one important element in any discussion of moral aspects of sanctions – but there are other relevant dimensions. As Ernest Lefever has pointed out: 'Moral choice demands calculation – an assessment of multiple causes, multiple alternatives, and multiple consequences.'[1] Moreover, decisions to impose sanctions are not necessarily motivated by 'moral choice'.

In his important contribution to normative political theory in international relations,[2] Charles Beitz identifies two major schools of thought which he characterizes as international scepticism and the morality of states. Hobbesian scepticism, 'based on a perception of a radical discontinuity between the normative order of domestic society and that of international relations',[3] is obviously linked with and reinforced by the realist views of leading twentieth-century scholars such as E.H. Carr[4] and Hans Morgenthau.[5] In contrast, the morality of states, expounded particularly by Pufendorf and other notable international jurists, postulates a different moral order between states from that obtaining within them. In international relations, according to these theorists, states play 'the roles occupied by persons in domestic society',[6] enjoying sovereignty and complete immunity from outside interference in their internal affairs. Beitz argues for a third view, which he labels 'cosmopolitan' in the Kantian tradition; this would reject international scepticism and also the fundamental importance of state boundaries. He notes that the 'effect of shifting from a statist to a cosmopolitan point of view is to open up the state to external moral assessment (and, perhaps, political interference) and to understand persons, rather than states, as the ultimate subjects of international morality'.[7] This mode of thinking is well exemplified by Stanley Hoffmann's recent consideration of the limits and possibilities of ethical international politics.[8] Contemporary concerns about international distributive justice also reflect cosmopolitanism.

Assuming that sanctions, as discussed below, may represent 'just' interference with the foreign and domestic conduct of states, and that the effects of sanctions may also raise issues of equity and justice, this chapter reflects cosmopolitan perspectives as well as cosmopolitan uncertainties.[9] It is presented as a basis for discussion of the ethical and practical aspects of international sanctioning and makes no pretence of providing definitive answers to the many difficult questions which are raised. Its premise is that there are no moral absolutes in foreign policy making, but that ethical considerations should be relevant, particularly where sanctions are threatened or imposed. But before proceeding further, clarification is needed on the meaning of the term 'sanction'.

Regrettably, in the writer's view, the word is being progressively drained of content in the international context, so that in popular and media usage (and also in the writing of scholars)[10] a negative sanction has come to mean no more than an influence attempt, i.e. an action by one or more states directed against another which the latter finds unwelcome. As will be discussed in more detail later there are difficulties in attaching authoritative status to international sanctions; they cannot always be characterized as penalties imposed by bodies which are authorized both to make judgments that rules have been broken and to enforce them. But to equate international sanctions with all injurious acts of foreign policy further confuses an issue which is already sufficiently confused. Negative sanctions must be a response to previous acts of impermissible or unacceptable behaviour, real or alleged, and it is in this sense that the term is used here.

In an attempt to order discussion in a logical sequence, the paper is divided into four parts. The first part considers the existence of moral or legal justification for the imposition of sanctions in the international milieu: the linked issues of the development of international standards of conduct and of processes for defending and enforcing them. The second part examines the motives and objectives of governments advocating or adopting sanctions and the third part the kinds of penalties which are appropriate for international use in relation both to the conduct which has provoked them and their likely effects. Here the main focus will be on economic measures. The final part of the paper will attempt a summary of salient issues. Limitations of space have dictated the restriction of discussion to government behaviour inside or outside international organizations. Other themes which could certainly have been included are the perceived misdeeds of non-governmental actors, particularly multinational corporations, and the efforts of non-governmental agencies and groups to influence and chastize them by organizing protests, boycotts and other kinds of negative pressure.[11] Unofficial boycotts adopted voluntarily by individuals or groups are not dealt with in this chapter; sanctions as public policy are its specific concern, although these may, of course, be prompted by internal or international pressure group activity.

THE STATUS OF INTERNATIONAL RULES OF CONDUCT AND THE LEGITIMATION OF SANCTIONS

It is a truism that there is no international authority capable of enforcing compliance with rules of conduct which is in any way comparable to the typical structures of national governments, whatever many of these may lack in terms of democratic accountability and legitimacy. But the twentieth century, with the impetus of two World Wars, and the haunting fear of a third, has seen progressive efforts first to lay some foundation for peace, security and world order by providing frameworks for international co-operation, and secondly to establish norms of behaviour in relation to the use of military force between states and to minimum standards of human rights within them. The basic rule of international law that states are bound to fulfil obligations which they have, themselves, accepted (*pacta sunt servanda*) has been institutionalized by the establishment of international organizations in which the duties of membership are spelled out in the founding treaty and developed by consent through the work of the organization.[12] This has introduced some limitations on traditional precepts of domestic jurisdiction, non-intervention, and the right to go to war; it has also provided some mechanisms for determination of rule-breaking and a collective response to deal with it. The League of Nations Covenant provided for automatic diplomatic and military sanctions if prescribed procedures for dispute settlement were not followed. The sanctions of Article 16 were intended to deter rule-breakers, or, if they failed to do so, to bring rapid compliance by their punitive effect. Economic weapons, particularly if wielded collectively, were expected to pack a powerful punch.[13] But, as is well known, League sanctions were only invoked once, following Italy's invasion of Ethiopia in 1935, and they did not succeed in halting it. Indeed, by the time they were lifted in July 1936, the conquest of Ethiopia was complete and its annexation by Italy was soon to be widely recognized.[14] The League was discredited by this episode but, of course, it had other major shortcomings, especially in respect of membership and its failure to provide mechanisms for peaceful change.

In fact, the Covenant's restrictions on the use of force by states were not sweeping: they called for prior use of diplomatic or judicial procedures and a delay of three months after the publication of a League Council Report or Court decision.[15] Nor did the Covenant directly address questions of human rights, which were considered to be a matter of domestic jurisdiction. However, in setting up the Mandate system, members of the League accepted some international responsibility for the rights of colonial peoples in ex-enemy territories.[16] Article 23 of the Covenant also recorded members' endeavours 'to secure and maintain fair and humane conditions of labour for men, women and children . . . in their own countries' and elsewhere, and an undertaking 'to secure just treatment of the native inhabitants of territories under their control'.

The horrors of the Second World War and the excesses of the Nazi regime brought new incentives to establish a firmer and more comprehensive framework for international co-operation, setting limits on state behaviour in external relations by prohibiting war and also by emphasizing justice and welfare goals in the domestic environment. In regard to war, the United Nations Charter was much more ambitious than the League Covenant, spelling out that force should only be used for individual or collective self-defence in the face of armed attack (Article 51) or with Security Council authorization under Chapter VII (Article 43). The obligation for individual members of the UN was to refrain from the use of force as a foreign policy instrument (Article 2(4)). Members accepted important binding commitments: to carry out decisions of the Security Council (Article 25) and to seek peaceful resolution of disputes (Article 33). They also pledged themselves to uphold and promote human rights within their own jurisdictions (Articles 55 and 56), and to promote the advancement of non-self-governing peoples in their own colonial empires as well as in the colonial territories of defeated states (Article 73). League mandates (with the exception of South-West Africa/Namibia) became UN Trust Territories under a system which brought them to independence within a relatively short space of time.[17]

Emphasis on human rights continued to be a prominent feature of United Nations activities. The 1948 Universal Declaration of Human Rights expanded on Articles 55 and 56 of the Charter and a convention on Genocide was adopted by the General Assembly in the same year.[18] In the 1960s, when newly independent countries began to exert strong influence in the General Assembly, further important declarations on group rights were forthcoming, particularly the Declarations on the Granting of Independence to Colonial Countries and Peoples[19] and on the Elimination of All Forms of Racial Discrimination.[20] In 1966, international covenants on civil and political rights and on economic, social and cultural rights were ready for signature and entered into force ten years later. Significant progress had also been made in Europe, through the European Convention on Human Rights, and to a lesser extent in the Western hemisphere under the auspices of the Organization of American States. Where rights are guaranteed by international treaty, they set up legal obligations for contracting parties. One might also suppose that a moral obligation to protect human rights has been formally acknowledged when governments support General Assembly declarations, or other non-binding documents, such as the 1975 Helsinki Final Act.

There is, therefore, no doubt that legal as well as moral

commitments exist at the international level requiring peaceful settlement of disputes and the protection of human rights. Rules have also been drawn up and accepted in functional areas of co-operation: in the International Monetary Fund (IMF), World Bank, General Agreement on Tariffs and Trade (GATT), World Health Organization (WHO) and numerous other agencies, and on a regional basis in bodies like the Organization of American States (OAS), Organization of African Unity (OAU) and the Arab League.

Unfortunately, the world around us does not reflect general adherence to Charter principles of peace, justice and human dignity. Conflict within and between states and persistent and gross violations of human rights within state borders are commonplace. There is no need to reiterate that the contemporary international system is marked by deep cleavages and asymmetries: major East–West and North–South divisions, as well as a myriad of racial, religious, cultural and other differences, make the prospect of consensus on values remote. International organizations are hamstrung: they can only regulate state conduct where the majority of their members are abiding by the rules and are willing to take some enforcement measures against those who are not. Chapter VII of the Charter gives the Security Council authority to declare any situation a threat to the peace, breach of the peace or act of aggression (Article 39) and to order non-violent measures to restore international peace and security (Article 41). But the UN reflects the world as it is and has no inherent power to control resort to violence or to enforce implementation of human rights standards. Failure to react to violations of human rights may seem somewhat paradoxical, given the expenditure of effort and apparent success in developing new norms of international behaviour based on ideas of justice and human dignity. The explanation, of course, is that general statements of principle do not require any sacrifice of national interest. They are cost free; better still, they sound good.[21] On the other hand, judgment of the behaviour of other states and, *a fortiori*, action to punish or change it, present much harder choices for decision-makers. Moreover, standards are themselves subject to varying interpretations, and are ranked in different order of priority. The Soviet Union refuses to accept international standards of individual civil and political rights; the United States supports repressive regimes because of their opposition to Communism; third-world countries claim that redress of their economic and social grievances must take precedence over the protection of other rights and are unwilling to criticize or condemn others in their group. Although the only case of comprehensive UN mandatory sanctions was directed at the violation by the Smith regime in Rhodesia of the new international norm of racial discrimination, many glaring cases of abuse of human rights have gone unpunished, and even uncensured. In a recent monograph, Samuel Kim provides a table of seven post-holocaust cases of genocide, each of which 'managed to escape collective sanctions'.[22]

Majority support which can be readily obtained in the General Assembly for standard-setting is rarely forthcoming to condemn standard-breaking, while Security Council action, subject to the veto of any one of the five permanent members in defence of their own or their clients' interests, is even more elusive. Despite flexible wording of Article 39[23] no consistent sequence of orders for sanctions could be expected from that body. Far from being predictable as certain or likely, international sanctions are predictably unlikely; in these circumstances they do not function as indicators of the limits of permissible behaviour, nor do they motivate behaviour by presenting the prospect of penalties for exceeding those limits.[24] It is obvious that the UN's inability to produce consensus leaves a vacuum at the 'top'. And it is not just a question of the veto, i.e. of one great power objecting, because that would be seen as self-serving if the remainder of UN members condemned misbehaviour and recommended sanctions by overwhelming majorities on a consistent basis. But ideological divisions, different perceptions of right and wrong, and solidarity with group positions have produced selectivity in condemnation and discriminatory judgment, and the status of the UN as a fount of moral or legal authority has been seriously undermined.

Emphasis shifts to the regional or sectional level where consensus may be easier to obtain. But without the top (UN) layer, problems quickly surface in attempts to identify wrongdong and impose sanctions. Regional positions may be totally rejected elsewhere in the world and the determination of offences, offender and penalties in a regional context may reflect the views of a hegemonial power who can resort to pressure to induce lesser powers to see things its way. The Brezhnev doctrine, which purported to assert a regional norm permitting intervention to preserve 'socialism' in the Soviet bloc,[25] echoed in some degree pronouncements of the OAS that Communism has no place in the Western hemisphere.[26] Whatever sanctions at the regional level may be designed to achieve – motives for imposing sanctions are discussed in more detail in the second part below – it cannot be assumed that the support of world order or justice will be enhanced.

The absence of an effective international authority structure and of the political will to organize an international response to perceived wrongdoing means that states have recourse to self-help, using military as well as economic instruments of policy. Since 1979 there have been several notable cases of retaliation using economic sanctions: against Iran, the Soviet Union, Poland and Argentina.[27] Against Argentina, economic measures were ancillary to the use of force. None of these sanctions was authorized by the Security Council; measures were adopted voluntarily by individual governments, acting in uneasy concert. In each case there was open disagreement about the need to take action and the specific penalties which should be adopted.

One may ask whether in cases of high politics it is useful to postulate the existence of authoritative international sanctions, that is, measures taken constitutionally by members of an international organization against a fellow member who has exceeded the limits of permissible behaviour defined by that organization. The Security Council can provide the maximum international legitimation by issuing binding orders, but it has only done so in two instances: for general sanctions against Rhodesia after UDI[28] and for an arms embargo against South Africa in 1977.[29] One can also note that in two recent cases there was Security Council condemnation without any order for sanctions. In the Tehran hostages case, the Soviet Union vetoed a draft resolution for 'effective measures' presented by the United States;[30] in the Falklands crisis, Britain did not seek an order for sanctions.[31] Security Council condemnation may provide some moral reinforcement for the retaliatory action taken by injured states, who can thus claim to be defending universal values as well as their own interests. But the larger the negative or abstaining vote in the Security Council, the less can such an effect be adduced.[32]

Generally Assembly resolutions are not binding and may simply reinforce a Security Council position. But if they deal with cases where a Security Council resolution has been vetoed, they provide some evidence of majority opinion as backing for action taken by individual states. Early in January 1980 at an emergency session called under the Uniting for Peace Resolution,[33] the General Assembly voted overwhelmingly to condemn the Soviet military intervention in Afghanistan; almost thirty years earlier, in February

1951, the Assembly had condemned the People's Republic of China as an aggressor for its intervention in the Korean War.[34] It may also be argued that if condemnatory resolutions are heavily supported by UN members and reiterated over a long period of years, they may have a cumulative delegitimizing effect in respect of the censured state. This would be true of resolutions condemning South Africa's apartheid policies. But except for representational penalties, as in the General Assembly's refusal since 1974 to accept the credentials of the South African delegation, the practical implementation of penalties recommended in General Assembly resolutions will be entirely within the discretion of individual members. Suspension or expulsion from the UN requires action by the Security Council as well as the General Assembly (Articles 5 and 6 of the Charter).

It may be noted that in cases of colonialism, apartheid, and the continued control of Namibia by South Africa, UN condemnation has been supported by Western powers, but action rejected. Israel has also been the object of General Assembly condemnation,[35] but the United States has vetoed condemnatory resolutions presented to the Security Council and threatened retaliation against the UN if moves to exclude Israel are proceeded with.

It is also worth noting that UN agencies can also provide a subsidiary source of sanctioning authority in a context limited to their activities. Penalties can be imposed on members for non-compliance with agency rules: concessions, funds or privileges may be withheld; voting rights may be lost; and in more serious cases suspension or expulsion may be imposed. For instance, GATT's Article XXIII (2) permits the contracting party or parties to suspend concessions under the Agreement. Another example is provided by the IMF Agreement, which permits the Fund to declare a member ineligible to use its general financial resources if that member is judged not to be fulfilling its obligations under the Agreement.[36]

UN agencies are also bound to carry out Security Council enforcement decisions in respect of their members, except that the IMF and the World Bank are required by their Articles of Agreement to remain above politics. Two comments are relevant here. First, the Security Council rarely takes enforcement decisions. Secondly, the proceedings of all UN agencies are subject to political influence and reflect the political will of their member states. The IMF and the World Bank are no exception. There is still dispute over the extent to which US influence delayed or prevented World Bank loans to Chile during the Allende years, but in 1972 the Gonzalez

Amendments required US representatives in multilateral financial institutions to oppose loans to countries which had expropriated American corporations without paying compensation.[37] Politicization of UN agencies has reached the point where, in line with General Assembly recommendations, exclusion of South Africa has been engineered from a number of agencies, including the World Health Organization and the International Labour Organization, despite the lack of Security Council support for expulsion from the UN itself.[38]

With regard to regional bodies, it is important to distinguish internal action directed against members as a penalty for constitutionally determined rule violation from external action directed against non-members. Examples of the former would be the diplomatic and economic sanctions imposed by the OAS on Cuba from 1962 to 1975 and the Arab League's suspension of Egypt from membership following the 1979 Israel–Egypt Peace Treaty. Examples of the latter would be the oil embargoes imposed by the Arab members of OPEC in 1973–4 and economic measures adopted by European Community members against Argentina in 1982.

The authoritativeness of regional measures is not in question if the Security Council has made an appropriate determination and ordered sanctions. Uncertainty arises when it has not, which is the usual situation. It should be emphasized, however, that use of an organizational framework against *non-members* is no more than a convenient means of co-ordinating retaliation. Non-members are not bound by the terms of a regional agreement and their 'sins' must therefore be cast in terms of the violation of universal values, probably with reference to the UN Charter. Claims to be defending such values will be more convincing if the Security Council has condemned the target state's behaviour or has failed to condemn or to order sanctions by one permanent member's veto, and/or if the Assembly has passed condemnatory resolutions recommending sanctions by a very large majority.

Collective measures taken outside a *regional* organizational framework are not distinguishable in terms of authoritativeness or legitimacy from organizationally sponsored measures against non-members, although the possibility of some legitimacy being derived from UN sources cannot be ruled out. Unilateral retaliation is also possible and may be justifiable in terms of a prior wrong committed by the target state against the retaliator.[39] The United States could not fail to make some response to the seizure of its embassy and diplomatic personnel in Tehran, whatever the reaction of the rest of the world. But in addition to the increased impact expected from a collective response, states characteristically seek to associate others with their sanctioning efforts in order to strengthen the image of wrongdoing attracting punishment.

In summing up the discussion thus far, we must acknowledge that state practice has not generally been supportive of collective action to support or maintain standards which have been set in legal or moral terms, nor has the apparent recent increase in governmental propensity to resort to collective non-violent measures been associated with a trend to sustained or increased authoritativeness for their imposition.[40] All that can be said is that on a case-by-case basis it may be possible to ascribe some status to the rule which has been broken and some degree of international legitimation for those imposing sanctions. In particular, despite the decline in the status of the UN, a Security Council resolution condemning state conduct is still significant, and a mandatory order from that body remains the fullest justification for international sanctions which can be achieved.[41]

One can also say that the existence of international standards does enable some kind of judgment to be made that sanctions would have been justified, even if they are not put in place. It is not seriously disputed that there were gross violations of human rights in Uganda and Kampuchea, and the regimes responsible are generally judged to have fallen well below acceptable standards. This is a far cry from saying that moral or legal principles govern, or even strongly influence, international relations, but it may be better to have some yardsticks rather than none at all. In his thoughtful study, *The Moral Issue in Statecraft*, Kenneth Thompson wrote: 'Even the fact that states possess an awareness of injustice indicates the possibility of justice in foreign affairs, for a sense of injustice presupposes categories of justice to which leaders have recourse.'[42]

THE MOTIVES AND OBJECTIVES OF STATES INITIATING SANCTIONS

The discussion in the previous section suggests that even where standards of behaviour exist and are clearly being violated, ethical considerations rarely prompt states to take action. It must also be acknowledged that the motives for imposing sanctions are not necessarily confined to 'righting wrongs' or punishing unacceptable behaviour. Typically governments will present their rationale for sanctions in language which stresses, on the one hand, the bad behaviour of the ostensible target, using connotations of morality and/or legality (e.g. 'aggression must not pay') and, on the other, their own role in defending community values at some cost to themselves,[43] but a more complex set of intentions usually needs to be unravelled. Defence of community values, even where these have clearly been violated (for instance Italy's invasion of Ethiopia in 1935), may be one of several objectives sanctions are designed to serve, and not necessarily the most important.[44] In some cases, the declared purpose of supporting an accepted norm may be a cloak for the pursuit of self-serving goals, of domestic as well as external relevance. Indeed, sanctions may serve a number of objectives in their initiators' home environment. They are a means of satisfying influential sections of the population who demand retaliation for the conduct of foreign states;[45] they can give an image of governmental purposefulness and strength; they may improve electoral popularity and prospects. Prestige and national honour are elusive concepts, but they should not be discounted as significant political factors, and repeated failure to respond to perceived external challenges may suggest a lack of will or resolve on the part of national leaders which will be particularly unwelcome at the great power level.

Target-related goals can also be complex. Total success for the League would presumably have meant that Italy gave up its designs on Ethiopia. In the case of UN sanctions against Rhodesia, the Smith regime would have abandoned UDI and moved rapidly to share power with Rhodesian Africans. In the Tehran hostage case, the Iranian government would have released the hostages as soon as – or soon after – the United States retaliatory measures were announced. But governments initiating sanctions have usually been more cautious in stating their expectations:[46] 'success' may be no more than attaching a price to the offending policy whether it is Cuba's Marxist–Leninist orientation or the Soviet military presence in Afghanistan.

In addition to coercive and punitive impact, there is also a demonstrative role for sanctions: they signal disapproval. The European Community's economic sanctions against Argentina in the Falklands crisis signalled strong disapproval of Argentina's resort to force, and willingness to incur some inconvenience to make the point.

Beyond the ostensible target, part of the motive for retaliation may be exemplary in demonstrating to other states the likely costs to them of behaviour similar to that of the target; more commonly a relevant third party goal seems to be that of extending support to friends and allies. As a motivating factor in the initiation of sanctions, the breach of an international norm, or the desire to defend it, may be less important than pressure from an ally. The reluctance of West European governments to take measures against Iran and the Soviet Union in the wake of the crises in Tehran and Afghanistan was patent, and a powerful factor in inducing them to take any action at all was clearly the expressed wish of the US Administration that they should do so.[47]

It is also possible that the action of one state may present an opportunity or pretext for others to satisfy wider foreign policy goals of their own by resort to retaliatory measures. 'Sanctions' can be a tactic in an on-going policy strategy rather than a discrete response to a discrete and illegal act. Action against Argentina by Britain, the United States, the European Community, and Commonwealth countries was specifically linked to the seizure of the Falklands, in the same way that League of Nations sanctions against Italy were occasioned by Mussolini's invasion of Ethiopia. These sanctions were imposed reluctantly by governments which, other things being equal, would have preferred to remain on friendly terms with the target state. Indeed, the concern of leading League members to retain Italy's friendship in the face of the German menace weakened their inclination to impose severe measures. Similarly, some EEC members quickly dropped measures against Argentina.

In contrast, action against the USSR for its connection with the Polish crisis can be viewed as a new stage in the Cold War which has characterized superpower relationships since the end of the Second World War. From this perspective the measures which the US imposed and tried hard to persuade its allies to support represented an intensification of the controls on East–West economic relations which have existed since 1947, but which were progressively relaxed in the years of detente. Co-ordinated by COCOM, a NATO committee, these controls have sought to prevent, or at least to hinder the growth of the Soviet economy and to limit Soviet military capability; as such they are weapons of economic (cold) warfare.[48] One can say that by denying the Soviet Union high technology items the West, under US leadership, is in a sense penalizing the Soviet Union for seeking certain ideological and strategic goals, but this is linked to the wider US foreign policy goal of containment, not to breaches of international law or moral lapses. For the Soviet Union, the United States has no monopoly of morality.

To sum up this brief discussion, it is obvious that some mix of objectives and intentions is likely to be present in all cases of sanctions, but the trend to *ad hoc* retaliation outside organizational frameworks, while perhaps inevitable, means that the specific domestic and foreign policy goals of individual states, particularly powerful states, can exert more influence than moral or legal considerations.

THE CHOICE OF MEASURES

This part of the chapter examines ethical and practical considerations which may influence the choice of particular measures as sanctions. In relation to the 'offence', one might look for a proportionate response – an effort to make the punishment fit the crime. But there are other operative factors. As noted in the previous section, the initiators will certainly take their own objectives into account, and these may be complex and self-serving; moreover, the consequences of different measures, in so far as these can be predicted, require careful consideration.

Perhaps the first point to be made is the obvious one that economic measures are less lethal than military measures. As E.H. Carr put it, 'there is a sense in which dollars are humaner than bullets even if the ends pursued are the same'.[49] In the inter-war period it was widely believed that economic pressure would be an effective deterrent as well as an effective means of coercion, and although much of this optimism has been dispelled, economic measures are still seen as the major alternative to force. Their costs, in terms of the hardship they inflict on initiators, targets and third parties, must be set against the higher cost of military measures.[50] Indeed, on ethical grounds one would expect to find a preference for non-violent sanctions which include diplomatic, political and cultural sanctions as well as a wide range of commercial and financial measures. (A typology is attached as an Appendix.)

A further point is worth making in comparing economic and military measures. Based on experience, the argument is usually made that economic sanctions do not produce political results quickly or at all; they are seen as 'long-haul' measures which may prolong an unsatisfactory situation which military intervention could end promptly even at the cost of some loss of life.[51] Presumably US intervention in Grenada in October 1983 was based on a judgment of this kind by the Reagan Administration (although Britain, Canada, and other Commonwealth countries favoured economic sanctions and diplomacy).[52] It will be recalled that African governments persistently pressed for the use of force against the Smith regime in Rhodesia, although the British government ruled it out from the beginning. The unsavoury regimes of Idi Amin in Uganda and Pol Pot in Kampuchea were eventually terminated by military intervention from Tanzania and Vietnam respectively. But opting for a quick military 'fix' instead of slower acting non-violent pressure can bring other problems. Given the existence of contested value systems, who is to decide – and on what basis – that intervention is justified and necessary? What are the dangers of proceeding at once to the use of force? What if the quick 'fix' does not work and further effort has to be expended at increasing cost in human and material terms? And can democracy or respect for human rights be guaranteed by military intervention? It is too soon to judge results in Grenada, but neither Uganda nor Kampuchea inspire much confidence on this score; other examples are discussed by Sam Nolutshungu in his chapter. Given the trend towards the use of sanctions *outside* the framework of the UN, advocacy of resort to force rather than to milder, non-lethal measures, seems a very risky proposition. Indeed, just as it is important to consider economic sanctions in the context of a military alternative, so perhaps should political and diplomatic measures be considered as being less damaging than economic sanctions. This point is taken up in the concluding section of the paper.

Assuming that economic measures have been selected by the initiating state(s), and are intended to have some economic effect on the target, one would expect these measures to relate to its vulnerability, for instance, trade embargoes, denial of credit, or suspension of aid. But here one encounters the problem raised in the introductory paragraph of this chapter. Except in such cases as the Nuremberg and Tokyo war crimes trials after the Second World War, the personnel of governments cannot be put on trial internationally, and sanctions – whether military or economic – hurt people. Given the propensity of governments not to yield to external pressure, is it justifiable to subject a whole population to a long drawn out process of economic deprivation? This is an important question not only because the majority of countries are classed as 'developing' and already have massive economic and social problems to contend with, but also because the impact of economic sanctions may fall, or be shifted by the target government, on to sections of the population least able to bear additional burdens. In Rhodesia, under UN sanctions, the white minority government of Ian Smith took prompt and effective action to protect the white farmers from the devastating effects of the collapse of the export market for tobacco, but little was done to assist the African population who were already seriously disadvantaged. Many of them were driven back to subsistence agriculture because the market economy was progressively less able to provide adequate employment opportunities. It is possible, of course, that increased unemployment and rural misery may have helped to recruit guerrillas for the forces of ZANU and ZAPU, but this was presumably an unintended consequence of sanctions.

Arguments have been made that the Rhodesian economy was both harmed and helped by sanctions. External trade suffered, but serious shortages were averted by rerouting of exports and imports through South Africa. Initially, impetus was given to the growth of secondary industry and agricultural production was diversified.[53] It is generally agreed that the economic sanctions, even if they had some 'bite', were not in themselves decisive in bringing an end to the illegal regime and precipitating a new political order based on majority rule. They may have contributed something, but guerrilla warfare, the withdrawal of South African support after the coup in Portugal, and the grant of independence to Angola and Mozambique, were more influential. If this is a correct assessment, and if one also attributes importance to the universal non-recognition of Rhodesia, which was reinforced by declarations and resolutions in the United Nations, the Commonwealth and other international fora, can one argue that economic sanctions were unnecessary? Or did they, in spite of their imperfections, contribute to an overall sense of isolation – a system under siege – which eventually brought concessions from the white minority, even if much African suffering occurred in the years from 1966 to 1980? These are not easy questions to answer – indeed they may be unanswerable – but in a discussion of the ethics of international sanctions they cannot be ignored.

The argument that economic sanctions hurt those whom they are meant to help has also been made in respect to possible action against South Africa. South Africa's exclusion from UN agencies and its forced withdrawal from the Commonwealth have prevented its participation in international organizations; but to date no more than a mandatory arms embargo has been imposed by the Security Council, despite the fact that the sanctions issue has been heatedly debated over a period of nearly forty years and calls for economic sanctions have been made repeatedly in the United Nations. The Anti-Apartheid Movement, church groups and other unofficial bodies have also pressed Western governments to take action of this kind.

It may be that the latest moves towards normalization of relations between South Africa and its neighbours, particularly Swaziland, Mozambique and Angola, herald an era in which demands for international sanctions will be muted. If it is their economic dependence on South Africa for desperately needed help, as well as their vulnerability to military incursions by South African forces to deal with guerrilla groups, which has brought these countries to adopt a more accommodating posture, they are hardly likely to continue pressing fiercely for international action which would damage the South African economy.[54] Obviously they have not become supporters of apartheid, a uniquely odious system which attracts universal condemnation, but their leaders have had to put their own national interests ahead of the interests of the South African blacks who would benefit from the easing or ending of apartheid induced by external pressure. But what if economic sanctions were to be imposed on South Africa? Would they 'work'? Would the poorer sections of the population who are not white but black, coloured and Asian, suffer the most? And would this be acceptable to them? Spokesmen for African nationalist movements do not consider this to be a problem, but do they represent public opinion? And are they perhaps influenced by the thought that more misery might be a spur to revolution?

In a review of possible international action against South Africa, Clyde Ferguson and William Cotter conclude with these words:

Finally we must be careful of the oft-repeated argument that Western pressures . . . will hurt the country's blacks most. Yes, increased pressures will hurt blacks in South Africa but they will affect the still-complacent white community most fundamentally. Blacks have little to lose – and they know it.[55]

It is not immediately obvious that whites would be affected 'most fundamentally'; they certainly have much more to lose politically, but the assumption that external economic pressure will work to produce political gains for Africans which will more than offset their economic loss is open to question.

Lech Walesa, speaking for the Polish people in January 1984, claimed that Western sanctions were causing unnecessary suffering and should be lifted; he also advocated massive economic relief for Poland.[56] Certainly, in this case, the basis for sanctions is far less clear than in the case of South Africa, which not only practises apartheid but also continues to administer Namibia in defiance of UN and International Court rulings, yet questions about the burden of personal hardship which sanctions can cause are common to both.

Discussion of the direct impact of economic sanctions on targets leads to questions not only about expected economic effects, and whether these will be translated into desirable political effects, but also about the ethics of denial of basic necessities. In the League's consideration of economic measures as alternatives to the use of force, denial of strategic minerals, and particularly oil, was seen as a key factor in limiting an aggressor's war-making capacity.[57] South Africa's vulnerability to an oil embargo has also been stressed as a means of inducing change,[58] although over the years conservation and development of oil from coal have probably reduced this vulnerability. Food sanctions, however, have not featured prominently in the general discussion of economic pressure. To deprive people of food and perhaps starve them to death seems an inappropriate penalty to be imposed by international bodies concerned with governmental failure to maintain international standards.[59] Nor does food as a commodity entering into international trade have obvious utility as a 'weapon' for collective or unilateral use: there are a variety of substitutes for staple grains, as well as problems of perishability and unpredictable harvests. But food and 'food power' came to the fore in the decade following the Arab oil embargoes of 1973–4, with considerable discussion of the possibility that the United States could use its massive grain surpluses as an effective retaliatory device.[60] President Carter did indeed impose a limited grain embargo on the USSR following Soviet military intervention in Afghanistan, but its effects were nullified by exports from other suppliers, particularly Argentina. President Reagan lifted the embargo in April 1981, fulfilling a campaign promise to do so, and it was not reimposed in the wake of the Polish crisis. Protests from American farmers provide the main explanation, but in general it would seem that morality should be a constraint on the use of food sanctions, particularly in view of the danger of scarcity being shifted on to the poorer people in the target state. Moreover, food shortages have become a serious world problem and to add to them deliberately seems crazy. Henry Nau has commented that 'even the use of food for the most exemplary purposes involves environmental consequences . . . All uses of food, therefore, entail non-food or larger social and economic consequences'.[61] The food weapon could do excessive damage in relation to the objectives it is intended to serve in the target.

But even if sanctions are confined to non-food items entering into the import trade of the target there will be some hardship, and the effects of embargoes on exports, or on loans and credits which reduce available foreign exchange, can also mean heavier burdens for the disadvantaged than for the élites, as well as the interruption of economic development. Increasing the economic and financial difficulties of Argentina or Poland may not contribute to a desirable change of policy by the regime, or to a desirable change of regime.

This leads directly to consideration of the wider effects of economic measures. The effects on the initiators' economies need not be a prime concern in this chapter, although initially and for as long as the sanctions programme continues they will certainly form part of the cost–benefit calculations of their governments. Effects on third parties are certainly relevant, however.

It is obvious that in some cases bystander states may be beneficiaries. As noted above, Argentina sold grain to the Soviet Union to make up the shortfall caused by the US embargo, and there are often markets to be gained and profits to be made by those remaining outside a sanctions effort. In the context of ethical considerations, it is a matter of concern that third states can be very seriously affected by sanctions imposed on their neighbours or trading partners. Skeletal provisions for possible burden sharing in the UN Charter (Articles 49 and 50) provide a basis for claims from adversely affected states in the case of UN sanctions: Zambia, and Mozambique (on gaining independence), both applied for help as a result of sanctions against Rhodesia. Their need was well-documented[62] and some aid was forthcoming from UN and Commonwealth sources, but overall the economy of Zambia probably suffered more damage than that of Rhodesia. Outside the framework of international organization formal claims for compensation cannot be made. Can such damage be justified, particularly where impoverished third-world states are concerned? What would be the further effects on Mozambique, and indeed on Zimbabwe and Zambia, if economic sanctions were imposed on South Africa?

Finally, one must consider the systemic effects of economic sanctions. The vulnerability of the world economy to disruption of trade, investment and monetary flows has come sharply to the fore in recent years, and it is obvious that resort to economic weapons of foreign policy by major economic powers for whatever reason is likely to have repercussions throughout the system. The United States, in particular, is still a dominant influence. The interrelationships between OECD countries, and between OECD countries and the the Third World, are particularly close so that shock effects are transmitted throughout the whole network and may gain momentum as they travel along 'fault lines', while trade and credit relations between Western Europe and the Soviet Union and Eastern European countries have grown steadily in recent years and are also susceptible to mutual damage. In addition, Western bank lending on a lavish scale, especially to Latin American and Eastern European governments, has introduced a new element of vulnerability to the international financial system.

It is obviously very difficult to make accurate estimates of the effects sanctions may produce. It is hard enough to predict the effect of negative measures on the target against whom they are directed: to predict wider ramifications is even more problematical. Such intangible factors as confidence may be crucial particularly where problems of massive international debt are concerned. But the possibility that pressure on a debtor country, the target of sanctions, could produce default, precipitating disaster for the whole international banking system, or that the level of confidence which is crucial to the continuation of orderly financial transactions could be fatally undermined by an assets freeze, should not be discounted.[63]

There are other worries. Trade and/or financial sanctions against a developing country can force it into a new and unwelcome dependence on another major power, perhaps exacerbating political as well as economic tensions at the regional or even the global level. Rhodesia was certainly driven into a much closer relationship with South Africa under UN sanctions, while Cuba's dependence on the Soviet Union hardly needs stressing. Is it in Western interests to force Poland back into closer integration with the Soviet Union?

Some of these problems only arise in cases of sanctions imposed by a limited group of states, but others could be present even if a general sanctions programme were approved by the Security Council. In other words, more authoritativeness does not automatically mean the absence of dangerous 'spill-over' and 'ripple' effects for the international system.

Part of the problem would seem to be the impossibility of applying discrete penalties to discrete acts of illegal or unacceptable conduct in the international milieu. Neither 'act' nor 'response' can be effectively separated from the continuing cascade of international events. Even if the act is reasonably clear-cut, as was Argentina's seizure of the Falkland Islands, the responses become part of the outcome, together with other developments. And where one is dealing with an ongoing situation, like South Africa's apartheid policies, or the existence of repressive regimes in the Soviet Union or Poland, there is much greater difficulty in making 'penalties' credible. One can argue that sanctions are best seen as a contribution to the solution of a problem – influential, if not decisive. But they may well become part of new set of problems which make the peaceful resolution of disputes more rather than less difficult.

ASSESSMENT

Armed conflict inevitably brings the destruction of individual human rights, as well as being a possible violation of international law under the UN Charter. A major nuclear war would mean the annihilation of all life and all rights. But human rights are also violated by governmental repressions: the denial of fundamental freedoms; the use of torture and cruel and inhuman punishment; and the practice of racial, religious and sexist discrimination. It is to prevent or counter the unnecessary resort to war and the unnecessary suffering produced by inhumane regimes that collective sanctions can justifiably be employed. And in the late twentieth century the basis for resort to sanctions, on legal a well as on moral grounds, is far stronger than in earlier times, when not only domestic but also colonial policy was outside the purview of international regulation, and war between states was an accepted instrument of national policy.

But even at this level of analysis, relating to justification for some form of retaliation, serious problems are encountered. Efforts to outlaw war have been unsuccessful: the concept of self-defence has been inordinately stretched to meet perceived security needs, and the use of force to overthrow colonial regimes has been virtually legitimized by the United Nations. Efforts to develop a system defining and protecting human rights might be seen as more successful, but different interpretations of principles and norms have meant the dilution of standards. It should be easier to judge failures to live up to commitments which have been freely entered into by states, but where these commitments are cast in general terms, governments can contend that they are, in fact, upholding them. They can also claim that national emergencies justify the suspension of freedoms. Controversy over the meaning of particular rules also makes it easier for other governments to disclaim responsibility for sitting in judgment or for responding with sanctions. Where individual governments attempt to make the protection of human rights a major plank in their foreign policy, they are likely to run into serious problems.[64]

In spite of these difficulties, however, government policy can be judged illegal or immoral. Gross and persistent violations of human rights can be collectively condemned. Grounds for international sanctions can exist.

But second-level difficulties arise when those threatening or imposing sanctions have self-serving interests which go beyond the support of law or principle. Enforcement is virtually absent at the UN level; at the regional level its legal or moral basis is often questionable. Where self-help is the order of the day, the status of sanctions is lowered. Motives for retaliation may be less than principled.

Even if there is at least a discernible goal of checking aggression, as with Italy's invasion of Ethiopia in 1935, or of ending inequality and injustice, as in Rhodesia after UDI or in South Africa today, and this goal is not offset or undermined by other goals of sanctions-initiating states, third-level difficulties are produced by the measures themselves. What kinds of penalties are appropriate? Should they demonstrate disapproval? Or punish by imposing physical and psychic deprivation which hurts the target? Or seek to coerce it into changing its policies? Or seek to topple the government responsible for those policies? Will resistance rather than compliance be the result?[65] If one takes the Tehran hostage case as an example of uncontestable wrongdoing by the Iranian government,[66] were *economic* penalties advisable? Western European governments were reluctant to impose them; the United States itself resorted to a (spectacularly unsuccessful) military rescue attempt. What should have been done?

Questions have also been raised in this paper about the distribution of economic hardship caused by sanctions. Who suffers most? Does the infliction of economic hardship, even if it fails to bring political results and despite its possibly damaging effects on innocent bystander states and on the wider international system, serve some purpose in reinforcing international standards at lower social cost than military measures?

These questions have no easy answers for scholars or policy-makers. But an awareness of their relevance and discussion of their implications are surely important. Alternatives to economic sanctions exist: diplomatic and political measures; severance of communications and cultural and sporting ties;[67] and exclusion from membership or participation in international organizations. These measures are less damaging in impact and less likely to produce unwelcome spill-over effects. But do they, in contemporary jargon, make a statement of sufficient strength? On the positive side, there can be dialogue and diplomacy, incentives to reform, and assistance to refugees. David Baldwin's reminder of the policy implications of neglecting positive measures and focusing exclusively on negative sanctions is still timely.[68]

In a world where equilibrium at the security level is maintained through deterrence and mutual fear of annihilation, where international financial equilibrium is precariously based on confidence, and where international economic interdependence is increasing, negative sanctions, even for the most convincing of ethical reasons, need to be most carefully and thoroughly reviewed in the light of alternatives and consequences.

APPENDIX

TYPOLOGY OF NEGATIVE NON-VIOLENT SANCTIONS

1. Diplomatic Measures

(i) Protest, censure, condemnation.
(ii) Postponement, cancellation of official visits, meetings; negotiations for treaties and agreements.

(iii) Reduction, limitation of scale of diplomatic representations:
      (a) status of post:
      (b) number of diplomatic personnel;
      (c) number of consular offices.
(iv) Severance of diplomatic relations.

2. Cultural and Communications Measures

  (i) Reduction, cancellation of cultural exchanges (scientific co-operation; educational links; sporting links; entertainment).
 (ii) Ban on tourism to/from target country.
(iii) Withdrawal of visas for nationals of target.
(iv) Restriction, cancellation of telephone, cable links with target.
 (v) Restriction, suspension, cancellation of landing/overflight privileges.
(vi) Restriction, suspension, cancellation of water transit/docking/port privileges.
(vii) Restriction, suspension, cancellation of land transit privileges.

3. Economic Measures

(a) *Financial*

  (i) Reduction, suspension, cancellation of aid: military, food, development, funding of technical assistance.
 (ii) Reduction, suspension, cancellation of credit facilities:
      1. at concessionary rates;
      2. at market rates.
(iii) Freezing of bank assets of target government.
(iv) Confiscation of bank assets.
 (v) Confiscation of other assets belonging to the target.
(vi) Ban on interest payments to target.
(vii) Ban on other transfer payments to target.
(viii) Refusal to refinance, reschedule debt repayments (interest and principal).

(b) *Commercial and Technical*

  (i) Quotas on imports from the target.
 (ii) Quotas on exports to the target.
(iii) Restrictive licensing of imports/exports.
(iv) Limited, total embargo on imports.
 (v) Limited, total embargo on exports.
(vi) Discriminatory tariff policy (includes denial of most favoured nation status).
(vii) Restriction, cancellation, suspension of fishing rights.
(viii) Suspension, cancellation of joint projects, industrial ventures.
(ix) Cancellation of trade agreements.
 (x) Ban on export of technology to the target.

(xi) Blacklisting.
(xii) Reduction, suspension, cancellation of technical assistance, training programmes.

4. Measures Relating to Status in International Organizations

(a) *Membership and Participation*

   (i) Vote against admission. (NB this may amount to a veto.)
  (ii) Vote against acceptance of credentials.
 (iii) Vote for suspension.
 (iv) Vote for expulsion.

(b) *Benefits*

  (i)   Vote against loans, grants, technical assistance, etc.

NOTES AND REFERENCES

1. E. Lefever (ed.), *Ethics and World Politics* (Baltimore, Md.: John Hopkins Press, 1972) p. 16.
2. C.R. Beitz, *Political Theory and International Relations*, (Princeton, NJ: Princeton University Press 1979). See too 'Bounded Morality: Justice and the State in World Politics', *International Organization*, 33 (1979), pp. 405–24.
3. Beitz, 'Bounded morality', p. 407.
4. E.H. Carr, *The Twenty Years' Crisis 1919–1939*, 2nd ed. (New York: Harper, 1945).
5. H.J. Morgenthau, *Politics Among Nations*, 5th ed. (New York: Knopf, 1973).
6. Beitz, 'Bounded morality', p. 408.
7. Ibid., p. 409.
8. S. Hoffmann, *Duties Beyond Borders* (Syracuse: Syracuse University Press, 1981). See too M. Howard's thoughtful article 'Ethics and Power in International Politics', *International Affairs* 53, (1977) pp. 364–76; S. Kim, *The Quest for a Just World Order* (Boulder, Col.: Westview Press, 1984).
9. Beitz, 'Bounded Morality', pp. 409–10.
10. Cf. R.S. Olson, 'Economic Coercion in World Politics', *World Politics* 31 (1978–79), who rejects legalistic definitions of sanctions and suggests that 'coercion' should be interchangeable with 'sanction' (pp. 472–4). G.C. Hufbauer and J.J. Schott define economic sanctions as 'the deliberate government-inspired withdrawal, or threat of withdrawal, of "customary" trade or financial relations' for foreign policy goals, i.e. 'changes actually and purportedly sought by the . . . country imposing sanctions in the political behaviour of the target state'. *Economic Sanctions in Support of Foreign Policy Goals*, Institute for International Economics, Policy Analyses, no. 6. (Washington DC: MIT Press, 1983) p. 2.

11. Two recent examples of campaigns to delegitimize behaviour in the private sector come to mind. The first was conducted by activist groups and co-dinated by the Infant Formula Action Committee (INFACT) over a seven-year period. Through a boycott of Nestlé products, it successfully persuaded the Swiss multinational to bring its advertising and marketing procedures for infant formula in developing countries into line with the World Health Organization code. The charge against Nestlé was that promoting formula feeding led mothers to abandon more hygienic and nutritious breast feeding, with resultant damaging effects on their health and that of their children. See T. Lemaresquier 'Beyond Infant Feeding: The Case for Another Relationship Between NGOs and the United Nations System', *Development Dialogue* (1980) pp. 120–5. The second example is the campaign directed at the Canadian seal hunt, and particularly the killing of baby seals whose beguiling furry faces provide a powerful image assisting pro-wildlife activists. Here too, a threat of a widespread consumer boycott – in this case of Canadian fish products – has prompted the Canadian Sealers' Association to ask for an official ban on the clubbing of seals (which has apparently not been practised since 1982), but the Canadian government is still hesi-tant to 'surrender' on this issue. See report in the (Toronto) *Globe and Mail*, 10 March 1984.

12. For more detailed consideration of these developments see M. Doxey, *Economic Sanctions and International Enforcement* 2nd ed. (London: Macmillan for the Royal Institute of International Affairs, 1980).

13. Cf. Sir A. Bertram's comment; 'The economic weapon, conceived not as an instrument of war but as a means of peaceful pressure, is the great discovery and the most precious possession of the League'. 'The Economic Weapon as a Form of Peaceful Pressure', *Transactions of the Grotius Society* 17 (1931) p. 169. Sir Anton was at pains to point out, however, that the League had not solved the problem of 'making the economic weapon effective' (ibid.).

14. See G.W. Baer, *The Coming of the Italo-Ethiopian War* (Cambridge, Mass.: Harvard University Press, 1967); F. Hardie, *The Abyssinian Crisis* (London: Batsford, 1974); Doxey, *Economic Sanctions and International Enforcement*.

15. Articles 12–15. Failure to observe this three-month 'cooling off period' was the technical breach of the Covenant for which Italy was punished in 1935.

16. The well-being of these people was described as a 'sacred trust of civilisation' in Article 22 of the Covenant.

17. The Pacific Islands of the Marianas, Marshalls and Carolines are still administered by the US as 'strategic' trust territories.

18. The Genocide Convention entered into force in 1961.

19. General Assembly Resolution 1514 (XV) 14 Dec. 1960. Voting 89:0, with 9 abstentions (Australia, Belgium, Dominican Republic, France, Portugal, Spain, South Africa, UK, US).

20. General Assembly Resolution 1904 (XVIII) 20 Nov. 1963. Adopted unanimously.

21. Cf. Hoffmann's comment, 'A community of vocabulary is not the same thing a a community of values', *Duties Beyond Borders*, p. 20.

22. *The Quest for a Just World Order*, p. 239. Table on p. 217. It should be recorded that the Carter Administration imposed a unilateral trade ban on Uganda in October 1978, six months before Amin was ousted. See J. Miller 'When

Sanctions Worked', *Foreign Policy*, no. 39, Summer 1980, 118–29. The article begs the question of whether or not sanctions 'worked'.

23. It can be argued that this discretionary power has proved a mixed blessing, permitting too much latitude in Security Council decisions.

24. Cf. H. Kelman, 'Patterns of Personal Involvement in the National System; A Social-Psychological Analysis of Political Legitimacy', in J.N. Rosenau (ed.), *International Politics and Foreign Policy*, rev. ed. (New York: The Free Press, 1969), p. 287n.

25. The 'Brezhnev' doctrine was formulated in a *Pravda* commentary on 26 September 1968 and reiterated by the Soviet Foreign Minister at the UN General Assembly on 3 October.

26. The unacceptability of Marxist–Leninist governments in the Western hemisphere was enunciated at the 8th Meeting of Ministers of Foreign Affairs of the OAS, Punta del Este, 31 January 1962. On the linkage between the two 'doctrines' see T.M. Franck and E. Weisband, *Word Politics: Verbal Strategy among the Superpowers* (New York: Oxford University Press, 1972).

27. Brief accounts of these episodes are given in M. Doxey, 'International Sanctions in Theory and Practice', *Case Western Reserve Journal of International Law* 15 (1983) pp. 273–88.

28. Security Council Resolutions 232, 16 December 1966; 253, 29 May 1968; 277, 18 March 1970.

29. Security Council Resolution 418, 4 November 1977. The arms trade with South Africa was defined as the 'threat to the peace'.

30. On 9 November 1979 the Security Council had called for the release of the hostages in Resolution 457; it subsequently threatened 'effective measures' in Resolution 461 of 31 December 1979. The draft resolution calling for economic sanctions was vetoed by the USSR on 13 January 1980. East Germany also voted 'no'; China did not participate, and Mexico and Bangladesh abstained.

31. Security Council Resolution 502, 3 April 1982, determined that a breach of the peace existed in the area and demanded an immediate cessation of all hostilities, the withdrawal of Argentinian forces and a diplomatic solution. Voting was 10:1 (Panama) with Poland, Spain and the USSR abstaining.

32. See W.M. Reisman, 'The Legal Effect of Vetoed Resolutions', *American Journal of International Law* 74 (1980) pp. 904–7.

33. General Assembly Resolution E/62. Voting was 104:18 with 18 abstentions.

34. General Assembly Resolution 494 (V), 1 February 1951. On 18 May there was a further Resolution (500 (V)) recommending a voluntary embargo in shipments to China and North Korea of arms, ammunition and strategic minerals, including petroleum.

35. Notably in General Assembly Resolution 3379 of 10 November 1975 which determined that 'zionism is a form of racism and racial discrimination'.

36. Article XXVI, sec. 2(a), 1976 revision. A decision to declare a member ineligible requires a simple majority of (weighted) votes in the Fund; a decision to expel requires 85 per cent of total voting power.

37. See P.E. Sigmund, 'The "Invisible" Blockade and the Overthrow of Allende', *Foreign Affairs* 52 (1973–74) pp. 322–40. In 1976 the Harkin Amendment required US representatives on the Inter-American Development Fund to vote against loans to governments guilty of gross violations of internationally

recognized human rights. See G.D. Loescher, 'US Human Rights Policy and International Financial Institutions', *The World Today* 33 (1977) pp. 453–63.

38. For instance, the World Meteorological Organization (WMO) found South Africa's policies of racial discrimination and continued control of Namibia to be inconsistent with the obligations of all members of the agency to promote technical and scientific co-operation in fulfilment of WMO's objectives and to co-operate with the UN in all possible ways. Resolution 38 (Cg–VII) 7th World Meteorological Congress, 1975, reprinted in F.L. Kirgis, *International Organizations and their Legal Setting* (St Paul, Minn.: West Publishing Co., 1977) pp. 526–8. On action against South Africa by UN agencies see E. Osieke, 'The Legal Validity of Ultra Vires Decisions of International Organizations', *American Journal of International Law*, (1983) 77 pp. 239–56.

39. See D.W. Bowett, 'Economic Coercion and Reprisals by States', *Virginia Journal of International Law*, 13 (1972) pp. 1–12. The Hickenlooper Amendment, in force 1962–73, required the automatic suspension of US bilateral aid to governments which nationalized US companies without paying prompt compensation. Extension of this sanction to multilateral lending institutions through the Gonzalez Amendments has already been noted. See C.H. Lipson, 'Corporate Preferences and Public Policies: Foreign Aid Sanctions and Investment Protection', *World Politics* 28 (1975–6) pp. 396–421.

40. Afghanistan, the Iran–Iraq war, the Israeli invasion of Lebanon, the Falklands War and Grenada may suggest an even more disturbing trend to the use of military measures in international relations.

41. Tom Farer's comment that the United Nations and the OAS act as claim appraisal agencies is relevant. See T.J. Farer, *The United States and the Inter-American System: Are there functions for the forms?* American Society of International Law, Studies in the Transnational Legal Policy, no. 17 (St Paul, Minn.: West Publishing Co., 1978).

42. K. Thompson, *The Moral Issue in Statecraft,* (Baton Rouge, La.: Louisiana State University Press, 1966) pp. 77–81. But perhaps Thomas Franck's comment that 'Tending principles only once in a while is probably worse than abandoning them altogether' should also be borne in mind. '*Dulce et decorum est*: the Strategic Role of Legal Principles in the Falklands War', Editorial Comment, *American Journal of International Law* 77 (1983) p. 123.

43. The British government's justifications for military intervention in Egypt in the 1956 Suez crisis can serve as a particularly unconvincing example. In Britain, the protection of British nationals and their property was emphasized, while at the UN intervention was described as a police action to separate Israel and Egypt and safeguard the Canal. See Robert R. Bowie, *Suez 1956: International Crisis and the Role of Law* (New York: Oxford University Press, 1974) p. 67.

44. Cf. J. Barber, 'Economic Sanctions as a Policy Instrument', *International Affairs* 55 (1979) pp. 367–84. Barber distinguishes between primary, secondary and tertiary objectives.

45. For instance A. Schreiber notes that economic coercion was applied to Cuba 'because it met public demand for action against Castro'. 'Economic Coercion as an Instrument of Foreign Policy', *World Politics* 25 (1972–3) p. 405.

46. Harold Wilson's oft-quoted and ill-founded prediction that sanctions would end the Rhodesian rebellion in a matter of weeks is exceptional in this regard.

47. In the Tehran hostage crisis, Douglas Hurd, Minister of State at the British Foreign and Commonwealth Office, reported in evidence to the Parliamentary

Foreign Affairs Committee that the alternative to imposing economic sanctions on Iran was not to do nothing but 'to go back to the President of the United States and slap him in the face'. 5th Report of the Foreign Affairs Committee, 1979–80: *Afghanistan: the Soviet Invasion and Its Consequences for British Foreign Policy*, House of Commons Paper No. 745, 30 June, 1980, p. 194.

48. The Arab oil embargoes of 1973–4 fall into a similar category of economic warfare.

49. E.H. Carr, *The Twenty Years' Crisis*, p. 131.

50. This point is argued forcefully and cogently by D.A. Baldwin in his paper 'Economic Sanctions as Instruments of National Policy', presented to the International Studies Association 25th Annual Convention, Atlanta, 27 March–1 April 1984.

51. Similar arguments about prolonging a dispute rather than settling it have been made about UN peacekeeping.

52. See J.N. Moore, 'Grenada and the International Double Standard', *American Journal of International Law* 78 (1984) p. 147.

53. The Rhodesian sanctions experience is analyzed by H.R. Strack, *Sanctions: the Case of Rhodesia* (Syracuse: Syracuse University Press, 1978).

54. As noted in an address given in Cape Town by the South African Deputy Minister of Foreign Affairs, Mr D.J.L. Nel, there are a number of areas in which South Africa plays a major role in southern Africa. For instance, South Africa is a major food exporter to 13 African countries; it provides essential transport services to Mozambique, Malawi, Zambia and Zimbabwe; it provides contract work for approximately 300 000 foreign blacks. Report in *South African Digest*, 24 February 1984.

55. C. Ferguson and W.R. Cotter, 'South Africa: What Is To Be Done', *Foreign Affairs* 56 (1977–8) p. 274.

56. See report in *The Times*, 14 January 1984.

57. Cf. Sir T.H. Holland, 'The Mineral Sanction as a Contribution to International Security', *International Affairs* 15 (1936) pp. 735–52.

58. In June 1978 a study published by the UN Center against Apartheid called for a mandatory oil embargo against South Africa, and the Special Committee on Apartheid endorsed this call in September of that year.

59. In the inter-war period the idea of food sanctions evoked great repugnance. See J. Foster Dulles, 'Practicable sanctions', in E. Clark (ed.), *Boycotts and Peace* (New York: Harper, 1932). In another chapter, E.C. Eckel declared trenchantly: 'For effectiveness and for moral standing, a really successful food embargo ranks well in advance of torpedoing hospitals ships and is somewhere near the class of gassing maternity hospitals.' (p. 257).

60. See M. Doxey, 'Oil and Food as International Sanctions', *International Journal* 36 (1981) pp. 311–34; *Data and Analysis Concerning the Possibility of a US Food Embargo as a Response to the Present Arab Oil Boycott*, US Library of Congress, Congressional Research Service, 93rd Cong., 1st session, committee print, 21 November 1973.

61. H. Nau 'The Diplomacy of World Food', *International Organization* 32 (1978) p. 780.

62. *The Front Line States: The Burden of the Liberation Struggle* (London: Commonwealth Secretariat, 1978).

63. See R. Carswell 'Economic Sanctions and the Iranian Experience', *Foreign Affairs* 60 (1981–2) pp. 247–65; K. Lissakers, 'Money and Manipulation' *Foreign Policy* no. 44 (1981) pp. 107–26.

64. Cf. Jimmy Carter, *Keeping Faith: Memoirs of a President* (New York: Bantam Books, 1982) particularly pp. 141–5.

65. Cf J. Galtung, 'On the Effects of International Economic Sanctions with Examples from the Case of Rhodesia, *World Politics* 19 (1966–7) pp. 378–416, and many other studies of sanctions.

66. See case concerning US Diplomatic and Consular Staff in Tehran (United States of America v. Iran) 1980, ICJ *Reports*, 3. The erosion of diplomatic immunity and of adherence to the standards of behaviour required of those claiming it, is a particularly disquieting feature of contemporary international life.

67. Commonwealth Heads of Government meeting in London in 1977 issued a statement of determination to end all sporting contacts with South Africa so long as apartheid persists. Termed the 'Gleneagles Agreement', this is still the official Commonwealth position, although there have been some lapses particularly in regard to South African 'Springboks' playing rugby in New Zealand.

68. D.A. Baldwin, 'The Power of Positive Sanctions', *World Politics* 24 (1971–2) pp. 19–38.

6 Non-intervention: Ethical 'Rules of Disregard' and Third-World Conflicts

S.C. NOLUTSHUNGU

The Third World provides the privileged theatre of intervention. This reflects not only the interests that great powers have, or seek to develop, in third-world countries, but also the fact that in their day-to-day existence third-world countries can do very little for themselves without a great reliance on external support. In many case state budgets still cannot be balanced without external aid, and even with aid many state functions are performed inadequately or not at all in substantial areas of the national territory. Because of the pervasive economic influence of large states on their everyday lives, such countries can barely contemplate significant initiatives in political development without a very considerable involvement of external influences.

In this light, the principle of non-intervention, which is based on a sharp distinction between internal and external affairs, would seem particularly unreal. Yet third-world states and political movements generally insist upon it as though it were more precious precisely because they are weak, vulnerable, and externally dependent. They value sovereign statehood and the related, though not always compatible principle of 'self-determination', not only as providing an arena in which life's aims may be struggled for,[1] but also as a resource with which to fight for their own share in a world of states. The ambivalence about non-intervention which is widely felt in the advanced countries, and reflected in the theoretical literature, is, however, evident in the Third World also.[2] Governments and opposition movements alike find it difficult in practice to uphold non-intervention consistently, even when they are not themselves

131

embattled or in any direct way affected by a conflict in another country in which intervention has occurred. Often their response to intervention in a particular case is conditioned by their general alignments in world politics.

No coherent statement of the exceptions that would appeal to various categories of third-world political forces has ever been elaborated, and it seems unlikely that such a task could ever be satisfactorily performed. Attempts by Western theorists to define conditions in which intervention may be morally permissible tend to reflect Western preoccupations and appear even less helpful than an absolute prohibition in regard to third-world realities, interests and conflicts. Yet examination of these attempts may help to clarify the problem of intervention or, rather, the ethical issues involved in formulating rules for disregarding the principle of non-intervention in the Third World. I shall consider in turn the main features of the arguments advanced by Michael Walzer,[3] Charles Beitz,[4] and Ralph Miliband.[5] Both the doctrine of non-intervention and the proposed exceptions to it raise conceptual problems which we separate from those relating to their application to specifically third-world situations. The first part of the present discussion is largely devoted to such issues, while the second part reflects on the specific features of the Third World and its conflicts which ought to be taken into account more fully in the ethical discourse on intervention. The aim is to show through this critical discussion, with concrete examples, some of the specific characteristics of third-world situations which relevant ethical theory ought to take into account, and to suggest non-relativistic reasons why a universal ethical standard or set of rules for disregarding non-intervention is likely to turn out to be a chimera.

Walzer proceeds from the point of view that it is not possible to uphold an absolute prohibition of intervention and still remain true to the larger concerns and values which that principle is intended to serve. Exceptions to the rule of non-intervention ought, however, to be truly exceptional and a heavy onus of justification falls on whoever chooses to violate the norm. From a somewhat modified version of Mill's 'anti-paternalist' argument he deduces three types of situation in which intervention may be undertaken: (a) secession; (b) where there has already been intervention: and (c) 'when the violation of human rights . . . is so terrible that it makes talk of community or self-determination . . . seem cynical and irrelevant, that is, in cases of enslavement or massacre'.[6]

The central idea is that of the 'self-determination' of a 'political community'. In the first case, that of secession, intervention takes place because there is more than one 'political community' within a set of boundaries. Intervention to help the seceding 'community' promotes national liberation and self-determination. In Kantian language the following rule would be appropriate: 'Always act so as to uphold communal autonomy.' In the second case, the prior intervention of a foreign army means that the political community is not self-determining and counter-intervention therefore does not violate that condition. Once undertaken, counter-intervention must operate to counterbalance the first intervention, so as to restore the original balance of contending domestic forces. It is not clear how the third case is derived from the principle of communal autonomy, or why 'enslavement' (which strictly speaking is rare nowadays and in some cases less odious than other much more common abuses) and 'massacre' (which is typically an event rather than an enduring condition) are singled out.

The fundamental problem is with the rather vague notion of 'political community', which seems to be an improvement on the more familiar 'nation' – presumably for the obvious reason that 'nationhood' is so elusive a concept. 'Political community' is no less so; for, whatever it might be taken to mean, in the vast majority of cases it cannot be taken as given or unchangeable, and may, in a sense, be created by the civil strife itself.[7] In third-world countries the states are new and nations are being built, and the communities that would secede have rarely better claim to being a political community than any of the other conceivable groupings within the larger state, except to the extent that they are mobilized for secession. Most often secession is a response to a particular experience of oppression or exploitation perpetuated by a particular regime, and it is chosen because it is easier to achieve (compared to reform or revolution within the larger entity), easier precisely because of the material frailty of the parent state. It may also be preferred by a group facing the loss of a previously dominant position. It may have much less to do with 'arduous struggle'[8] or self-determination than other conceivable forms of opposition, reform or revolt. It may preempt and foreclose the emergence of alternative political communities. The attempted secession of Biafra from Nigeria illustrated each one of these points. When the Nigerian federation was reformed in response to the Biafran challenge and new states were created, new 'political communities' began to form around these new states at the same time as a larger, stronger Nigerian 'community' emerged. Walzer's rule on secession would have favoured one line of political development which emerged largely because a section of the Nigerian army preferred it and was in a position to fight to achieve it. Walzer, like Mill, attaches very considerable weight to the fighting achievements of claimants to 'national liberation'. The ability to fight legitimizes the cause.[9]

Post-colonial African states, avowedly strong champions of national liberation, are well known for their great hostility to seccessionist movements because they are all vulnerable to such threats, since the colonial boundaries they inherited are arbitrary. Although the arbitrary nature of the boundaries (and its importance) is much overstated, it remains nevertheless true that there are particular problems of national integration in these new and often desperately poor states. What is more important, however, is that it is extremely doubtful that any imaginable redrawing of boundaries would be any less arbitrary, the resulting 'political communities' less artificial and, therefore, less prone to fission. Acute conflict has occurred in supposedly homogeneous states like Lesotho and Swaziland, and political integration has been no more successful in homogeneous Somalia than in larger, more diverse countries like Kenya, Zambia, or even, despite its civil war, Nigeria.

The theoretical problem is, of course, that the notion of 'political community' is a vague one, especially where, as in Walzer's analysis, the unifying feature, apart from political will, is not specified.

Walzer's rule of disregard in the case of counter-intervention is based on an astonishing misapprehension, namely, that counter-intervention can ever restore an original balance. What, in any event, is to be balanced apart from military might? The more likely result is that a balance may be struck between the contending intervening armies at a higher level of destruction of the persons and resources of the country in conflict, and in circumstances in which the respective strengths of the original parties in relation to their external supporters may well remain, or become, greatly unequal. Counter-intervention does not restore innocence and autonomy but threatens both and, what is more, entails escalation ruinous to the population of the host country. Competitive intervention in Angola can barely be said to have served the interests of Angolans. To the contrary, it has produced a process of aggression that has exposed other countries in southern Africa to violent destabilization and a certain loss of autonomy. In any event, it is difficult to see what merit there would be for the local population in a return to square one, i.e. the original 'balance' between the three movements, which, it may be recalled, was itself the key cause of armed conflict and the interventions it entrained. Counter-intervention cannot be justified with regard to the autonomy of the community or communities in strife; it makes more sense as a rule of 'fair play' in the balance of power game among would-be intervenors.[10] In an ethical theory of intervention the notion is particularly odd since it implies a spurious moral equality among all claimants to power – so long as they can demonstrate some capacity to fight or establish a following with a section of the population or a region of the country. By this reasoning it was right for Libya to counter-intervene against the Tanzanian intervention in Uganda.

Walzer's stipulation that counter-intervention aims at 'holding the circle, preserving the balance, restoring some degree of integrity to the local struggle' overlooks two considerations. First, the 'local struggle' arose in the case of Angola out of a colonial war in which the various movements formed their positions and strengths abroad and thus were helped and hindered from the outset by forces that were 'external' to the local struggle. Secondly, there would have been no way of relating the original military strengths of the movements to the relative strengths of conflicting popular interests, beliefs, etc., at the beginning of the war in the near total absence of an antecedent political process. The fact of the matter is that there never was an 'original balance' in which a local struggle enjoyed some degree of 'integrity', whatever that might mean.

The counter-intervention formula is even less applicable to the conflicts in Central America (or Latin America, generally) where at the outbreak of armed conflict between government and revolutionaries – the moment of the original balance – the power of the forces on the right in no way reflects their strength in terms of domestic political support or 'legitimacy' but is the result of very considerable external support over many years. In many cases, intervention short of the actual dispatch of foreign combat troops has been the normal condition for decades. Private foreign interests, as well as agencies of foreign governments, perform such a decisive role in the maintenance of such governments that it is difficult to see what 'the integrity of the local struggle' could mean apart from the *status quo ante*.

It is true that Walzer's counter-intervention and secession

arguments could be used to justify support for popular movements against US-dependent regimes on the grounds either that such movements were engaged in 'national liberation' from a species of imperial domination, or that intervention on their behalf would be no more than counter-intervention to the US's generalized but effectively interventionary presence in the Latin American state – let us say Nicaragua or El Salvador. The trouble with this line of reasoning is that the notion of national liberation loses precision and the real nature of the conflict, which is a class one, albeit within a context of neo-imperialism, is unhelpfully distorted. Virtually all third-world revolutions could in this sense be placed in the category of national liberation. In any event, the notion of a counter-intervention against the United States intervention, restoring local integrity to Central American civil wars, sounds even more fantastical in this case.

There are several weighty objections that can be raised against Mill's 'anti-paternalist' argument on which Walzer bases his defence of the non-intervention principle itself. Some of these have been forcefully put forward by Charles Beitz, whose own views we shall presently consider. I shall not, however, deal with the antipaternalist argument for non-intervention for reasons of economy, my main concern being the rules of disregard and their bearing on the Third World. I do however believe that it should be possible to advance far better arguments for non-intervention than the Millian argument. The latter is based on highly questionable assumptions regarding what is most deserving of international support (the principle of 'communal autonomy') and the ways in which freedom actually is or is not attained (the simple-minded emphasis on 'arduous struggle'). I am concerned with the efforts to define rules of disregard because they represent the search for a more definite ethical basis for intervention and an attempt to apply, in a modern sense, political theory to the field of intervention, more so than most of the arguments generally of a legal or quasi-legal form that have been advanced for and against the norm of non-intervention.[11]

Although his stance becomes less clear as his arguments for disregard develop, Walzer represents a fairly strong non-interventionist position. In contrast, Beitz advances the view that the moral case for the general prohibition of intervention is very weak, although he might concede that in most cases intervention would not be desirable. While the criterion he recommends for permitting intervention would in principle allow for intervention in a great many more cases than those allowed for by Walzer, there is no doubt that Beitz does regard the practical problems of intervention as being such as to make it an infrequently desirable course of action.[12] The norm, one may suppose, would still be non-intervention but qualified by a general principle of justice from which specific rules of disregard might be derived.

Non-intervention appears to Beitz as a rule of unlimited toleration among states that is founded upon respect for state autonomy, an autonomy that can and often does work against the rights of persons.The principle can only be morally justified if it serves to uphold the rights of persons, which alone can provide the ethical basis of state autonomy. Beitz does not, however, proceed to examine whether or how intervention can be used to secure and advance those personal rights but concerns himself with trying to specify the conditions in which states ethically lose their entitlement to toleration. This is an unfortunate emphasis because it makes the loss of immunity seem a punishment meted out to states for wrongful behaviour and disregards intervention that is not directed against the state (in the sense at any rate in which Beitz uses 'state'[13]). The criterion of toleration is a state's conformity with principles of justice appropriate to its situation, justice itself being defined according to a modified version of Rawls' theory of (domestic) justice.[14] A state may be tolerated if it seems likely to conform to such principles, but there is no requirement to intervene if it does not; nor is it clear what is to be done when there is no clear evidence that either the state or its challengers have much likelihood, with or without external pressure, to further justice. Leaving aside the problem of defining 'appropriate principles of justice', there is the additional difficulty that a prediction has to be made as to whether a state is likely to develop just institutions with or without intervention. It is difficult to see how such a judgment might be made, and what timespan we should have in view. There is an argument that unjust institutions – like those based on slavery and feudalism – not only led to but were essential to the development of Western societies that many now regard as just. On the other hand, just institutions – as may have existed in many small pre-colonial societies – may well have stood in the way of a growth of economic and military strength that could have spared those societies from the depredations of more powerful states.[15]

More important, however, is the fact that in most third-world civil wars the issue is not the state or its institutions but particular governments, parties, or even individuals. To be sure, there may be radically different conceptions of the state, and different institutional development patterns may follow the success of the one or the other contending group, but it is simply not the capacities of a state's institutions for which people lay down their lives but hostility towards a concrete, presently felt antagonist. In Zaire, under Mobutu, it is not the state or its institutions, such as they are, that have provoked armed opposition but the men who preside over them. There is simply no merit in speculating on whether the state, as distinct from Mobutu, is likely to develop institutions corresponding to appropriate principles of justice. Similar observations might be made of Uganda under Amin or the Central African Republic under Bokassa, to mention only a few examples.

The difficulty with Beitz's opposition of state to personal rights is that it works only when the civil strife can be characterized as a total opposition between the state and persons whose rights it undermines. Where persons threaten each other's rights and the state is merely an arena or context of such conflict, it is difficult to make sense of this justification of intervention. Chad provides a concrete historical illustration. Here, since the early 1970s at least, all parties have been more or less agreed in their critique of the inherited colonial state as they have been largely agreed in their determination to maintain its essential unitary character. Since 1973 control of the state has changed hands among various armed movements, the state functioning both as the focus of conflict and as a resource in the conflict among a multiplicity of factions representing different social interests. The state has been in a substantive sense autonomous: in the sense that it continued to function, minimally, regardless of who was in power, and that even in disintegration it was the univerally sought resource by groups of persons, both in and out of power, who were locked in mortal combat. Intervention was hardly a simple matter of backing either the state or persons, but some occupants of state positions and some rebel factions simultaneously.[16] As for institutions, little could be said about these that was not already common cause among most of the internal forces.

In such cases the view of non-intervention as a reward to states for just behaviour seems unhelpful. The principle of state autonomy could here be related to a real and substantive autonomy of the state in social conflict.[17] There are interests which all groups (in all cases except secession) share in the continued existence of their country, its territorial integrity, its external recognition as sovereign, and indeed even in the particular form of state it has.[18] The state then can be a resource not only competed for by the combatants but valuable to others who may not be involved in fighting – a common enough occurrence in third-world conflicts – as the principal means by which they can enjoy the benefits of international life. To a considerable extent even the personnel of the state, or most of them, can and are used as a more or less neutral resource – at any rate, a malleable one within certain limits – by different claimants to power as they alternate in office. The value of statehood, which means nothing if not a powerful presumption of toleration by other states, derives not only, or, rather, not so much, from the fact that statehood is a first step to 'self-determination' but from the more negative yet more decisive consideration that to the people of any country no other state is likely – except perhaps for a very small privileged minority of the population of a third-world country – to serve their interests better than their own. It is the presumption that no foreign state will serve their interests better that must be defeated before the principle of state autonomy and the doctrine of non-intervention to which it gives rise can be discarded. Refugees know that depending on the 'international community' or a host state is no substitute for secure citizenship; the one shows an intermittent and somewhat capricious interest in their affairs, the other puts the interests of its own citizens before their own. In the long run, preserving the autonomy of the state, and therefore its existence, preserves the possibility of its eventual reform. While in exceptional circumstances foreign domination could, as in the case of the United States in Japan after the Second World War, accelerate economic development and enlarge liberty and democracy, the Japanese could hardly have wished their own defeat. In the perspective of history they would have had little warrant for the expectation that they would fare better under foreign tutelage than in a state of their own which continued to enjoy autonomy in international affairs. In most cases the foreign state is more predatory and the price of its civilizing mission high.

Any doctrine that opposes persons to states must also address the potential, substantive autonomy – relative autonomy, to be sure – of the state in social conflict. In their war against, as it seems, the whole Arab world, Iranians may be defending not just Ayatullah Khumayni or the revolution associated with him, but a heritage more valuable and more permanent, yet one which, as Lebanon has lately shown, cannot be taken for granted and can under certain conditions face total disintegration.

The moral here is that conflict typically occurs, in the first place, between groups of people and it is on behalf of one or other group that intervention is contemplated or undertaken. In such cases the potentialities of the state to develop in a just way in the present or at some remote date are not always a central topic of conflict. To be sure the state is not typically autonomous even in a relative sense. But it is tied to 'persons' with contested conceptions of how and through what institutions justice may be achieved. It might be more relevant to address those claims and to examine the claimants themselves, rather than the state and its institutions, to arrive at a conclusion as to where justice lies in any particular case, or, indeed, what may be 'appropriate principles of justice'. In such cases it is not the question of whether or not the state as such is entitled to toleration by other states that is at issue but the comparative merits of opposed groups within its jurisdiction.

For the rest, the problem of Beitz's analysis is twofold. First, the criterion of justice as advanced is so abstract that it is difficult to see how it could be used to decide conflicting claims – leaving aside the practical, procedural and empirical problems he often appears to regard as somewhat extraneous to ethical theory. Secondly, when the practical implications of adopting and acting upon his more permissive criterion of toleration are looked at, it is by no means clear in which types of real world cases interventions are to be allowed, when any actor is entitled to intervene, whether anyone has a duty to intervene or to counter-intervene, or what say various groups in the population of the affected state should have. To Walzer's self-determination, Beitz opposes 'justice' as the crucial ethical consideration but provides little guidance as to where, in the real world, justice is likely to be found and how.

By contrast with both Walzer and Beitz, Ralph Miliband approaches intervention from a specifically socialist point of view, and considers the conditions in which intervention on behalf of non-capitalist movements ought to be accepted by socialists. Although Miliband is largely concerned with intervention by the Soviet Union and its allies, he does not consider these regimes as socialist or as even being on the way to socialism. If there is any possibility that socialists might treat their actions on a different footing from those of the capitalist big powers (for whose interventions they can have absolutely no sympathy) it is because, despite its lack of socialism, the Soviet Union stands to benefit from and does, therefore, help progressive movements in the Third World. Miliband allows two 'sets of conditions' in which military intervention 'poses no problems' for socialists.

The first set of conditions is where 'a more or less progressive government' with 'a large measure of popular support' is seeking to repel a 'counter-revolutionary internal movement' in conditions of civil war of near civil war or faces attack from abroad 'which is clearly designed to overthrow it'.[19] He presents two examples of such situations – the Spanish Civil War and the Angolan Civil War.

The second set of conditions is where a movement 'of opposition or liberation' with 'a substantial measure of support' is waging a military struggle 'from its own liberated bases' against 'an authoritarian and reactionary regime' representing 'landed, commercial and financial oligarchies, foreign concerns, multinational corporations, and backed by the US and other Western powers'. Miliband's qualifications and reservations in the immediately ensuing paragraph indicate, however, that this is not a case which 'presents no problems' for socialists. The basic point of uncertainty is that such a movement is less likely than a government to retain its autonomy if intervention takes place.

In virtually all other cases support for 'more or less progressive' movements and regimes must, of course, occur but should not include military intervention. Even humanitarian intervention against a genocidal regime is excluded because of the encouragement that such a concession would give to other interventions and because of the dangers of counter-intervention and international conflict. It is difficult to see why these dangers are greater in the case of humanitarian intervention than in the cases which evidently 'present no problems' for socialists.

Miliband's rules of disregard turn on three kinds of consideration, which in the light of his own conclusions from the facts of civil conflicts and intervention also justify a strong anti-interventionist position. The first relates to popular support. Here the argument is not that it is in itself wrong to govern without popular support, or that it is right to tolerate all governments which have popular support, but rather a consequentialist one: socialism is unlikely to be securely established if it is externally imposed on an unwilling people. If a movement or regime does not have substantial popular support, it is more likely to become a mere puppet of its external military supporters who, as already observed, are not in any sense socialist. Given the weight that Miliband accords to popular support one would suppose that the only object of intervention would be to secure 'free and fair elections', but he does not go that far. Indeed, the formula of substantial popular support is somewhat odd. Why not the more familiar criteria – 'the majority' or the 'overwhelming majority'? The extent of popular support a movement enjoys is notoriously difficult to gauge in such circumstances, and, in a socialist perspective, it is difficult to see how one can ignore the quality of support – the extent to which people have had a chance to know and understand the alternatives, what they are prepared to do to give substance to their support, and, above all, what classes they belong to. None of these questions is raised by Miliband.

In the Angolan case, which apparently fits into the first set of conditions, it was decidedly not the case that the MPLA had more persons marching under its banner, nor is it by any means certain that it would have won 'free and fair elections' had it been possible to hold these, given the highly regional character of support for each of the major movements. The socialist justification for supporting the MPLA could only be that it was the only socialist, or aspirant socialist movement fighting against organizations that were either avowedly tribalist or known to be hostile to socialism and which, moreover, were supported by those same foreign countries which had aided Portugal's colonial war. In addition, the Angolan case illustrates the limitation of the formula of 'substantial support' since each movement had in some sense a numerous popular base, and yet none was either able or willing to share power or to settle their differences by holding elections. In any event some external force would have had to assume the military (as well as political and administrative) responsibility of conducting or supervising such elections.

Yet MPLA supporters knew better than their opponents what they were supporting – their movement had an ideology and policies – and the MPLA more than any other had sought to make itself a national rather than merely tribal or racialist organization. Moreover, it had a structure of internal organization that was infinitely more democratic than the personal dictatorship that characterized its challengers. If the others had won there might have emerged a regime not much worse than some African regimes with which we are already quite familiar, but the MPLA would have been eliminated and the wider cause of liberation in southern Africa could hardly have benefited thereby. It is difficult to believe that such considerations could be less important for socialists than its popular support, which was probably no greater than that of other movements.

The second important consideration for Miliband is the degree to which a movement or regime will be able to preserve its autonomy while being aided by military intervention. The problem is real enough, but perhaps even more complicated than Miliband allows. First, no state will commit its troops and incur risks if it cannot exercise control over the way they are used or the purposes for which they are used. It would hardly be reasonable to expect otherwise. On the other hand, it is true that while the host regime is often disregarded in the conduct of the war, quite often it also enjoys great autonomy as regards political policy. Thus, for example, despite continuous Soviet urging the military regime in Ethiopia has moved extremely slowly towards allowing the emergence of a socialist or Communist party, and basing power more broadly. Cuban efforts in the late 1970s to encourage negotiation with the Eritrean movements were, reportedly, discountenanced. Indeed, the Soviet Union has been criticized by the left for not making a change of the Derg's policy on these questions a condition of its military support.[20] At the other end of the ideological spectrum, American governments have had great difficulty in committing the regimes they support to undertake reforms even when it might have been of mutual advantage for the regimes to do so. The presidency of Jimmy Carter is replete with examples of such failure. The French, whose interventions in Africa are sufficiently known, have undertaken three interventions in Chad, and until the late 1970s maintained a substantial military presence there; yet they have been signally unsuccessful in their attempts to stimulate policies of reform and accommodation.[21] It could be argued that in all these cases the intervenor has not been insistent enough or consistent in his own commitment to reform or conciliation. That may well be true, but the fact remains that beneficiaries do not readily submit to dictation on vital questions of political policy. Khaddafi has found that to be the case with Chadians and Palestinians, as no doubt Stalin did with the Chinese Communist Party.

Yet the problem remains as to what obligations, if any, intervenors have to ensure that the struggle they are supporting remains true to principles which they can endorse and, much more important, does not lead to consequences elsewhere that would defeat the common cause. 'Socialist internationalism' is simply incoherent if it is a one-way street.

The third issue for Miliband is the future international consequences on the prospects for peace and war that are likely to follow from military intervention. As already suggested with reference to humanitarian intervention, it is difficult to see how these are determined by the internal merits of the struggle that is being supported by military intervention, such that the cases which raise no problems for socialists (because of the character of the internal conflict) should also be less threatening to peace. However, concerns for world order, legality and mutual non-provocation among powers are proper constraints on intervention. In disregarding the non-intervention principle one necessarily disregards these values as well to some degree – a disregard presumably justified by the end in view, or the magnitude of actual wrongs to be put right, or the promised amelioration if a particular movement or government triumphs in the civil war.

The main argument underlying Miliband's position is a kind of consequentialist one: apart from those pertaining to the cases where non-problematic conditions exist for socialists, military interventions are not likely to aid the achievement of socialism but may thwart it, even to the extent of producing the 'Soviet-type' regimes that he deplores. This points to a problem which would appear insuperable. Where, in a way, Miliband's concern with socialist principles of intervention and non-intervention seems precise and therefore more practical than the more general and abstract Beitzian criterion of 'justice', it does nevertheless raise intractable problems. The first one is the very idea of what is or is not socialist or 'more or less progressive', and how one decides in the real world what is leading to 'socialism' or to something less wholesome without taking on board the historical baggage of anti-Soviet Western socialisms. The second problem, by no means less important, is that of removing from serious consideration a vast range of situations where the principal intervenors may not be the United States or the Soviet Union, and where oddly the intervention of non-socialist or even capitalist powers might actually be sought by 'more or less progressive' movements. Britain's intervention was sought by nationalists in Zimbabwe and was crucial to the eventual installation of Mugabe; France's overthrow of Bokassa served no socialist purpose but it would be difficult not to place it among the more useful things done by a French president who once described the Emperor as 'mon cher parent'.[22]

In recent years, intervention undertaken by relatively minor powers has increased and occasionally involves conventional military confrontation between two states of comparable power. In many of these cases the intervention does not fall under any pure heading but includes a combination of motives. Vietnam's action against the Pol Pot regime and Tanzania's ousting of Amin were of this kind. There was a humanitarian purpose in the overthrow of a genocidal regime, but there were also concerns relating to Vietnam's own security in the face of attacks by the Khmer Rouge undertaken with increasing encouragement from China. There may have been an equal concern not to allow Indo-China to come under Chinese sway at a time when China was showing little patience with 'Hanoi's policy of equidistance as between itself and Moscow'.[23] For Tanzania there were also security reasons involved. Uganda had attacked Tanzania and was expected to do so again if Amin remained in power. Most states that were involved in the Angolan Civil War could not possibly have kept out of the reckoning questions relating to the future of Namibia, Rhodesia, and South Africa. Yet each would also have had reasons of national policy and self-interest for doing what it did. As Walzer correctly observes, an action does not cease to be humanitarian simply because there may also be an advantage for the intervenor in undertaking it. Moreover, the national interests served are not *ipso facto* incompatible with the causes that intervention may be proclaimed to be intended to serve, i.e. justice, socialism or humanitarianism. For such complex cases, the standards set by Miliband do not provide any grounds for intervention: nor do they by any accessible argument provide sufficient grounds for excluding it. All that can be said is that his principles are essentially insensitive to these concerns.

When all this has been said, it may still remain the case that, for practical reasons, intervention may yet not be a suitable means in all, or most cases, for achieving the ends in view. But that is a matter that cannot be settled *a priori* in advance of the facts; nor does it provide a means of choosing between competing criteria (or moral imperatives) for disregarding non-intervention, since, as I have argued, these criteria themselves do not establish cases or types of cases that inherently differ in the practical consequences that would follow intervention. Angola, which appears unproblematical to Milliband, has still not been stabilized; aggression and destabilization continue. Heng Samrin's regime was undoubtedly a kind of deliverance for the Kampuchean people, but while neither it nor Vietnam can be blamed if others have found occasion to intervene and sustain their various protégés, such in practice are the likely consequences of intervention.

The three positions that I have reviewed, all too briefly and not without some oversimplification that might do less than full justice to their exponents, have much in common. Each illustrates in its own way the difficulty, from a moral point of view, of accepting an absolute prohibition of intervention. Yet each recognizes – Beitz, perhaps, less strongly than the others – that intervention on moral grounds could only be justified in rare, exceptional instances. None of the authors attempts to show how the moral exceptions to the rule might be accommodated in international law, or indicates how far such exceptions would be consistent with the interests of world order. The present discussion also puts aside the problems of law and world order to focus on specifically ethical questions, subject, however, to two considerations.

First, it is safe to presume that from the point of view of law and the interests of world order, the simple, absolute prohibition of intervention is to be preferred to any qualified norm that has yet been proposed if for no other reason than that it is clear, even with such generally accepted legal exceptions as self-defence and invitation by a competent authority. This is a presumption for which I shall not argue.

Secondly, it may also be presumed that it is highly desirable from a moral point of view that what little law and order exists among states should as far as possible be upheld. But order and legality do not exhaust the interests of morality and it may occasionally be that the law prescribes a course of action (or inaction) that, taken on the merits of the particular case under consideration, may be morally perverse. International law and the international legal system are simply not sufficiently developed to resolve such anomalies when they arise, and the correspondence between what is legally right and what men judge to be morally right, indeed, incumbent upon them to do, may be less strong in international than in internal affairs.

Ethical reflection undoubtedly reveals many instances in which intervention is hard to condemn, or unlimited toleration among states (which is, as Beitz insists, the meaning of the rule of non-intervention) hard to justify. That is why the need is often felt for rules for disregarding the prohibition. Yet it is difficult to see that this applies uniquely to the principle of non-intervention. If a state does not merit toleration in this way it is difficult to see how it might deserve to be tolerated through, for example, the general extension of all the other benefits of international law to it. Some states might not deserve to exist any more than they deserve to be immune from external interference. However, international life would be more difficult and more dangerous if states' rights were made to reflect their moral deserts.

The problem with attempting to define 'rules of disregard' is that, first, if a rule is accepted there is the danger that it may no longer be exceptional cases that are tolerated but varied situations which may be far too numerous for our general preference for a severe restraint on intervention to continue to have any meaning – the thin end of the wedge. Secondly, the genuinely sympathetic cases for intervention are more numerous and of more different kinds than any of the rules proposed allows for. As historical events they may be better understood as unique instances in which different moral considerations – or mixes of moral factors – apply. There may be merit in treating each case as exceptional in the strict sense that it sets and can set no precedent for any other. After all, civil conflicts differ, as countries themselves differ in their histories and their world-political contexts.

Whether we should, if we proceeded in this manner, end up with many more exceptions than we would if we followed one or other of the rules proposed is not a matter that can be settled *a priori*; but the fact that each case has to be justified on its own as an exception against the background of clear law should have a restraining effect. It would still be necessary to know what ethical considerations should weigh most heavily in such justifications, but it is not clear that these should be expressed in rules or be any different from the normal range of moral considerations that the people affected by the conflict and by any possible intervention consider important and relevant.

Humanitarian motives for intervention are the stuff of international ethics. States, however, do not generally accept the existence of a right of unilateral humanitarian intervention though they may, occasionally, acquiesce in such action. Similarly, intervening states hardly ever justify their actions on such grounds but restrict themselves to legal or quasi-legal justifications – such as having been invited by a competent authority or acting in self-defence – or to political arguments of the balance-of-power type that are likely to be more persuasive with friends and allies – such as restoring regional security or countering a prior foreign intervention or subversion.

Whatever the value or principle to be furthered by such intervention, the practical problems of institutionalizing or legally permitting it are well-nigh insuperable. In addition there is the danger of weakening the general prohibition of intervention at law. Above all, there is the problem of credibility. Since it is generally unlikely that a state would intervene in another without some hope of advantage for itself, there would always be room for scepticism about any claims that an intervention was inspired primarily by humanitarian concerns. Even if such a claim were accepted as the motive which inspired the action, there would still arise practical problems as to how the intervening state should be kept strictly to its humanitarian mission. There would be the problem of what to do if a 'humanitarian intervention' failed to achieve its aims, or was ineptly executed in any of a number of ways, e.g. in terms of its cost in human life and resources to the host country, or refugee problems created for neighbours, or a militarization of the host state which might change a regional balance of power. How, and by whom, should corrective action be taken, and should such remedial interference include the possibility of the use of force against the first intervenor?

Collective intervention would, on the face of it, appear to be one way of getting round these problems. After all, truly humanitarian concerns ought to affect all, or nearly all states. The collective involvement of the international community should provide some safeguard against the pursuit of selfish ends by a single intervening state or group of states. However, the United Nations, which alone could give universal character to such collective action, is simply not suited to such tasks. First, there would be great difficulty in finding agreement that any particular cases warranted humanitarian intervention and what form that should take. Secondly, the deliberative process would probably be too slow to be of any use in some situations (as in cases of massacres and genocidal pogroms, etc.). Thirdly, there would be little agreement about operational control and day-to-day, on-the-spot political decision-making during the course of the intervention. Fourthly, the problem of sharing the costs and burdens would be a major one. Fifthly, such actions would tend to impart to the UN supranational powers which many states do not believe it should have. Finally, and, perhaps, most important, such humanitarian intervention would virtually always be feasible only against the weaker states and never against the great powers. Any rule or principle allowing for intervention, however 'neutral' in pure conception, would in practice be far from impartial as between strong and weak.

If ethical 'rules of disregard' of the non-intervention principle are hard to translate into legal rules or quasi-legal norms that can guide state behaviour satisfactorily, it may be wondered if the quest for 'rules' is not in any case misplaced. For the problem is not simply that of choosing the 'principles' or 'values' that are most important, but also of ensuring that they are helpful to those concerned in the civil conflicts that actually arise. A consideration of the diversity and complexity of third-world conflicts that attract intervention discourages hope that much may be gained from a search for 'rules'. It encourages the belief that the proper task of ethical inquiry should be to uncover the full range of moral concerns that ought to be taken into account when a judgment is made on an intervention, prospective or actual, and that such moral evaluation ought to be particularly sensitive to the specific characteristics of the conflicts which actually occur.

Theoretical discussion of intervention is mostly focused on armed intervention involving the dispatch of troops into a country in civil conflict to decide that conflict in favour of one movement or coalition of interests against others. That is also the situation that most causes alarm among states and ordinary people alike. Yet it is one form of intervention among many and it is often merely the culmination of previous acts of interference, pressure and coercion. It could be a necessary consequence of those other forms of intervention.[24] Evidently, military intervention in the Third World cannot be regulated, or ethical rules defined for it, without regard to the characteristic relationships of the Third World with the states which typically intervene either directly or through their allies.

However one characterizes the relationship between third-world countries and the West, it is undeniable that the economic power and political influence of the major Western countries is such that any political or social change that is disapproved of by the West has great difficulty in succeeding, and almost no chance at all without the country concerned developing an abnormally high dependence on the socialist bloc. And even then, it suffers with the socialist bloc the punitive discrimination of those few countries which dominate the world economy. Cuba bears testimony to this.[25]

In the case of popularly based armed revolution against non-socialist regimes, there has not been a single case in the post-war period where the West has not in one way or another sought to thwart it. For revolutionaries the problem of intervention is essentially that of coping with an almost always expected interference – particularly in the 'Western Hemisphere' – and of neutralizing the foreign factor, which is often the only real obstacle to success. Only very rarely has it been possible to secure military intervention on the side of popular forces and often, as in Angola and Kampuchea, that has in due course been followed by counter-intervention at a higher level of violence.

For conservative pro-Western regimes, the problem is one of securing assurance of intervention when their own efforts at counter-insurgency have failed. Increasingly intervention is called for not only by the embattled right-wing forces within the country concerned but by right-wing neighbours who assert, evidently with Western encouragement, a *droit de régard*. Thus intervention was requested by neighbours in the case of Grenada, and destabilization and Chinese military pressure on Vietnam and Kampuchea have been 'legitimated' by some of the ASEAN countries.[26] Gabon has led an anxious caucus of right-wing states, strongly backed by the United States, in its insistent demand for decisive French military action in Chad since July 1983.

The opposition between revolutionary and anti-revolutionary positions, with all its international ramifications, is so radical and by now so well established in many parts of the Third World that it is difficult to see how any norm of intervention, sensitive to the needs and concerns of third-world people, could fail to embody a substantive ethical commitment on this central issue.

Since external involvement is always implicit, and armed intervention a permanent possibility, in social revolutions, it is quite evident that the belief that global balance-of-power issues are extraneous to third-world conflicts needs to be qualified. Certainly local concerns are central, and certainly great powers impose their own global concerns on such 'internal conflicts'. Yet third-world movements and regimes engaged in conflict are never indifferent to the state of the balance of power. Soviet intervention in Angola and Ethiopia might not have been possible had the Americans not been restrained after Vietnam; had the United States held its position in Iran, the Soviet response to developments in Afghanistan might have been different. Without the Iranian débâcle, Nicaragua's revolution could conceivably have met a milder response in the United States, and so on. One does not need an ideological globalism to see the interrelation of world power positions and the possibilities of revolutionary success or failure in any country, particularly one that is considered important.

Given that the global distribution of power underlies that interdependence which more than anything else forms the basis of international moral discourse, the state of that 'balance' cannot be a matter of moral indifference. Once again, a set of norms on intervention which does not embody substantial moral commitments on the rightness or wrongness of the 'balance' or indeed on how 'balancing' should be done, would seem incomplete.

Pervasive though the issues of social revolution, reaction and imperialism may be, it is decidedly not the case that all significant conflict in the Third World takes place between unambiguous protagonists of these positions, or that it provokes responses of a decisive kind from the powerful countries. Many bloody conflicts are 'parochial', and in many instances the powers watch passively as the gruesome drama of fratricide unfolds, often sustaining it only with limited supplies of arms and economic aid, often through intermediaries. In such situations the danger lines in both passive detachment and an over-eager cosmopolitanism on the part of outsiders. Sometimes, the global and the parochial are combined, as in the Horn of Africa, where undoubtedly socialist and anti-socialist interests, East–West rivalry, revolution and reaction are involved, but there are also national and nationalities conflicts which, however they are resolved, are unlikely in themselves to make much difference to the condition of the rest of the world. While the conflict continues, in some cases between movements that all avow socialist anti-imperialism, more basic loyalties to kith and kin and one's own immediate community dictate the behaviour of most combatants. In Chad, a war has been fought for seventeen years with foreign arms, and victories have been decided, or reversed, by foreigners. Universal ideologies of 'socialism', 'free enterprise' and 'Islam' have found echoes in the utterances of the combatants, but these are only remotely related to the real issues of the fight and the practical concerns of the fighters, which are more immediate and more basic.[27]

In African conflicts, perhaps more than in any other, some basic, almost pre-ideological 'parochial' issues are always involved: the very existence of the state and whom it will include; finding the state form that can work at the most basic level of being able to perform the functions of government and exercise authority over its entire territory; in the keen contest for extremely scarce resources, giving the state sufficient neutrality between powerful claimants so as to make possible the pacific resolution of disputes. In the case of the Nigerian Civil War such issues were central, and precisely because they were so 'parochial' military intervention would almost certainly not have occurred even had it been requested by either party. In Chad many neighbouring states believe that a Chadian state must survive in the form it had at independence since its disintegration or disappearance might carry dangers for many other states as well. In Angola and Ethiopia over and above the conflicting ideological positions of the different parties, the fragility of statehood and citizenship in itself provides opportunity for others to fish in troubled waters and creates a need on all sides for massive external support. The issues combine in different measures with different effects in different conflicts.

State formation and national integration require material resources, including military means, in order to be accomplished. In virtually all cases the need cannot be met without external assistance, and in some cases that may include military intervention. Stretched beyond its economic capabilities and faced with aggression from South Africa, Mozambique's Frelimo government would have been in a very different position today had it been possible to obtain direct military assistance against its enemies. Poor states not only govern beyond their means, they also fight that way given the nature of their new states and the realities of world politics. The ethics of non-intervention cannot properly exclude those realities either.

Revolutions raise particular problems in this context. Most contemporary discussion of international relations tends to be based upon the notion that there is interdependence between the Third and other worlds, or more strongly, a moral unity in terms of which all people have obligations to all other people.[28] However, revolutionary struggles in an interdependent world necessarily challenge fundamentally the structure of interdependence and its apparent values. They are among the principal means through which power relationships both international and domestic can be drastically changed, and it is often revolutions that force a reappraisal of international norms. European decolonization might have occurred in any case, but the Algerian and Indo-Chinese upheavals, following so shortly upon the Chinese revolution, accelerated the process. Similarly, without the Cuban revolution the impulse toward reform in the United States' relations with its Latin neighbours might have been much feebler. What was at stake in each case was not only the overthrow of local misrule but the reordering of relations among states as well. Revolutions properly so-called are international as well as national both in their causes and their consequences.

While ethical 'rules of disregard' of the non-intervention principle owe their appeal largely to the belief that they may promote values that are or ought to be universally, or nearly universally accepted, and which are neutral as among the different ideologies to which most people actually subscribe, moral concern in international politics may itself be a source of conflict. Indeed, revolutionaries often have an intensely moral view of politics, domestic and international, on the basis of which they make their claims for international support. Yet, the support they need and demand is a partisan one as between themselves and their antagonists. General principles of 'justice', 'communal autonomy', and 'socialism' are involved in revolutionary claims but the protagonists are seldom unequivocal embodiments of such values. Indeed, humanitarian appeals of the same kind can often be made both against the old order which the revolutionaries seek to overthrow and against the excesses of the revolutionary process itself. The ethical challenge of such situations is not met by the enunciation of general principles but by their translation into more specific political positions of support for or opposition to revolutions directed not only against domestic enemies but also to some extent against the international system.

At the same time, it is all too easy to exaggerate the voluntary element in revolutions. People are often caught up in revolutionary crises which they have not themselves designed or planned for, and which present them with options of internal and external alignment and policy which are much constrained. Thus, every revolution in this century has not conformed more than approximately to the demands of even its own ethical theorists.[29] Those who sought to overthrow the Shah of Iran for Marxist or liberal reasons had to work with the mullahs as assuredly as the Ayatullah Khumayni relies on the support and arms of non-believers to defend and consolidate the Islamic revolution.

The element of determinism means that the conflict cannot be ordered at will in such a way that the opposed positions represent faithfully universal, moral or ideological positions. Often what revolutions do is to create the opportunity for moral ideals to be more seriously debated and struggled for, though the opportunity is sometimes temporary or even illusory. A tragic sense of history might suggest that the opportunity is itself all that one can be assured of, all that is worth dying for – and intervening for.

A general 'neutral' principle is then often an externally imposed criterion that is difficult to relate to the actual choices facing a particular population or to the inner logic of the revolution, which may be difficult to discern while conflict rages. It is impossible to know what the eventual outcome of the Nicaraguan revolution will be, just as it would have been impossible to foretell in 1949 the present character of the Chinese revolution.

It may be possible to pass judgment on revolutionaries and their programmes, but if revolutions themselves are in large part determined one could hardly ask the various revolutionary groups in Afghanistan, say, to restore the monarchy or to cease their struggle because none of them was or, given their historical circumstances, *could be* true to the demands of Marxist theory or Rawlsian justice. It would be possible though not morally demanding to pronounce 'a curse on both their houses'. Otherwise one is ethically committed either to support or to subvert the revolutionaries more or less as one finds them, and more or less within the limitations imposed by the terms of their own historical situation.[30] Anything more may border on usurpation, or imperialism. Although that might conceivably produce a happier issue than could the original internal conflicts – e.g. by imposing 'peace' and 'progress' on a conflict-ridden community, and perhaps even uniting them against the intervenor – it envisages an international order quite different from the present one, which is more or less typically presupposed in the debate on the ethics of intervention.

Revolutions depend for their success on favourable international contexts while they almost invariably attract some measure of external opposition because they upset existing regional or international power balances, or because they threaten to encourage revolutions elsewhere by the force of their example, or because they undermine the material interests of powerful states where they occur. On the other hand, it is often extremely difficult to consolidate revolutionary state power without considerable external support including military intervention. Examples include Angola where there is armed counter-revolution, and Mozambique where, despite the popular support enjoyed by the revolutionary regime, the state simply lacks the military capacity to maintain internal and external security even against a small though well trained counter-revolutionary force. In both cases, there has, of course, been a considerable South African involvement also, but even without the direct intervention of South African troops these states are vulnerable. The alternative to inviting external military intervention may well be capitulation to anti-revolutionary enemies, given that power-sharing and mutual accommodation between such opposites are often quite impossible.

In theory it might be possible to specify types of revolution for which the prohibition of intervention (on the side of certain types of claimants to power) might be disregarded, but in practice this is likely to be a futile exercise since each situation and its international context are in an important sense unique. Yet, just as municipal law cannot legislate for its own suspension in the event of a revolution, so too is it unthinkable that there could be a coherent international law that contained provisions for its disregard in the case of revolutions. At such times the moral battles are not decided within the confines of law but largely outside and often against it. Yet that is no reason for not having clear law.

If in international law there is much to be said for a simple norm of prohibition of intervention, and if by contrast ethical reflection shows that morally no such position is possible, it is nevertheless virtually impossible to formulate clear rules for intervention. In a sense there is the logical problem of devising rules for exceptional cases. But much deeper lies the objection that each position on intervention calls for a clear moral position on other issues.

The rules must bear some relation to the actual position of third-world countries in the international system and must take account of the nature of its conflicts.

Any rule of non-intervention and every exception to it must take full account of the fact that the struggle to advance any significant moral or political values in third-world countries often involves not only domestic change but also a hard struggle against traditional international relationships which underpin and sustain those very domestic structures that call for reform or even destruction. Moreover, the economic weakness that hampers social and political advance also undermines the capacity of such societies to resolve internally all major crises, including political and military ones, relying on their own resources. Evidently this is truer of some than of others and depends on the crisis and its international context. After the civil war, Angola might have managed its own conflicts and brought them to a definite outcome were there no Namibian problem, and had Western powers not become more indulgent in their attitude towards South Africa with the election of President Reagan. Without a tense Sino–Soviet relationship the internal development of the Vietnamese revolution following the American withdrawal might have been different. In such conjunctures the boundaries between internal and external conflict become blurred.

The civil conflicts which arise differ both in their articulation to international relations and in their local dynamics. The moral issues do not always fall under any convenient theoretical heading, e.g. the furtherance of justice, or autonomy, or socialism. It is not cultural relativism but distance and detachment from these crises, as lived by those in the grip of civil war, which seem to ensure that the concerns of ethical theorists are hardly ever those of the conflict-ridden societies themselves. It might be that the real challenge for international ethics lies precisely here, in bridging the gap between abstract ethical theory and the enunciation of rules for international behaviour on the one hand, and the pressing concerns of people actually caught up in civil wars and revolutions on the other. The contribution of ethical theory may then lie not in rules which it decrees for foreign participation or non-participation, but in the extent to which through its *engagement* in the struggles of the day it is able to increase our sensitivity to the actual needs, concerns and moral preoccupations which inform actual civil conflicts. Often that may require not such neutrality as may be embodied in general principles but a partisanship in the conflict, not only as among third-world combatants but also between the external, international forces that favour alternative resolutions to the conflict.

Law in itself is clearly not capable of incorporating and accommodating the demands of morality in all such cases. The task of morality is not to imitate the law by seeking to devise law-like rules that may be applied to all cases over and above those extremely limited prescriptions that the law itself imposes. There are good reasons why international law is sparse and treads warily in the area of enforcing morals. One reason is that for considerations other than those of cultural relativism, but rather having more to do with our different situations and political engagements, we agree much less among ourselves on morality than on law much of the time.

Every conflict, especially when it involves a fundamental social upheaval, produces its own ethical discourse, even within that common distinctness of the condition of third-world states. It is only by taking up a substantive position within that discourse that one can form an ethical view which is neither abstract nor irrelevant on whether, in the particular case and circumstances, having regard to the ethical interest in legality and the restraint of force, external military intervention is or is not appropriate.

NOTES AND REFERENCES

1. M. Walzer, *Just and Unjust Wars: A Moral Argument with Historical Illustrations* (New York: Basic Books, 1977) p. 89.
2. See, for example, R.J. Vincent, *Nonintervention and International Order* (Princeton, NJ: Princeton University Press, 1974) *passim*; Martin Wight, 'Western Values in International Relations', in H. Butterfield and M. Wight (eds) *Diplomatic Investigations: Essays in the Theory of International Politics* (London: Allen & Unwin, 1966) pp. 111–20.
3. Walzer, *Just and Unjust Wars.*
4. C. Beitz, *Political Theory and International Relations* (Princeton, NJ: Princeton University Press, 1979) pp. 71–129.
5. R. Miliband, 'Military Intervention and Socialist Internationalism', *The Socialist Register 1980* (London: Merlin Press, 1980) pp. 1–24.
6. Walzer, *Just and Unjust Wars*, p. 90.
7. If secession fails one 'nation' could develop; if it succeeds two will exist.
8. Mill's idea that freedom cannot be imposed but is earned by 'arduous struggle', quoted by Walzer, *Just and Unjust Wars*, p. 87.
9. Ibid., p. 88, pp. 98–9.
10. However, this can be part of a doctrine of 'the moral interdependence of people' one of whose tenets, according to Wight, in 'Western Values in International Relations', p. 116, is that 'in a moral scale, to maintain the balance of power is a better reason for intervening than to uphold civilized standards, but to uphold civilized standards is a better reason than to uphold existing governments'. The difficulties of the doctrine are, I think, quite obvious.
11. Cf. Vincent, *Nonintervention and International Order* and T.J. Farer, 'Harnessing Rogue Elephants: A Short Discourse on Foreign Intervention in Civil Strife', *Harvard Law Review* 82 (1969) pp. 511–41, and 'Intervention in Civil Wars: A Modest Proposal', *Columbia Law Review* 67 (1967), pp. 267–79.
12. Beitz, *Political Theory and International Relations*, pp. 90–1.
13. That is, almost as a synonym for 'government' or 'regime'.
14. J. Rawls, *A Theory of Justice* (London: Oxford University Press, 1972).
15. Ethiopia's oppressive economic system and its militarism were important factors in its managing to escape colonization.
16. See, among others, C. Bouquet, *Tchad: genèse d'un conflict* (Paris: Éditions L'Harmattan, 1982); R. Buijtenhuijs, *Le Frolinat et les révoltes populaires du Tchad 1965–1976*; M. N'Gangbet, *Peut-on encore sauver le Tchad?* (Paris: Editions Karthala, 1984).
17. Consider the view of the role of the state and its 'potential autonomy' put forward in T. Skocpol's, *States and Social Revolutions* (Cambridge: Cambridge University Press, 1979) pp. 24–32.

18. Presumably also a potential idea behind secessionist movements is any sense that the 'community' will be self-determining. The 'self' is defined in the first place against *foreign* domination. This is also what makes possible patriotic appeals by movements of radically different ideological or class character.

19. Miliband, 'Military Intervention and Socialist Internationalism', p. 2.

20. Cf. R. Lyons, 'The USSR, China and the Horn of Africa', *Review of African Political Economy* 12 (1978) pp. 5–30. See also, *Africa Contemporary Record*, 1980, p. A136.

21. At one time a Mission of Administrative Reform was actually sent to Chad, but it is now only remembered for digging boreholes, and for the kidnap of the wife of one of its directors, Françoise Claustre; see, among Others, T. Desjardins, *Avec les ôtages du Tchad* (Paris: Presse de la Cité, 1975).

22. B. Loubat, *L'ogre de Berengo:'Bokassa m'a dit'* (Paris: Éditions Alain Lefeuvre 1971) p. 17.

23. *Revue Française de Science Politique* 32 (1982), virtually the whole issue but particularly P. Devilliers, 'L'Indochine et l'Asean en lutte pour le Cambodge', pp. 346–69.

24. I have deliberately set aside the problems of the definition of 'intervention' and of the boundary between 'military' and 'non-military', but as virtually every commentator has observed they are both difficult and important.

25. Cf. I. Wallerstein, *The Capitalist World Economy* (Cambridge: Cambridge University Press, 1967).

26. B. Baudouin, 'Le prince Sihanouk et la "coalition souple" devant les grandes manoeuvres sino-sovietiques', *Le Monde Diplomatique*, February 1983.

27. This is not to imply that these positions are not relevant or to deny that 'in the final analysis' this is what it may all turn out to be about, but to stress the immediate, concrete content of the struggles in the light of which 'ultimate' concerns have to be interpreted, and to highlight the specific circumstances in which they emerge.

28. Note, however, the contrasting emphasis in the doctrine referred to by Wight, 'Western Values in International Relations', and say, Beitz, *Political Theory and International Relations, passim.*

29. Cf. T. Skocpol, *States and Social Revolutions, passim.*

30. One is forced to back revolutionaries with questionable socialist theories and practices and barely a proletarian base, or anti-revolutionaries who are neither liberals nor democrats. The characteristics of both reflect aspects of the levels and forms of social and economic development in their country.

7 Confrontation or Community? The Evolving Institutional Framework of North–South Relations

JANE DAVIS

North–South issues in the 1970s clearly revived interest in the fortunes of international institutions. Until then the United Nations, for example, threatened to become increasingly peripheral to the challenges posed by global changes. However, the evolving North–South relationship, reflecting the changing priorities on the international agenda, provided considerable raw material for emergent theories such as transnationalism, *dependencia* and developmentalism. These encouraged reassessment of the role of international organizations in the global system and therefore of traditional thinking about international politics. North–South relations may be long on expectations and short on achievements, inflicting a new polarization and paralysis on the United Nations, but they have revitalised traditional issues of international politics and given a new lease of life to academic writing on international organization.[1] In this sense the North–South dialogue[2] can at least claim to have had a rejuvenating effect. But caution dictates that we should perhaps question the perspicacity of those writers who faithfully pin the flag of international organization to the mast of North–South relations.[3]

There are few significant issues in international politics which do not impinge on the North–South relationship and the institutional structures which attempt to give it some coherence. These structures are seldom unencumbered by the display of rival moralities or by competing impulses between what ought to be done and what prudence dictates. Moral judgments and predilections have become almost the *sine qua non* of the conduct and substance of North–South encounters. In the process, moral ambiguity and double standards[4] have only served to encourage scepticism as to the role and value of institutional proceedings where stated principles are compromised and intended goals are frustrated. This kind of criticism appears to be justified where an organization's authority is seen to have been devalued, or its legitimizing function (to say nothing of its credibility) sacrificed on the altar of majoritarianism.[5] The UN has been the least immune to such criticism: charges of hypocrisy and double standards have become part of the folklore of the organization. Admittedly, inveterate detractors of international institutions are well armed with damning evidence, but a more balanced and constructive approach might suggest that the very existence of these institutions at least testifies to a 'will' to organize, however nebulous that 'will' may appear at times. Because they are concerned to devise rules and procedures designed to improve order, stability and predictability in the world, institutions emerge as legitimate means by which to regulate and manage the international system, to mitigate problems, and perhaps implicitly to cultivate a sense of community, even a common morality. In this respect institutions indeed bear a heavy responsibility – nothing less than the promotion of an international community as the moral yardstick of their success.

Support for the idea of a global constituency is implicit in the argument that 'international organization is something more than a grouping of national governments, it is . . . an expression of the concept that there is an international community which has responsibility for dealing with matters which refuse to be confined within national boundaries'.[6] Whatever the motives and incentives for co-operation between North and South, whether these are seen in terms of 'milieu' or 'possession' goals,[7] it is the apparent absence of a universally accepted notion of morality, i.e. the lack of a generally agreed set of standards and priorities, which makes a 'confrontation of visions and principles'[8] inevitable within the North–South relationship. Confrontation can but hamper progress towards an international community.

If '*peace* is scarcely a shared value'[9] in the present century, then the likelihood of North–South agreement on issues as controversial as the right of full and equal participation by all members of international society in international decision-making processes appears remote. For the core of the North–South institutional dilemma concerns the prospects for genuinely shared *control* of the instruments of power. To this extent it might be argued that the North–South institutional framework is fatally and irrevocably flawed. It apparently promises more than it can realistically hope to deliver without resort to enforcement and the confrontation and conflict which that implies. If it claims to identify, or indeed actually reflects a need for 'common ground' and international community in a meaningful sense, the North–South institutional framework simultaneously demonstrates characteristics more symptomatic of an arena of confrontation. The challenge is to reconcile these incompatibilities and comprehend this apparently contradictory state of affairs. The challenge is all the greater given the ambiguity arising from perceptions of the international community as simultaneously a goal to be strived for and an existing condition to be managed.[10]

From its inception the North–South relationship has been most clearly expressed and understood in institutional terms. To the extent that it is a tangible phenomenon, it derives much of its identity from what Inis Claude calls 'the regulatory function of international institutions'.[11] At issue is the South's desire to devise and establish rules and practices which reflect their specific needs and interests, and the North's capacity and willingness to accommodate the consequences of the proliferation of autonomous third-world actors. For at the very least the South's interests require that international institutions confirm and promote their national identities.

International institutions may be suitable arenas in which to attempt to raise the moral consciousness of member states and their respective publics, but in reality they are somewhat less conspicuous for effective, practical implementation of agreed policies. Efforts to change attitudes, let alone to regulate conduct, inevitably invite resistance and all too often provoke disillusionment, cynicism and ultimately apathy. It is less than surprising that such conclusions are drawn, for international institutions, by definition, suffer from a congenital defect in the form of the sovereign state. From the point of view of collective decision-making it is an affliction which many observers are prepared to diagnose as 'terminal'. As long as defence and promotion of national self-interest remain the hallmark of the sovereign state, international institutions will necessarily reflect and contribute to the amorality which normally characterizes much of international politics.

Although the march of interdependence and the attractions of supranationalism and integration may have eroded the quality if not the sanctity of sovereign status, the existing institutional framework gives little indication that states have consequently developed a greater sense of mutual responsibility or that international society has been seized by higher moral instincts and principles of justice and reciprocity. It remains the lot of many institutions in international society to confront the difficulty of persuading their members to behave in a manner which transcends their own perceived self-interests in order to serve a larger good. Many issues in the North–South relationship are morally compelling on humanitarian grounds alone, but their institutionalization with its attendant 'politiking' constantly threatens to diminish, if not extinguish, incentives for moral behaviour.

From this broader perspective, North–South issues, ranging from decolonization to development and disarmament, have been responsible for much of the institutional proliferation since 1945. Yet this phenomenal growth rate has not necessarily been a harbinger of community-mindedness. In the North–South institutional arena, notably in the UN system, the negative aspect of organizational growth can all too easily outweigh positive attributes. Hence the squandering or mismanagement of resources, the duplication of roles, politicization, inefficiency and bureaucratic inertia are familiar charges levelled against the UN and its agencies.[12] The contention that institutional proliferation 'may express more disillusionment with existing bodies than enthusiasm for additional ones, and reflect the neglect of the former rather than the need for the latter'[13] has become particularly apposite in the light of the South's demands for different (new or reformed) instruments[14] in which to negotiate development issues. These demands have met with sustained resistance and much stonewalling by developed states anxious to avoid both substantial reform of existing Bretton Woods structures and the creation of additional fora less accommodating to their interests.[15]

The trend towards collective decision-making does not guarantee a greater sense of responsibility or a more stable and just world order. Similarly the pursuit of 'milieu goals' rather than 'possession goals' in shaping the international environment contains its own dilemmas.[16] In particular, the expectations raised may underestimate both the vagaries of perception and the calculation of interests in a volatile society, as well as the role which rationality plays in national decision-making. Ostensibly a philosophy which encourages states to shape their environment through collective decision-making offers greater opportunities for international institutions to undertake a more effective and credible role. However, the nature of contemporary international society, the resilience of the sovereign state and the requirements of national self-preservation serve to arouse competitive rather than co-operative instincts. It is worth noting that much of the antagonism between North and South arises precisely because each coalition seeks to shape the operational environment to suit its own requirements. Also, the competing demands of 'possession' and 'milieu' goals would presumably have an enervating influence on the community of states. As with efforts to classify 'North' and 'South', the subject matter does not lend itself to clear-cut distinctions.

Yet however diffuse and unproductive North–South decision-making processes may be, they are, for better or worse, infused with moral issues. The assertion that international institutions have a normative function is less than novel, but the institutional manifestation of the North–South relationship does have an intrinsically normative rationale. It is charged with adjusting as well as with establishing standards of international behaviour and with generating and legitimizing norms. The very conduct and substance of the North–South debate, and not least the associated rhetoric, are replete with such notions as justice, equality, rights and obligations. In appealing to these concepts the developing countries have proclaimed a new focus of concern, a new set of priorities. Development, egalitarianism and distributive justice have replaced established concern with the disparities of power, wealth and technical know-how between North and South. This new focus is most evident in institutional fora, particularly within the UN 'family', which has nurtured the new ethos emerging out of third-world assertiveness. In doing so it has posited a new 'morality', thereby challenging the congruity of Thucydides' observation that 'in international affairs the strong do what they can and the weak suffer what they must'. Within the UN the strong can no longer assume that they have a monopoly of power nor that the weak will be content to remain the meek. Moreover, the South's challenge to the 'might is right' formula has been issued within an institutional framework which was initially both reflective and supportive of

Northern values and interests. This fact alone has compounded the discomfort of the developed states.

A further consequence of the changing emphasis of the international agenda has been to place the concept of interdependence, with its connotations of community, at the forefront of the North–South relationship. Interdependence is neither an intrinsically 'good thing', nor is its institutional manifestation a panacea.[17] Indeed, in practice it can be a double-edged sword capable of various, and therefore of misleading interpretations which do not necessarily presuppose or promote harmony. Neither is interdependence a solution to the problem of conflicting perceptions, particularly the kind which are induced by entrenched superiority or inferiority complexes. The North–South dialogue has been notable for the conflicting approaches which have constantly frustrated attempts to promote a more equitable global economic system. There was an element of this in the wake of the 1973–4 oil crisis when such Western politicians as Henry Kissinger, having undergone a remarkable conversion, claimed to acknowledge common interests between developed and developing states. They presumed the existence of an interdependence which compelled co-operation and acceptance of a common destiny[18] but one which was strictly *within* the established order.

The notion of interdependence may have sharpened awareness of common and conflicting interests, and of the advantages and disadvantages of complex interrelationships, but for the South it only underlines the Third World's position of weakness, a condition perpetuated by injustices emanating from the *status quo*. For developing countries, the 'northwestern'[19] interpretation of interdependence resembles a wolf in sheep's clothing – beguiling, but synonymous with and an excuse for more of the same. For the developing countries such interdependence is merely a euphemism for asymmetrical dependence, whereas their conception of interdependence[20] embodies the desire to negotiate on an equal basis with industrial countries, and to prevent any undermining of third-world solidarity in the attempt to reconstruct the international system. Such divergence suggests that the constant hammering home of the qualities and potential of interdependence has actually accentuated the division between North and South, between the 'haves' and 'have-nots', unjustifiably raising expectations. Interdependence does not of itself promote a more equitable system, nor close the 'gap' between North and South. To this extent it has heralded a false dawn.

Clearly the 'will' to organize, manifest in institutional proliferation, can be seen as a consequence of intensified interdependence
and of the inadequacies and limitations of the traditional state
system. The severity and magnitude of security and welfare
problems facing states in the nuclear age have prompted both North
and South to sacrifice a measure of sovereignty and autonomy in
decision-making, to assume collective responsibilities, to incur
collective obligations, and to recognize that individual as well as
common interests dictate the need for collective action. In this
respect the 'community option' has been thrust upon states. Largely
denied the luxury of choice, they have sought to co-operate 'to
establish norms and habits of behaviour that will enhance the
orderliness of the system and the security and welfare of all its
members'.[21] Just as the perceived need for collective security
formerly 'stimulated the rudimentary development of a sense of
responsibility to a world community',[22] so multiple insecurities and
shared vulnerabilities in the contemporary era seemingly enhance
the prospect of community-building, strengthening the identity of
interest and the sense of involvement in the 'fate of mankind'. Yet to
judge by the disillusionment associated with the two attempts at
universal, general purpose organization in the twentieth century
that prospect has receded dramatically. Security, far more so than
beauty, lies in the eye of the beholder. Moreover, one of the
weaknesses of the concept of 'community' is its capacity to convey
dangerous connotations of homogeneity and universal common
interest.[23] Nowhere is this more apparent than in attempts to fashion
a form of collective economic security. If they achieve nothing else
these efforts have at least erased the image of the UN as something
more than a 'lateral extension'[24] of the existing states' system.

It is tempting to argue, despite obvious limitations, that the UN
Charter has, by its very existence, contributed something to the idea
of a community with a common morality.[25] After all, the UN serves
to formulate and express the 'collective will and judgment of states'[26]
and it is this 'collective' attribute with its legitimizing capacity which
largely determines its overall value and significance for member
states. But in some respects the UN has been a victim of its own
ambitions, particularly as far as its goal of universalism is concerned.
Inevitably the nascent international community which the Charter
sought to establish was largely rooted in Western custom and law.
The 'founding fathers' created a potentially universal organization
very much in their own image, so that the rights, obligations, rules
and practices associated with the UN were necessarily imbued with

Western notions of morality and hence generally uninfluenced by non-Western cultures. Yet if its universal pretensions were to materialize, the prevailing morality, if not the legitimacy of the organization in bestowing rights and imposing obligations, would be called into question sooner rather than later in the climate of rapid change and uncertainty which marked the post-war era. The problem was how to accommodate change and adjust to new realities so as to promote the general good yet sustain the relevance of the recently established institutional framework. As decolonization unleashed pressures for change from the developing countries within the UN, a variety of questions were posed: under what circumstances could reform be countenanced; at what point should concessions be made; how should national or sectional interests be balanced with the wider interests of the UN, if this proved possible let alone desirable? These were important questions, not least in so far as the answers would indicate where the power of initiative lay and reveal the divergent perceptions of the UN's value and role.

The assumptions underlying these divergent perceptions are vital to an explanation of the problems besetting the North–South relationship to date. Perhaps the most obvious is the asumption that both North[27] and South are homogeneous cohesive groupings. In fact neither label connotes a tailor-made constituency. In some respects the developed countries only belatedly discovered the diversity of and divisions within the South, despite overwhelming evidence to the contrary. On the whole, the global perspective of leading industrial states was conditioned by their preoccupation with the bipolar East–West axis. They tended to lump together all developing states as the 'Third World' or more recently the 'South'. In addition to reflecting the developed states' myopic fascination with 'geopolitics', this attitude towards the Third World was fuelled by their uncertainty over how to react to the claims of unity emanating from the Afro-Asian bloc, the Non-aligned Movement, or the Group of 77. Consequently, for convenience rather than for clarity's sake, the Cold War protagonists tended to ignore third-world diversity in their competition for influence over the developing countries. Nowhere was this more apparent than in the UN General Assembly, despite the fact that the variety of colonial experiences and legacies alone suggested the potential for political, cultural and ideological fragmentation. Another divisive factor was the differing needs and interests of the non-industrial states.[28]

This evident diversity was, and still is, regarded as a major source of weakness by the developing countries. Their stress on the need for unity is a clear acknowledgement of the divisions within their ranks and the disadvantages these fissures are seen to create. As a result, developing countries argue that 'strength through unity' (or more accurately, 'leverage through unity') is not only a prerequisite for achieving objectives but it also confers greater legitimacy on these. To this end the United Nations Conference on Trade and Development (UNCTAD), the United Nations General Assembly, the United Nations Industrial Development Organization (UNIDO) and the South's economic pressure group, the Group of 77, have been the preferred instruments in the South's bid to realize their aspirations. Shridath Ramphal has instructively warned 'Not By Unity Alone'[29] in presenting the case for a third-world organization for economic co-operation along the lines of the OECD. He perceives that such an organization would be the 'missing link' between strength and unity, and argues that its creation would be both 'a concomitant of unity and a precondition for unified [and by implication legitimate] action by the South'. So far unity has proved to be a frustrating mirage, more so for the South than for the North, and as such has been a relatively easy target for critics.[30] Moreover, institutional experience suggests that even in the most favourable circumstances unity and the ability to get one's way in the world are ephemeral qualities. The histories of OPEC and the OECD (among others) testify to this. If the Northern grouping is regarded as being less heterogeneous than the South, it may simply be because it has fewer 'inmates' and is more clearly polarized along ideological lines between two alternative systems. On the one hand, the North–South polarization over 'who gets what' in the international system is obvious, but the assumption that divisions and conflicts by definition only occur between North and South is clearly misleading. There is ample evidence to indicate that these are as likely to be *within* the increasingly diverse and heterogeneous groupings testifying to conflicting interests and incompatible objectives.[31]

Whatever the verdict on the North–South debate so far, the focus of attention remains the 'conflictual relationship' between North and South played out in the institutions which give global negotiations their structure and coherence. By the early 1960s a North–South axis had begun to emerge, challenging the preponderant East–West axis within the UN. The growing third-world presence there ensured that a new sense of urgency was brought to the expectation that rights be exercised and obligations fulfilled, i.e. to international accountability, in accordance with the will of the newly emergent majority. While the South continued to perceive a power-oriented world which was untempered by justice and in which it was necessary to seek redress, the North equally remained wedded to its perception that justice without order is misconceived, since without order there can only be the injustice which accompanies anarchy. Perceptions are never uniform and seldom permanent however. In recent years many of the more radical demands of the South have been modified to accommodate the vested interest of developing countries in stability.

It is nevertheless not surprising that the fundamental differences in the experience and expectations of North and South have been translated into contrary notions about the role and capacity of international organization as a technique for managing the global system. In the past the developed countries, particularly the Western industrial states, have tended to see international organizations as guardians, even guarantors, of the *status quo*[32] which serve both their particular interests and the more general interest of a stable international order. In consequence, the idea of restructuring the system is regarded by many in the North as at least untimely, if not unnecessary and undesirable. For the developed countries any change should be gradual and controlled by the North. The possibility that global security might be conditional on world economic development was a particularly difficult pill to swallow for those raised on a diet of undiluted 'realism'. But since 1960 the prevailing Western political ethos has not gone unchallenged.

Among the challenges to the North's preferred international order was the fragmentation and diffusion of power resulting from decolonization. This process caused dramatic changes in the institutional balance generally, but most significantly in the complexion of the membership, voting patterns and agenda of the United Nations. The UN was the arena in which the drama of rival legitimacies unfolded with, on the one hand, the developed countries seeking 'freedom to . . .' and, on the other, the developing states seeking 'freedom from . . .'.[33] The privileged North presumed the freedom to prevail as in the past; to preserve, operate and refine the existing system to its continued advantage, by determining the level and pace of global economic development, for example. As the South's 'will' to exercise dormant or undefined rights has grown, so the North's freedom of manoeuvre in exercising power over developing states or in exploiting their resources has declined. Meanwhile, the disadvantaged, 'have-not' states have sought freedom from exploitation and manipulation, sovereignty and control over their own natural resources, and a more equitable distribution of the world's wealth amounting to positive discrimination in their favour. It is the developing countries' perceived sense of common history, their presumed identity of condition, and their indignation at not being present at the creation of the established economic order (seen as containing the roots of injustice) which underpins their claim to unity and their original contention that international decision-making processes were largely irrelevant, anachronistic or injurious to their needs and interests. From this perspective international institutions are themselves seen as impediments to progress in the South.

Yet given their intrinsic weakness, the newly independent states had little alternative but to adapt to the existing order.[34] Having 'arrived', the developing countries adopted Trojan horse tactics. They have pursued their diverse interests by challenging the North's supremacy and instigating change 'from within', and to this extent they have strengthened rather than weakened the international institutional system.[35] As a result the institutional framework is both the instrument and the object of reform or, more ambitiously, of radical reconstruction intended to reduce or remove the North's inbuilt advantages. The considerable numerical strength of the developing states has encouraged them not merely to seek to change the rules of the game but to change those who make the rules. In this respect it was natural that the UN system should prove the most attractive arena for the South, but it became the prime focus of attention once the campaign for reform gained momentum in the wake of OPEC's fabled confrontation with Western industrial states in 1973–4. This time of crisis for the West represented a moment of opportunity for the South and the occasion for 'North–South relations to move from the level of petition to the level of negotiation'.[36] During the 1970s it became clear that essentially evolutionary structures were being confronted by revolutionary forces for change, a clash which was also precipitating a shift in the focus of world politics. Once access to decision-making processes became an explicit theme of the South's manifesto,[37] the campaign to halt and gain compensation for past exploitation by the North became as much a desire for shared political control as for the redistribution of wealth and resources. The point that the South seeks power as well as position is succinctly put by Robert Gregg. He asserts that the developing countries sought 'not only a larger slice of the pie' but also signalled their intention 'to have a hand on the knife that cuts the pie'.[38]

The UN's potential for promoting the spirit of international community depends on its success in dispensing collective legitimacy (giving the stamp of approval or disapproval to the policies and actions of member states)[39] and in exercising moral authority as a result. Ironically the UN's potential in this regard has been undermined by its very prominence as an arena of contested legitimacies, whether East–West or North–South. In fact there has been a lengthy transition period since the 1960s in which the established legitimacy associated with Western preponderance has been increasingly challenged but not entirely eroded by third-world purveyors of a new legitimacy. This shift from Western to Southern predominance in the UN has been matched by a shift in the type of principles invoked by the General Assembly, with the emphasis increasingly on political and economic self-determination, positive discrimination for developing states, and the 'common heritage of mankind',[40] to name but a few. By persistently asserting the right to self-determination, the South has succeeded in raising this to a moral and legal principle, aided by the 1960 Declaration on the Granting of Independence to Colonial Countries and Peoples.[41] The Declaration proved to be instrumental in the campaign to invalidate colonialism and establish international (by which was meant Northern) accountability. By similarly asserting the right to a more equitable distribution of the world's resources, the Third World gained universal recognition (if not approval) of these as 'legitimizing principles' which sustain new norms, help to redefine international relationships and prompt institutional change.

In pursuing its challenge to the existing system, the South has confirmed that power resides not only in the barrel of a gun, or for that matter in a barrel of oil,[42] but it can also be acquired (potentially at least) through the propensity of institutions to dispense collective approval or disapproval of the behaviour of states. In other words, power can be acquired through the barrel-organ of multilateral diplomacy, its cacophony of standards notwithstanding.[43] The problem for the UN has been how to avoid collective legitimization deteriorating into selective endorsement or disapproval; how to prevent its nascent moral authority from being undermined by the 'tyranny of the majority'.[44]

If the existence of a general consensus and of an apparent 'consent to be governed',[45] together with the encouragement of integration are among the criteria for membership of a community, these have not been much in evidence within the United Nations. Rather, the limitations on the UN's political role have been to the fore. Somewhat less clear is the impact of North–South decision-making processes on the UN as a source and stimulant of international law. Preoccupation with the New International Economic Order (NIEO) may have reinforced the organization's normative role and testified to a continuing need for an adjustment of standards, but the legal status of the principles and rules for international behaviour advocated by the Third World's programme has been called into question.[46]

Not for the first time this century existing modes of decision-making have been found wanting. In an effort to remedy the situation institutions have seen the principle of unanimity replaced by the principle of majority rule[47] and parliamentary diplomacy. More recently, as multilateral diplomacy has become increasingly North–South oriented, a further development has been identified. As a consequence of multilateral decision-making processes the interests of groups of states have tended to prevail over those of individual states. Efforts to promote equality have been conducted between coalitions rather than between states in the UN. The need to manage the complexities of interdependence, the dominant spirit of egalitarianism, and even a readiness to tolerate disadvantageous outcomes, have produced the principle of parity and consensus diplomacy as the potential, though not unchallenged successor to majoritarianism.[48]

As if to confirm that North–South decision-making is beset by a kaleidoscope of contending perceptions and rival moralities, the so-called dialogue has stumbled over such essentially mundane matters as the site and agenda of negotiations. Together with the fact that both coalitions have looked to the creation of additional organizations to support their respective positions, these differences have produced something akin to an institutional tug-of-war.[49] Despite incipient consensus diplomacy,[50] the South, in its anxiety to flex its numerical muscles, has preferred to negotiate in inclusive multilateral bodies where it can exert pressure for comprehensive discussions on a wide range of issues. In contrast, the North has sought negotiation on specific issues within the weighted voting agencies established at Bretton Woods where their in-built majority and control over agendas and finance at least provide some semblance of political and economic reality. It is the legitimacy of this position which has come under sustained attack from the developing countries. The South's perception of being denied the right to economic security and development by the Northern-dominated economic and financial institutional network caused the Bretton Woods institutions to be the prime targets of third-world pressure for reform. There is a certain irony in the fact that in the 1980s it is the South which is springing to the defence of the Bretton Woods institutions (particularly the World Bank and its affiliates) as these come under attack from critics in the North.

From the point of view of the South and its supporters, the moral imperative has always been a prominent feature of the North–South institutional relationship. It has been less obviously so for the North. Three institutional developments spanning the past twenty years illustrate this discrepancy. Each emphasised the role of rights and obligations in North–South relations, each had implications for the notion of international community, and each was progressively more ambitious in its goals, and hence more likely to generate and legitimize norms of international behaviour. The creation of UNCTAD, the proposals for a NIEO and the UN Convention on the Law of the Sea stand at the threshold of important phases in the history of the North–South relationship.

The South's efforts to change the rules of the institutional game remained muted until the UN's membership explosion. The first tentative steps in mobilizing collective action came in 1955 at Bandung. While the conference was more notable as a symbol of Afro-Asian solidarity than as a platform publicizing the development dilemmas of the South, Bandung at least signposted the intention to place development issues on the international agenda in the future. The 1950s saw modest requests for multilateral aid being met with equally modest responses from the industrial countries. The preoccupation with security concerns during the Cold War ensured that the economic implications of decolonization were largely ignored. Even the UN Charter, which had encouraged colonial emancipation, was heavily retrospective on economic and develop-ment issues. Initiatives which were attempted (e.g. the Special United Nations Fund for Economic Development) tended to be undermined by bilateral arrangements which consolidated the state of dependence of former colonial peoples. But on the whole it was the great powers' disregard for UN economic fora which weakened still further the organization's already limited role in this field, and which fuelled the dissatisfaction of the ex-colonial states. Not only were they aggrieved by their exclusion from Bretton Woods decision-making processes (particularly from the General Agreement on Tariffs and Trade), they were also disillusioned by the failure of the system to include a genuine international trade organization (ITO). For the newly independent states this was the most crucial of the triad of specialized agencies proposed at Bretton Woods. GATT was a poor substitute for a trade organization and of questionable legitimacy since it did not even fall within the purview of the UN. Instead, it was designed to perpetuate and serve Western interests and preserve a traditional trade policy which discriminated against the developing countries. Once it was clear that development would not be a focal point of the international economic agenda GATT became the particular *bête noire* of the 'have-nots'.

As the South's economic problems and disenchantment grew, so did its voting strength in the General Assembly and its calls for equality in rights as well as in obligations between UN member states. Admittedly movement towards recognizing the salience of development and economic security issues was gradual, but it gathered sufficient pace for the South to pressurize the North into limited reforms which acknowledged the linkage between trade and development. A dual strategy was adopted by the developing states. At first they sought to adjust existing mechanisms but subsequently also pressed for the creation of additional institutional fora. The fact that the Northern response to this pressure induced institutional proliferation was a harbinger of things to come. New institutions, including the International Finance Corporation (IFC) and the International Development Association (IDA), which were both affiliates of the World Bank, were designed to placate the increasingly strident developing states. Although tainted by association with the Bretton Woods system, these two agencies established a precedent which was subsequently to prove impossible for the North to reverse. The industrialized countries were simply fuelling the fire for more radical structural reform, assisting the emergence of a new legitimacy and contributing to the rising expectations of the South. The North's gradual awareness of the South's development problems may have been an inadequate response from the point of view of the poor countries, but combined with the tendency towards institutional proliferation it effectively represented the thin end of the institutional wedge for the industrial states. As their hesitant relationship developed, North and South, formerly occasional sparring partners, became entrenched protagonists. An era of frequently bitter confrontation ensued as the developing countries sought economic emancipation courtesy of the United Nations.

The 1950s didn't augur well for those seeking to advance the cause of international community through the UN. The organization, already constrained by the East–West impasse, plunged into a further cycle of polarization and confrontation, enhancing its reputation as the repository of rival moralities and competing notions of justice and fair treatment. As the decolonization process and the campaign against racism reached a crescendo (allowing development issues and nuclear disarmament to deepen still further the North–South cleavage) the UN appeared to be harbouring if not actively cultivating rival communities. The creation of UNCTAD did little to dispel this notion.

The Third World's assault on the established economic system and its effort to erase the last vestiges of unanimity and secure the principle of majoritarianism had been made possible by the campaign to 'delegitimize colonialism'.[51] The success and implications of the anti-colonial campaign[52] seemed to confer greater legitimacy on the South's objectives. Encouraged by this the developing countries, assisted by the socialist bloc, pressed for the establishment of UNCTAD as the institutional focus of their economic demands. Central to these was Northern recognition of the vital relationship between trade and development. Given the circumstances, it seems to have been inevitable that UNCTAD, the institutional expression of the South's solidarity, should institutionalize the North–South confrontation, not least through its subsequent rivalry with GATT.[53] Northern efforts to make GATT more appealing to developing countries and more representative of their interests and needs were too little and too late. The Geneva Conference of 1964 did more than merely launch a new centre of decision-making into the international arena. By adopting the principle 'from each according to his ability, to each according to his needs', third-world representatives imposed upon the Conference a moral obligation to provide aid to poor states. This was to become the dominant theme of the UN's First Development Decade.

UNCTAD clearly set an important precedent. Having begun with the scales weighing heavily against them, developing countries hoped UNCTAD would begin to tilt the economic and institutional balance more in their favour. They saw in UNCTAD a universal agency whose Secretariat was obviously sensitive to third-world needs, which could not only instigate and control policy but also translate that policy into rules and standards and then implement them.[54] In this sense UNCTAD was perceived by the developing states as having the potential to generate and legitimize new standards of international behaviour. Yet UNCTAD was not the equivalent of a Bretton Woods style ITO. It was a compromise solution and therefore only a qualified success for the South. It was, nevertheless, optimistically expected that the new organization would be a forerunner of a more powerful forum for North–South dialogue.

The formal emergence of the Group of 77 at the Geneva Conference as the Third World's economic pressure group encouraged optimism and enhanced UNCTAD's legitimacy for the South. This became more evident as the Group of 77's prominence in the assault on the North made it the backbone of the Third World coalition. It articulated third-world claims and became a troublesome thorn in the side of the industrial countries, reminding them of their obligations and responsibilities towards the world's poor states. UNCTAD enabled the South to clarify rights and obligations and to exploit the opportunity to advance a less discriminatory economic system. Equally, it was coalition enhancing. The Group of 77 and the system of regional groupings adopted by UNCTAD were significant institutional developments in terms of helping to promote identity of interest and a feeling of involvement within those groups. At the same time the group system has proved divisive and has undermined any prospect of UNCTAD emerging as a venture in international community-building.

UNCTAD has proved a disappointment for the South primarily because of its difficulties in implementing the results of its deliberations, i.e. in going further than symbolizing and articulating the plight of the poor states, and in preventing development issues from being submerged in bureaucracy and ideological rhetoric. For many in the North UNCTAD has always been disruptive of a wider community not least because it duplicates the work of GATT and impinges on the latter's area of jurisdiction. At most, the North conceded that UNCTAD should limit itself to instigating policy and leave practical application to GATT. Although UNCTAD has been hailed, somewhat untypically, as 'a turning point in the evolution of international organisation',[55] its effectiveness in promoting fair treatment has been limited by its own principles and *modus operandi* – most obviously by the principle of majoritarianism. UNCTAD was born out of political compromise and has since been compelled to deal in compromise. In this sense it has paid the price for institutionalizing the North–South divide. Together with the Group of 77, UNCTAD has been criticized for 'demanding commitment to principles before clarifying what the principles might mean in practice'.[56] Everything about UNCTAD suggests that it could not, and was never intended to effect reconciliation and harmony, or consequently to contribute to a wider sense of international community. The process of establishing a more just and equitable economic system, ameliorating grievances by intruding upon the *status quo*, and challenging and removing long-held privileges, was a recipe for acrimony and confrontation. At this stage the principle of distributive justice and the prospect of global community-building were antithetical phenomena. UNCTAD did not promise the concilation of differences. It opened an era of confrontation in which the South claimed the 'right to receive' while imposing on the North the obligation 'to provide'.

The South's demands for change, participation in decision-making, and for economic self-determination became more radical as its lack of power and resources to implement its policies became more apparent. However, in 1973 the full implication of the 'process of concession'[57] burst upon the UN. The origins of the demand for a New International Economic Order are not difficult to trace,[58] but its impact was certainly unexpected. This demand for the most comprehensive review of economic issues since Bretton Woods was both a response to the inaction of the North and a reflection of the South's newfound sense of power and status derived from the leverage acquired on it's behalf by the Arab oil-producing states. In consequence, the Sixth Special Session saw the peak of confrontation and acrimony between North and South in the General Assembly. In seeking sovereignty over natural resources, the right to aid, improved trade conditions and access to technology 'by law, as of right and without strings',[59] the Declaration,[60] Programme of Action[61] and subsequently the Charter of Economic Rights and Duties[62] indicated that the new order and projected rules of conduct would require new multilateral institutions. Predictably the instruments of control have become a central issue of the NIEO, important in its 'creation and content . . . in the manner and speed of its establishment . . . and [in] the legitimacy it enjoys'.[63]

Despite their concern to enshrine the principle of economic self-determination in international law, the developing countries were essentially proposing a political programme which spelt out the rights of the South and the duties of the North. The objectives and principles of this new economic and political order were expounded in the Declaration and the Charter. The Declaration sets out the South's aspirations for a better world which would be the basis of the international community, whereas the Charter goes further. It is explicitly concerned with principles of justice and equality and recognizes the need to establish or improve norms of universal application for the development of international economic relations on a just and equitable basis. It also calls for the participation of all in the international decision-making process in order to resolve the world's economic, financial and monetary problems.

The South's earlier search for preferential treatment had produced some concessions, e.g. GATT's modification of the traditional norm concerning the principle of free trade. But by attempting to reform or even replace the system which discriminated against them with one which discriminated positively in their favour, the South was explicitly seeking compensation for past exploitation by the North. The more vigorous and persistent the South's demands became, the less inclined the industrial states were to accept the duty of international co-operation proclaimed by the Charter. In any case, the demand for such fundamental change was essentially unrealistic given that the South needed the co-operation of the North in order to dismantle established privileges. Not surprisingly, the South's tactics put the industrialized countries on the defensive, encouraging them to close ranks (as in Kissinger's plan for a counter-cartel, the International Energy Agency). The resulting exacerbation of the North–South confrontation was ultimately detrimental to the cause of the developing countries. It deflected them from their central purpose, namely to bring about real changes which would reflect the requirements of the South. Polemics were no substitute for actions.

The issue of control, that perennial cause of division and discomfort within the UN, became the focus of the controversy over the proposed Programme of Action as it drew attention to the contentious egalitarian decision-making procedures which were to advance the NIEO. Majoritarianism and consensus diplomacy were anathema to the North, but more especially to the United States which rejected the imposition of obligations on states without their prior consent. Northern irritation with the assumption that the majority could change the rules simply by virtue of being the majority, lay behind the US complaint about 'the tyranny of the majority'. In many ways it is the prospect of losing control over resources and funding to a hostile majority which has proved particularly distasteful to the industrial countries, and so disruptive to the North–South dialogue. However, it has not been an insuperable problem as the compromise solution over the International Fund for Agricultural Development reveals.[64]

In contrast to the drama of the Sixth Special Session, a more constructive atmosphere was in evidence at the Seventh Special Session in 1975. Shocked out of its complacency by OPEC's 'alliance' with the poor countries, the United States found it expedient to respond to third-world grievances in order to at least mitigate confrontation. Washington's recognition of the principle of permanent sovereignty over natural resources and its acceptance of the linkage between energy on the one hand, and commodities and raw materials on the other, made possible the convening of the Conference on International Economic Co-operation 1975–7 (CIEC) in Paris. This raised third-world hopes for a more flexible and sympathetic attitude on the part of the North. These hopes were short-lived, however. Contending principles and differing priorities produced the familiar deadlock, as in the US's implacable opposition to the attempt by the developing states to erode the established principle that there should be no expropriation of foreign assets without compensation. If the failure of the CIEC after two years of deliberation challenged the already precarious assumption that 'dialogue was useful', it emphatically underlined the importance of 'control' for each coalition.[65]

The evolving debate over the NIEO has vividly registered the intractability of problems which are no longer the exclusive concern of the South. It is no coincidence that the more moderate tone of many of the South's demands accompanied a growing recognition by the North that the developing countries *do* have a legitimate claim to assistance, and that concern with international development *is* necessary for the continued functioning of the international system. Hence the emphasis on co-operation, mutual interests and obligations which characterized the Brandt Reports[66] potentially enhances the prospects for norm creation in this field. Also, it is significant that less than ten years after the South's demand for radical reform of the system and for aid 'as of right', Shridath Ramphal felt able to stress that the NIEO was about rules and arrangements to improve the order, stability and predictability of the international economic system, and that it was about 'shared management' rather than about economic assistance.[67]

Even so, conflicting perceptions continue to take their toll of tolerable solutions and the NIEO has remained largely an aspiration. Indeed, from its inception critics questioned the authenticity of the package served up by the South, arguing that the New International Economic Order was not new (most of its proposals had been made in the 1960s), not truly international (it was designed by the South in order to benefit the South), less an economic programme than a political manifesto, and a recipe for chaos rather than order. The impact of adversary politics robbed the idea of legitimacy and undermined its capacity to generate new universally applicable standards of international behaviour. The North's grudging acceptance of the principle of economic self-determination was a recognition of what had long been inevitable rather than the dawn of a new era. Moreover, far from enabling aspirations to be transformed into new rules of behaviour or legal principles, international institutions have often been an obstacle to the creation of a NIEO.[68] The requirements of the new order exposed the limitations of the South's Trojan horse tactics. Having been sucked into the prevailing economic system, the developing countries find it almost impossible to negotiate change and reform of the existing order from *within* that order.

In contrast, the UN Convention on the Law of the Sea[69] and the emergent global consensus it embraces appear to hold greater prospects for the creation and legitimization of norms, such as the concept of an Exclusive Economic Zone (EEZ),[70] and for community-building among states. The Convention represents the compromise outcome of the South's challenge to yet another traditional legal principle, namely the principle of the freedom of the seas. Predictably it is riddled with references to the rights and duties of states in relation to their activities at sea. But unlike the principles of equality, national self-determination or positive discrimination, the principle of the common heritage of mankind has emerged as a negotiated principle of international law. It embodies a general consensus and establishes new rules and standards of ocean practices which offer improved prospects for greater predictability in the maritime regime. The debate and concern aroused by the action of the non-signatories to the Convention only serves to emphasize its significance.

From the outset the Third UN Conference on the Law of the Sea

(UNCLOS III) was regarded by the South as a cornerstone of the NIEO programme. As a result it conveyed many of the tensions and divergent interests accumulated in an era in which the Third World collectivity challenged the *status quo*. UNCLOS III reflected the struggle between those seeking to bring about fundamental change in the ocean regime and those determined to resist such change. In doing so it encapsulated the conflicting philosophies and ideologies of North and South, but at the same time the issues under negotiation produced new alignments and competing interest groups within the established coalitions.[71]

The traditional maritime powers, concerned to protect their navigation rights, sought to preserve the principle of the freedom of the seas which sustained their dominant role. Yet for the South the existing regime was both anachronistic and discriminatory with the balance of rights and duties clearly favouring the developed states. Consequently the developing countries seized on Arvid Pardo's 1967 initiative[72] as an opportunity to redress the balance and close the gap between rich and poor. By invoking the established principle of sovereignty and promoting the emergent common heritage principle, the South sought a legal right to ocean resources and a new law of the sea which would establish norms to meet its demands for a more equitable distribution of global wealth. In this respect the debate at UNCLOS III was highly political. But it also involved a technical issue of international law. Just as in the South's campaign to 'delegitimize' colonialism, the General Assembly's competence to create binding principles of international law was questioned. The status of the various interpretations of the common heritage principle invoked by the 1970 Declaration on ocean use[73] became a particular bone of contention between North and South. Yet it was equally significant that the Declaration itself became an intrinsic part of the South's strategy for an NIEO: the South and supporters of UNCLOS III have claimed that it signalled a moral commitment to a wider legal regime for the oceans, and provided 'the basis for the generation of legally binding rules'.[74] The inclusion of the common heritage principle in the Charter of Economic Rights and Duties gave it even greater legitimacy as far as the South was concerned.

There was an important difference in the attitudes and perceived interests of the parties to the UNCLOS negotiations when compared with debates on the NIEO in the UN General Assembly. Both North and South (albeit for different reasons) came to accept the need for a new agency to deal with the conflicting claims of coastal states, to resolve the issue of sea-bed resources, and not least to define the rights and duties of all states in regard to the ocean and its resources. The degree of common interest between the main coalitions was compounded by their recognition of the concept of the EEZ. The acceptance of the EEZ was particularly crucial for the Third World's campaign to transfer resources from North to South and to achieve economic self-determination. This required the exclusion of developed states from the seas adjacent to developing countries. The fears of many of the maritime and coastal developed states as to the consequences and long-term implications of this 'creeping jurisdiction' were ultimately balanced by the recognition that many in the North had common interests with the South in extending their rights over their continental shelves. Once the costs of resisting the South were perceived to be outweighed by the benefits of co-operation, the developed states were prepared to accept the concept of the EEZ, thereby giving birth to a new norm relatively painlessly. Other issues, including the protection of the marine environment and transit rights, proved less easily amenable to compromise.

The crucial question of who should control the key decision-making instruments envisaged under the proposed Convention caused a serious rift between North and South, most notably on the issue of the resources of the deep sea-bed – the issue which lay at the heart of the common heritage principle. While the South envisaged the wealth resulting from deep sea-bed mining being used to close the gap between rich and poor, the free-enterprise oriented North argued for minimal interference in mining operations from the proposed International Sea-bed Authority. Not surprisingly those industrial states anxious to promote opportunities for their multinational companies were particularly hostile to the idea of a monopolistic Sea-bed Authority dominated by states which would ultimately reap all the benefits derived from Northern technology and investment. On this occasion the developing states' numerical preponderance was not enough, and the North's monopoly of technology and finance exposed the South's lack of leverage.

Critical evaluation of the performance of international organizations not infrequently suggests they are destined to underachieve, to dash even inextravagant hopes, and to undermine the most noble causes. Organizations which have universal pretensions in the latter half of the twentieth century, thereby attempting to embrace the diversity and ideological partisanship of North–South relations, almost by definition fail to live up to expectations. In this respect

UNCLOS III and the Convention opened for signature in December 1982 are no exceptions.

The Treaty's potential for norm creation is undoubtedly limited by the inevitable ambiguities characterizing a compromise political package which sought to accommodate all parties and interests. That potential is further reduced by the decision of major industrial states not to sign, and by their selective approach to the rights and obligations incorporated in the Treaty. By rejecting the Treaty the United States and the other non-signatories have shattered the global consensus so painstakingly evolved at UNCLOS III, and eroded the promise it held out as a community-building venture. It might be argued that the Treaty's potential in this respect was much overrated anyway given the new fissures which appeared within the Third World coalition at UNCLOS III. The ideological North–South divide not withstanding, conflicting interests within the Group of 77 removed the illusion of third-world solidarity during the protracted negotiations.

The disappointment of some at the limitations of the Convention hinges on its non-fulfilment of two criteria essential to its community-building function, namely the extent to which it enhances world order by promoting a just and equitable ocean regime for all, and the extent to which it encourages 'rational' resolution of maritime problems such as resource management 'by establishing appropriate legal regimes . . . within and outside national jurisdiction'.[75] Yet while critics bemoan the lost opportunities,[76] the UN Convention on the Law of the Sea can claim to promote the common interest and community objectives to the extent that it did achieve an accommodation of competing interests, even if the price of consensus was ambiguity. The dispute settlement provisions and the management of sea-bed resources through the International Sea-bed Authority were, in fact, singled out in advance as positive aspects which would make the Convention potentially precedent-setting.[77] Once a new maritime order became the objective of states, the pressures of political and technological change also exposed the need for consensus, compromise and in some cases acceptance of less than desirable outcomes. The adoption of the Convention, with its many innovations, potentially opened a new era in maritime and international law, and a new chapter in North–South institutional relations. If this materializes, the novelty will lie as much in the efforts expended to fashion a broadly acceptable maritime order out of an increasingly chaotic and unjust traditional regime as in the establishment of new norms. Also the acceptance of the common heritage principle will have created an important precedent if it stimulates collective resolution of other outstanding global problems. In the North–South arena it seems that some degree of confrontation, even acrimony, is a prerequisite for change.

The theme of rights and duties runs like a red thread through the North–South institutional relationship. If it has inspired rhetoric and been exaggerated at times, there have also been occasions where it has been overlooked to the detriment of all parties. On the whole it seems reasonable to conclude that moral values have proved a poor guide to the unravelling of North–South relations manifested in an increasingly intricate and complex organizational web. But, while they may obscure rather than illuminate proceedings, conflicting or contentious moral values do not, in themselves, explain why the North–South dialogue has made such slow progress and has so few achievements to its credit. However, a better understanding may be gained if it is recognized that 'in political affairs . . . morality is never simply a matter of principles, it always entails the weighing of consequences'.[78]

We might judge the success of international organizations on two levels. On the one hand, we can assess their contributions to the working of what Hedley Bull calls the 'more basic institutions' such as the balance of power, international law and diplomacy.[79] On the other hand, it is perhaps more meaningful to focus on what states can achieve through organizations, to assess their utility for states in gaining objectives and coping with change in international society. In terms of achievement the North–South institutional relationship has been found wanting at both levels. That North–South issues have made an impact on the global system cannot be denied, and the extent to which organizations satisfy their members will clearly depend on the goals set and expectations nourished. Nonetheless, after two decades of dialogue, the restructuring of the economic system remains a contentious and distant objective, with its ethical rationale as fragile as ever.[80]

Even the Law of the Sea Treaty, the most substantial and potentially far-reaching global institutional development since the 'founding fathers' penned the Charter of the United Nations, must be regarded at this stage as being at best a limited success. It may have been an ideological, or even a moral victory for the South, but it remains a hollow victory as long as the major industrial countries regard it as an inadequate legal framework for a maritime regime.

Although much depends on the rate of ratification at a later date, the Western refusal to sign has pulled the rug out from under the Third World. The conclusion of UNCLOS III promised to be a memorable milestone in the chequered history of the international community-building process, not least because by encouraging stability and predictability it supported values which have become as important to the South as they supposedly have always been to the North. By its concern to balance the exercise of rights with the corresponding fulfilment of obligations, the Convention shows considerable potential for realizing a just and equitable maritime order. It may even suggest that in a society which claims to acknowledge, however selectively or expediently, international law, the submission of states to legal authority may itself be seen as a moral obligation.

However, it is an abiding feature of international organization that ultimate success depends on the commitment of every participant to the common good, to the extent this can be ascertained. UNCLOS appeared, albeit fleetingly, to restore some credibility to the UN. But the genie of global consensus was only partially and temporarily released from the bottle. National and sectional interests seem to have removed the opportunity for the UN to be something more than the dispenser of a dubious legitimacy. Instead the hiatus over the Law of the Sea Treaty threatens wider and more lasting damage to the North–South relationship. The Western inaction may not merely undermine a tortuously negotiated maritime regime, it may also diminish the general commitment to multilateral co-operation still further. It this happens, a spill-over effect could polarize positions throughout the North–South institutional framework and evoke the kind of disillusionment which encourages authoritarianism and the search for unilateral advantage. It is precisely because the UN remains central to the establishment of standards of international behaviour that the North's declining confidence in the organization is so portentous in the post-UNCLOS-III era, not least because with the adoption of the Law of the Sea Treaty the UN, for once, has been seen to be in the business of solutions as well as resolutions.

NOTES AND REFERENCES

1. For a useful introduction to the literature on international organizations see C. Archer, *International Organizations* (London: Allen & Unwin, 1983) chap. 3. See also the journals *International Organization* and *Third World Quarterly*.

2. North–South negotiations were generated by the Third World's call for a New International Economic Order in the wake of the oil crisis of 1973–4. For a recent assessment see R.L. Rothstein, 'Is the North–South Dialogue Worth Saving?', *Third World Quarterly* 6 (1984) pp. 155–81.

3. See R. Jutte and A.-G. Jutte (eds), *The Future of International Organization* (London: Francis Pinter, 1981).

4. Note, for example, the Third World's enthusiasm for nuclear disarmament, but its reluctance to consider conventional disarmament at the UN.

5. For an illuminating analysis of the development, merits and politics of international majoritarianism see I.L. Claude, Jr., *Swords Into Plowshares* (London: University of London Press, 1964) pp. 113–31.

6. Ibid., p. 404.

7. A. Wolfers, *Discord and Collaboration* (Baltimore: John Hopkins Press, 1962) p. 73.

8. Rothstein, 'Is the North–South Dialogue Worth Saving?' p. 170.

9. A.B. Bozeman, *The Future of Law in a Multicultural World* (Princeton, NJ: Princeton University Press, 1971) p. 182.

10. For a development of this theme see R.A. Falk, 'The Trend Toward World Community: An Inventory of Issues', in A. Lepawsky, E.H. Buehrig, and H.D. Lasswell (eds), *The Search for World Order* (New York: Appleton-Century Crofts, 1971).

11. Claude, 'The Growth of International Institutions', in B. Porter (ed.), *The Aberystwyth Papers* (London: Oxford University Press, 1972) p. 297.

12. See the Reagan Administration's justification for its withdrawal from UNESCO in 1984 for example.

13. Claude, 'The Growth of International Institutions', p. 284.

14. See the second Brandt Report, *Common Crisis: North–South: Cooperation for World Recovery* (London: Pan Books, 1983). Also relevant are the South's demands for a new Bretton Woods at the Non-aligned Summit, March 1983, reported in *The Guardian*, 15 March 1983, and the call for reform of the international monetary system in a report submitted to the Commonwealth Finance Ministers, *The Guardian*, 9 September 1983.

15. Northern opposition to reform has been a feature of the summits of the seven richest Western industrial countries at Williamsburg in 1983 and London in 1984.

16. Wolfers, *Discord and Collaboration*, pp. 73–9.

17. D.A. Baldwin, 'Interdependence and Power: a Conceptual Analysis', *International Organization* 34 (1980) pp. 471–506; S. Hoffmann, *Duties Beyond Borders* (Syracuse, NY: Syracuse University Press, 1981) p. 176.

18. S.P. Varma, ' "Interdependence": The Third World Perspectives', in K. Misra and R.S. Beal (eds), *International Relations Theory: Western and Non-Western Perspectives*, (New Delhi: Vikas, 1980).

19. See H.W. Singer, 'The Brandt Report: a "Northwestern" Point of View', *Third World Quarterly* 2 (1980) pp. 694–700.

20. Varma, ' "Interdependence": The Third World Perspectives', p. 134.

21. Claude, 'The Growth of International Institutions', p. 294.

22. Claude, *Swords Into Plowshares*, p. 259.

23. But, as is contended elsewhere in this volume, the existence of an international community does not preclude the outbreak of conflicts within that community. See A.J.M. Milne, 'Human Rights and the Diversity of Morals', *supra*, p.31.

24. E.H. Buehrig, 'A Charter Dilemma: Order versus Change', in Lepawsky, Buehrig and Lasswell (eds), *The Search for World Order*, p. 279.
25. For an analysis of the pitfalls associated with this motion see Milne, *supra*, pp. 29–30.
26. Claude, 'The Growth of International Institutions', p. 297.
27. Although in many instances the 'North' is synonymous with the 'West', the term is retained largely because of the socialist bloc's anomalous position. Its interests coincide with those of the West on many issues.
28. For an elaboration of this argument see G.L. Goodwin, 'The United Nations: Expectations and Experience', *International Relations* 3 (1969–71) pp. 729–55.
29. S.S. Ramphal, 'Not By Unity Alone: The Case for a Third World Organization', *Third World Quarterly* 1 (1979) pp. 43–52.
30. Rothstein, 'Is the North–South Dialogue Worth Saving?', p. 170n.
31. In practice the composition of both categories is frequently changing.
32. This attitude has been modified with the proliferation of international organizations dominated by the developing countries.
33. I am indebted to Ken Booth for drawing my attention to this distinction. See his article 'Naval Strategy and the Spread of Psycho-legal Boundaries at Sea', *International Journal* 38 (1982–3) pp. 373–96.
34. H. Bull, 'The Third World and International Society', *Yearbook of World Affairs 1979* pp. 15–31; S. Gupta, 'Great Power Relations and the Third World', in C. Holbraad (ed.), *Superpowers and World Order* (Canberra: Australian National University Press, 1971).
35. For further analysis of this see ibid.
36. Ramphal, 'Not By Unity Alone: The Case for a Third World Organization', p. 45.
37. For the development of this theme see R. Gregg, 'The New International Economic Order as a Political Manifesto', *UNITAR News* 11 (1979) pp. 21–7.
38. Ibid., p. 22.
39. I.L. Claude, Jr., 'Collective Legitimization as a Political Function of the United Nations', *International Organization* 20 (1966) p. 372.
40. In 1967, Ambassador Arvid Pardo of Malta suggested that the resources of the sea-bed beyond the limits of national jurisdiction should be designated the 'common heritage of mankind'. This was subsequently adopted by the South as a cornerstone of the NIEO. UN GAOR C.1 (1515 mtg.) para 6., UN Doc. A/C.1/PV 1515 (XX) 1967.
41. UN General Assembly Resolution 1514 (XV) 1960).
42. Adapted from the title of an article by A.A. Mazrui, 'The Barrel of the Gun and the Barrel of Oil in North–South Equation', *Alternatives* 3 (1977–8) pp. 455–79.
43. The moral authority of the UN and hence the legitimacy of its decisions are largely determined by the nature of its members, many of whose domestic policies and records undermine the principles of equality and majority rule and the credibility of that same moral authority which they claim to promote and so frequently invoke. It has become apparent that the UN is essentially a community of governments rather than a genuine world community of peoples – despite the ringing declaration of the Charter's preamble.
44. A phrase attributed to a former US Ambassador to the UN, John Scali, which came to reflect US perceptions of a hostile General Assembly and by extension a hostile UN.

45. K. Deutsch, 'The Probability of International Law', in K. Deutsch and S. Hoffmann (eds), *The Relevance of International Law* (Cambridge, Mass.: Schenkman, 1968) p. 61.

46. For an interesting analysis see K. Tomasevski, 'The New International Economic Order and International Law: Progressive Development or Decline?', in Jutte and Jutte (eds), *The Future of International Organization*, pp. 146–57.

47. This generalization must be qualified. The UN system for example demonstrates restricted and weighted voting procedures.

48. G. Gottlieb, 'Global Bargaining: the Legal and Diplomatic Framework', in N.G. Onuf (ed.), *Law-making in the Global Community* (Durham, NC: Carolina Academic Press, 1982) pp. 108–30. Gottlieb sees efforts to negotiate change between groups of states of equal standing with each acting on collectively agreed positions, as the beginning of a new phase in multilateral decision-making.

49. For example, institutions established or favoured by the North include the International Energy Agency, and those favoured by the South include the UN General Assembly, UNCTAD and the Committee of the Whole (COW). UNCTAD and the General Assembly have competed rather than collaborated over management of the NIEO agenda.

50. UNCLOS proceeded via consensus.

51. The phrase is that of Inis Claude in 'Collective Legitimization . . .' p. 376. In many cases the principle of self-determination did not extend to the rights of minorities within the new states.

52. This was illustrated most notably by the reaction to and consequences of India's invasion of Goa in 1961, which was in violation of the Charter's norm regarding the law against the use of force.

53. See B. Gosovic, *UNCTAD: Conflict or Compromise* (Leiden: A.W. Sijthoff, 1971) for a detailed analysis of the rivalry between UNCTAD and GATT.

54. Ibid., p. 266.

55. R. Gardner, 'The United Nations Conference on Trade and Development', *International Organization* 22 (1968) pp. 99–130.

56. R. Rothstein, *Global Bargaining: UNCTAD and the Quest for a New International Economic Order* (Princeton, NJ: Princeton University Press, 1979) p. 24.

57. S. Weintraub, 'The Role of the UN in Economic Negotiations', in D.A. Kay (ed.), *The Changing United Nations* (New York: Praeger, 1977) p. 100.

58. The steady build-up of collective self-confidence and cohesion, combined with the feelings of resentment and radicalism, exploded in the call for an NIEO at the Algiers Non-aligned Summit, 1973.

59. L. Henkin, *How Nations Behave*, 2nd ed. (New York: Columbia University Press, 1979) p. 198.

60. *Declaration on the Establishment of a New International Economic Order* UN General Assembly Resolution 3201 (S-VI) 1 May 1974.

61. *Programme of Action on the Establishment of a New International Economic Order* UN General Assembly Resolution 3202 (S-VI) 1 May 1974.

62. *Charter of Economic Rights and Duties of States* UN General Assembly Resolution 3281 (XXIX) 15 January 1975.

63. R. Gregg, 'UN Decision-making Structures and the Implementation of the NIEO', in E. Laszlo and J. Kurtzman (eds), *Political and Institutional Issues of the New International Economic Order* (New York: Pergamon Press, 1981) p. 105.

64. Gregg, 'The New International Economic Order as a Political Manifesto', p. 25; I.F.I. Shihata, 'The North–South Dialogue Revisited', in A. Gauhar (ed.), *The Rich and the Poor* (London: Third World Foundation, 1983) pp. 81–100.

65. Weintraub, 'The Role of the UN in Economic Negotiations', p. 98.

66. *North–South: A Programme for Survival* (London: Pan Books, 1980); *Common Crisis* (see n. 14).

67. S.S. Rampal, 'North–South Cooperation: Why and How the South Must Persist', in A. Gauhar (ed.), *The Rich and the Poor*, pp. 101–38.

68. Gregg, 'UN Decision-making Structures and the Implementation of the NIEO', p. 112.

69. Adopted on 30 April 1982 and opened for signature on 10 December 1982.

70. One of several novel concepts given legitimacy by UNCLOS III embodying the principle that states should enjoy an exclusive economic zone (EEZ) of 200 miles from their coastline, in which they have the sole right to the food and mineral resources of the sea and sea-bed. Other states would have freedom of navigation and overflight rights in the EEZ, together with the rights to lay submarine cables and pipelines. The coastal states, however, would also be obliged to follow sound conservation policies in their EEZs.

71. Many issues raised at UNCLOS made the categories 'North' and 'South' even less meaningful than usual, as new group interests emerged bridging North and South, e.g. the landlocked and geographically disadvantaged states.

72. See n. 40.

73. *Declaration of Principles Governing the Sea-bed and the Ocean Floor and Subsoil Thereof, Beyond the Limits of National Jurisdiction* UN General Assembly Resolution 2749 (XXV) GAOR Supp. (No. 28) UN Doc. A/8028 1970.

74. E.D. Brown, 'Freedom of the High Seas Versus the Common Heritage of Mankind: Fundamental Principles in Conflict', *San Diego Law Review* 20 (1983) p. 545.

75. A. Pardo, 'The Convention on the Law of the Sea: A Preliminary Appraisal', ibid., p. 496.

76. Ibid., pp. 502–3.

77. J. Temple Swing, 'The Law of the Sea', in D.A. Kay (ed.), *The Changing United Nations*, pp. 128–41.

78. Hoffmann, *Duties Beyond Borders*, p. 152–3.

79. H. Bull, *The Anarchical Society* (London: Macmillan, 1982) p. xiv.

80. Less than universal efforts have evinced similar symptoms. Note the problems in negotiating Lomé III, concluded in December 1984.

Index